JOE AND THE PREACHER'S KID

Whiteboy Comedy on the Wind River Indian
Reservation

By Earl Batten

Copyright 2019
ISBN9781098606114

Cover: "Buffalo Hunt under the Wolf-skin Mask,"
George Catlin, 1832
Smithsonian American Art Museum

Table of Contents

v

CHAPTER 1 How the Preacher's Kid let the biggest fish get away

Red suspected that when people talked about him they called him the Preacher's Kid. Old people and friends could call him Red. When someone called out "Red", everyone knew who was meant. He was the only redhead in the whole school.

Joe Charbonneau, as Game Warden for this part of the Shoshone and Arapaho Reservation, worked from the Big Horn River all the way up to the Continental Divide in the Wind River Mountains. His job was to keep an eye on Red as he hunted and fished all over the Reservation. Red didn't know that there was such a thing as an Indian Hunting or Fishing License and was too young to buy one anyways. His Shoshone friends told him about Reservation Game Wardens, like Joe Charbonneau. Sometimes Joe's green Ford 4X4 pickup with the red light on the roof would raise a telltale dust cloud along the gravel roads that crisscrossed the area. Red may not have been breaking any laws when he walked around Fort Washakie and Wind River

1

shooting rabbits with a .22 rifle. He wasn't sure about pheasant, duck, and sage hen shots. In the trees of The Little Wind River, with a fishing pole, Red was impossible to find. Or was he?

From Hunt's Corner to the Ft. Washakie Agency were three Churches: Mormon, Episcopal, and Catholic. Next to St. David's Episcopal Church was the new Rectory which luckily replaced the old house at Wind River Agency shortly before the mysterious fire that leveled it. Across Highway 287 from Red's new house, Red could see Alan Beauclair's houses. There were many cars and trucks parked askew, showing a progression through time. The house closest to the highway was now being lived in and the newest car was being driven. Some cars had four flat tires and were sinking into the ground. Halfway along the debris field was one that had its hood up, waiting for completion of the repairs started years before.

Rick and Alan lived in their little house with Grandma, Alan's Mom, older brother Chester, Little Rick, and Alan's goodlooking sister, Nora. Some other Uncles came and went and Red never did understand all the relationships. He had never been inside their house. Alan's Uncle Rick was Red's baseball coach. He had a really nice 1955 Mercury two door hardtop. Up to 6 Little Leaguers could crowd into Vic's car and smoke Lucky Strikes and Viceroys all the way to the games and back. Alan sometimes slipped through the two barbwire fences that lined highway 287 and walked over the gravelly weed patches to Red's house. They could start a fishing or hunting trip instantly just by walking out the door.

Alan suggested they go fishing up the North Fork of the Little Wind River. They walked into the canyon with no food or sleeping bags. The fishing was so good that they clamored higher and higher up, scrambling around jutting cliffs. They found the fish would bite anything; currants, leaves, bubble gum, and even a bare hook. The Boys just couldn't quit so they found it getting dark when they were past the point of no return.

"Let's start a fire," said Alan. "We can top out the canyon tomorrow and walk to the road."

So, they lay in t-shirts and Levis through the cold night. With no breakfast, they continued cliff-climbing and fishing upwards. Alan caught a scary strange big fish that had a whale size head on a midget body. They didn't know what it was. When the Boys topped out of the canyon they were exhausted. Walking down the sandy road, they heard someone coming. It was Joe, in his great big green Game Warden truck. For the first time, Red felt glad to see him. Alan asked him about the Big Headed Fish.

Joe looked at it, "It's a lake trout from one of the lakes up above. It got caught down in the falls and has been starving. How many fish you guys got?"

"I caught 120," said Alan.

"How 'bout you, Red?"

"I didn't catch any."

"Oh, too bad. What you doin' holding that pole, practicing?"

"It's Alan's back-up pole."

Indians could take any amount of fish they wanted. There was no point arguing about fishing limits.

Joe was checking the mountain lakes for fishermen. He didn't have time with the Boys aboard to drive to all them, so he revealed one of his tricks. At the start of a dirt trail into a lake, Joe would get out, grab some branches and sweep away all the tire tracks. Obviously, this would allow him to come back later and see if anyone had driven in since his last visit.

After setting all these tell-tales, Joe gave them a ride down off the mountain. They reeked of campfire smoke and obviously hadn't eaten or slept for two days. The fishing had been too good to quit.

*   *   *

4

A short time after this, a bright red Jeep CJ-5, without a lid, appeared at Alan's house. This was the vehicle that most excited Red, as he had just started to come into the Age of Awareness. This was the vehicle that could get them anywhere they wanted to go in the Wind River Mountains. This was a dream.

Alan told Red the history of the Jeep. It was his Uncle Charlie's. Charlie was partying and needed money. Whenever he was in this position, he sold his Jeep to Rick for $25.00. Later, he would buy it back for $25.00. This was a regular affair, so for the time being, the Jeep was available. In fact, Alan was already planning a fishing trip.

"Do you want to go up to Timmoco Creek with us?"

"Yes!" yelled Red, realizing that he didn't know where Timmoco Creek was. He knew the North Fork of the Little Wind River, the South Fork, and Trout Creek. There was Ray Lake, Alkali Lake, Bull Lake, Diversion Dam, and the Big Wind River. There was Moccasin Lake and Mary's Lake, but that was off the Reservation.

The next day, Charlie, still functioning, drove Alan, Larry, and Little Rick into the Episcopal Churchyard. Red jumped into the Jeep with his fly pole. As was their style, they had no coats, no hats, no food, and no water. Well, Red did have a pocket full of bubble gum and Little Rick was already chewing something. Red passed around his gum.

As they drove by the Old Post Office building, Joe Charbonneau passed them in his big Game Warden pickup with the red light on top. He saw Red glowing white with his T-shirt and red hair in the middle of four brown Shoshones with coal black hair. The only things the Jeep riders had in common were white T-shirts, Levis, Flat Top haircuts, and a big chew of bubble gum in their mouths. The tips of five fishing poles were sticking out behind the jeep and flicking around in the wind.

No Game Warden would waste time following one White Boy in a Jeep full of Shoshones. Joe drove east and the Jeep continued west with puffs of cigarette smoke and bubble gum breath streaming behind and mixing with the billowing dust cloud.

Somewhere up the South Fork Road, Charlie headed off to the South. They snaked around through the trees and had to four-wheel up some steep hills. Then they dropped down into another little valley with a creek flowing through it. Willows and small trees lined the water except where it cut through some rock outcrops and made small overhanging cliffs.

Charlie stopped the Jeep and they all jumped out and readied their fishing poles. Red noticed that they all had spinning poles.

"You guys all going to use spinners?" he asked, holding his fly pole delicately.

"Yep, yep, and yep." Nod. Their red/white striped and silver hammered spinners would look like a minnow going through the water and excite the bigger trout. Needle sharp treble hooks twirled behind the spinners.

Then there was some discussion about which way everyone should go. The Indian Boys proposed to send Red up to the best fishing hole and pointed repeatedly upstream where the canyon narrowed and the water was fast.

"Everyone split up, so we won't get in each other's way," said Charlie. "Red, you head up there."

Then they darted into the brush along Timmoco Creek and tiptoed along the bank to the bad holes left for them.

Red slipped into the Willows and worked his way up along the meanders. He started casting his fly upstream and letting it float along the surface over the shade covered bends in the creek.

The time of year and low water in the streams had made Red bet on flies. Spinning tackle would be okay on the lakes, but not here, he thought. He hadn't brought a single spinner with him for emergency use with a fly rod. Nor did he have worms, the universal fish catcher.

Red worked the creek thoroughly. He cast and cast. Not a single strike. He tried several different flies; a bee, a mosquito, a mayfly. Finally, he turned around and fished his way downstream to see how the others were doing. He caught nothing on the way back.

He found Charlie first, standing on a shallow bank and casting across the stream into a deep pool cut under a redrock cliff. Wham! - he caught a huge trout and reeled it in. Red went further downstream and found Alan at another cliff.

"Alan," Red whispered, "How ya doin?"

Alan put his finger to his lips and waved Red over to him. When Red got beside him he saw three huge trout lying in the shallow water with a willow fork running through their gills.

"You got those on a spinner?"

"Yep."

Red didn't know what to do. He had the wrong fishing gear for this creek on this day. It was the best fishing he had ever seen and there was no way that he was ever going to catch a single fish.

Alan wondered if Red was going to ask him if he could borrow his spinning rod. To occupy Red, he suggested he help him land the monsters. They didn't have a landing net and his 10 pound test line was overworked by these big fish. Red set his useless fly rod down and stood near Alan, who was smiling with so much pleasure that he drooled his bubble gum out into the water.

The second his pink wad of gum hit the water, a giant lunker grabbed it and disappeared. They both let out loud, "Holy shits!"

The silver flash and the brilliant iridescence of the rainbow stripe hypnotized them. Then Alan nudged Red out of his dream and said, "give me your gum."

Red took his wad of bubblegum from his mouth and gave it to Alan, who reeled his spinner in and mashed the gum onto the treble hook. Then he cast it upstream beyond the deep hole in front of them.

With just two cranks on his reel, Alan got a strike and they both saw a big flash in the water. Alan set the hook and then carefully worked the fish toward the shore. When it came into sight they both whispered, "oh shit".

Alan knew he needed help with this fish. One tail flip in the shallows and he would break the line. Red had never met a Trout this big in person. He was going to help his friend catch it. He leaned over and thought about whether to grab the fish, the spinner, or both. Alan reeled the fish into the shallows at their feet. Red kneeled down and reached for the fish. He realized that he had never grabbed a fish for someone else before and never one this big. The giant flashed silver in the sun. The iridescent rainbow stripe confused him. A fierce eye pierced into Red's eyes and hypnotized him. The hook in the big mouth was bloody.

The big trout went still. Red grabbed. The fish flipped. The hook came bloody out of his mouth and stuck in Red's thumb. Red found the fish quite slippery. Alan felt the line go slack. The fish found Red's touch undesirable. He flipped again and splashed free. Red watched it as if in a movie.

Red felt funny. He knew something enormous had happened. He looked at Alan. Alan didn't say anything. Red looked at the mixture of his blood and the fish's blood on his thumb.

"Want to be Blood Brothers?"

"Yah."

Alan grabbed the bloody treble hook at the end of his spinner and punctured his thumb. They mashed their thumbs together for a few seconds, bonding Preacher's Kid, Shoshone, and Trout.

"Brother."

"Brother."

Alan cast his spinner again and kept on fishing. Red backed away and sat down on the bank in the shade.

As the sun got lower, the fishing slowed. The other fishermen congregated at Alan's fishing hole and showed off the monsters they had caught. Red said that he should have brought his spinning pole. No one said a single sarcastic word. Four of the five were all bright and happy and joked as they scrambled over the fenders into the open Jeep.

Charlie wanted to drive up to the cliffs above the South Fork of the Little Wind River, so they bounced around the rocks switchbacking higher and higher until they got close to the giant cliffs. They got out and walked toward the very edge. The wind increased, moaning and shuddering until it shook them back and forth and made them crouch down as they approached the drop off to the river thousands of feet below. You could see for 100s of miles. Red listened to his Shoshone friends.

"The Little People live in caves in these cliffs."

"Very few people have ever seen them."

"Sometimes they will help you."

"If you believe in them."

"The Shoshones used to bury the dead in these caves years ago."

For a few silent minutes they gazed on the massive cliffs of the canyon to the west and the redbeds and sagebrush basin to the east.

"Want to go to the edge?" Alan asked Red.

"Sure!"

"Give me your hand." Alan reached for Red and they interlocked their hands. Then Alan reached uphill and grabbed Charlie's hand. Then Larry and Little Rick got in the chain. They crouched and tiptoed carefully toward the face of the cliff. The rocks were treacherous but the unpredictable back and forth hammering of the wind was more dangerous. Red held on tightly so the blast wouldn't flick him over the edge.

"You're a Thunderbird, Red!" yelled Alan into the wind, "lean out and take a look!"

Red stepped to the ragged rocky edge, tightened his grip on Alan's hand, and then leaned out over the face. He could look straight down the jagged stone and see the tiny thread of the South Fork wandering below. The gusts of wind shook him and he held his free arm out as if he was a Thunderbird.

He yelled and whooped. The wind shattered his voice and the Indian Boys thought he was yelling quits. They dragged Red back from the edge and they all sat down for a smoke.

12

"You guys going to try it?" Red asked them, looking around the circle.

"Na" "Nah" "Nope" "She-it". They indicated there was nothing to it and they weren't interested. The ceaseless wind made their smoking unrewarding. Gusts would shoot hot ashes into their eyes. They flicked the butts away. Red spit on his first.

Then they hopped in the Jeep and headed back toward Fort Washakie. The Indian Boys bragged about their big fish and how many they had caught. Everyone wondered how the Preacher's Kid liked going all day without a single nibble on his hook. He was happy though. He had been a Thunderbird. He congratulated them on their fish.

"I caught the biggest one on a Viceroy filter tip," said Little Rick.

"Aww, geez," said Red.

The next day, Red walked down to the Sacajawea Service Station to buy some Bull Durham. On the way home, Joe Charbonneau drove by in his big pickup truck and noticed that Red was sunburned a bright pink on the arms, neck and face and seemed to actually be glowing.

Ft. Washakie Quadrangle, USGS, 1951

14

Ft. Washakie, 1883

CHAPTER 2 Joe

Joe thought back to the first time he had seen the Preacher's kid with flaming red hair. It was on the Opening Day of the Fall Deer Hunt.

* * *

Joe saw two deer come over the ridge from the south. He leaned against the hood of his great big green game warden truck and swung his spotting scope toward the animals. He saw a buck and a doe pause after topping a high point. Their ears flicked in the direction of the path ahead. Something startled them and they bounced over the sagebrush down to the clumpy junipers at the bottom of the ravine. They were probably on Indian Land. The Reservation boundary wasn't fenced here on the sandstone ledges and steep foothills.

Joe suspected hunters were driving the deer in front of them. On opening day of the deer season on White Mans' Land, half the population of Lander would be out chasing the deer over the hayfields and up into the hogbacks and ridges. There was no hunting season limiting the Shoshones and Arapaho. An Indian could take game or fish on the reservation any time he wanted and in any quantity.

Joe was here now near the reservation line to see that Whites didn't hunt on the reservation.

Joe had gone to school at Ft. Washakie and Lander. He went to the State of Wyoming's Game Warden Academy in Lander. He was also a Deputy Reservation Policeman and Volunteer Fireman.

*   *   *

The 1868 Ft. Bridger Treaty had given land to the Eastern Shoshones and Chief Washakie. That was later trimmed to exclude Wind River Mountain gold fields, Thermopolis hot springs resorts, and the Riverton Reclamation Project. Now, 3,000 square miles were left, about the same amount of land set aside in 1872 for Yellowstone Park. Joe saw the potential for great humor in this coincidence and had mentally filed away some appropriate jokes and one-liners.

In 1877, the Eastern Shoshones competitors, the Northern Arapaho, were also settled on the Wind River Indian Reservation. The two tribes owned everything in common, a White Man's term. There were many sore spots. The Shoshone had settled in the western area where the streams flowed out of the Wind River Mountains. The more numerous Arapaho settled further east. Constrained and isolated with meager rations and minimal healthcare, TB and measles raged.

While the Tribes were poor they were buoyed up by Church and Government programs. Joe's Grandfather was trained to be a carpenter, but once the cookie cutter White Mans' houses had been built up and down the little valleys – there was no more work.

Then, as part of a program to make Indians become Farmers, Allotments of reservation land were granted as Homesteads to individual Indians. Big reclamation projects were begun; rivers dammed, canals cut. More hardscrabble farms came. But, it took more than 160 acres and a 140 day growing season for the inexperienced to farm in Wyoming. Some Indians sold their Allotments and their water rights to Whites.

The Wind River Canyon through the Owlcreek Mountains was a clear Indian boundary. The Reservation was surveyed with its own Wind River Meridian as a baseline. Sections and ¼ Sections had been surveyed as was customary to encourage homesteading and settlement. Local people generally knew when they were or weren't on the Reservation.

*   *   *

A movement caught Joe's eye. Someone was tracking the deer and had topped the ridge. They stopped to catch their breath before closing in on

18

the deer. Joe looked through his scope. He saw two Indians, a man and a boy, with rifles and a White Boy with a rifle. He recognized John and Beazel Hardin but — who could that White Kid be?

John Hardin motioned the two boys to go both left and right to encircle the deer. Joe watched through the scope while the White Boy went up the mountainside and crossed over to the next ridge. Young Beazel Hardin went downhill and then cut back over to the next ridge. The boys began walking toward each other, flanking the deer. All this time, John stood unmoving on the deer trail. If the two boys had successfully surrounded the deer, he would have a good shot when they ran back towards him.

The plan worked perfectly. The two boys came within a good 30-30 shot of each other and then turned south to John. They walked towards him. The deer in the ravine bolted south up the slope. "Boing, boing, boing."

"BANG!" A shot rang out and the buck fell down. Was it on the Reservation? If so, had it been there long enough to be Indian? What if the deer slept near Lander and only ate lunch on the Reservation? Did the White Boy or one of the Indians shoot it? The buck jumped up and ran away. "BANG!" Another shot rang out and the deer fell again. Off or on the reservation? Maybe there was

19

one Indian bullet and one White bullet in the deer's heart.

The three hunters met at the downed animal. They started to dress it. Joe watched John perform a certain surgery and then stand up holding a piece of meat. The two boys stood while John spoke some words. Joe knew this was the ceremonial eating of the liver – when you kill your first deer. John handed the piece of raw liver to the White Boy and he ate it. He danced around a little bit and John laughed.

Then John disappeared, apparently to get his truck, while the two boys finished cleaning out the deer. They were a mess. Joe, through the scope, saw bloodstained hands and faces. Then Joe witnessed another ceremony. The boys examined their fingers and their knives and then got into an animated discussion. Each one punctured a finger with his knife. They held their deer-bloodied fingers together and Joe knew what they were doing – they were becoming blood brothers.

The Brothers completed their task and then smoked. They milled around for a while and then decided to build a fire. Joe watched them try to cut sagebrush. It just bounced around when chopped with a hatchet. It was too tough to cut with a knife. They tried breaking it. Nothing seemed to work. Then, the White Boy found that he could worry off a branch of sage by twisting. He grabbed a branch about a foot off the ground. Then he turned backwards to the bush and began to spin around and pull. This required him to lift his legs over the branch on every rotation. He whirled like a dervish until the gnarly sage split and came free. When they had a big, springy pile of branches, they tried to light it. This proved to be nearly impossible. Only because they had cigarette lighters did they manage to get a fire started. They tried to break off dead wood rather than fresh springy wood. They finally got a fire going but it was a miserable and uncooperative thing. It had to be three times the size of a normal fire to put out any heat, the branches holding up big airholes in the pile. Gathering new branches and feeding the fire was a fulltime job. They let the fire die down.

Now, Joe knew that John Hardin wouldn't be able to drive close to where the deer was down. Sure enough, here came John back on foot. There was some discussion and then John whacked off the deer's two hindquarters.

The three hunters working together were able to lift the front half up onto the White Boy's back and he slipped into the deer's rib cage and held onto the front legs flopping over his shoulders. John and Beazel then each helped each other lift a ¼ each onto their own backs. Off they trudged – the Hunter, his Son, and their pack mule. Joe giggled and watched the gangly white boy disappear with his bloody load, "Who the hell is that?" he thought, "and where did he come from?"

Mule Deer

CHAPTER 3 The Preacher's Kid arrives in the back of a pickup truck

In 1805, Lewis and Clark visited the Walla Walla Tribe near the Columbia River. Walla Walla means "many waters". The Shoshone Indian girl, Sacajawea, helped translate the Indians' language for the Americans.

In 1836, Marcus and Narcissa Whitman, medical missionaries, started a mission six miles south of the future town of Walla Walla. In 1847, a measles epidemic killed one half of the Cayuse Tribe being attended by the Whitmans. The Whitmans and 12 others were killed and 53 hostages taken by the Cayuse.

* * *

Reverend B. served early in his missionary career on Pelee Island in Lake Erie, home of the Caldwell Band of Chippewas. This was his first assignment, where he took his young wife, Beatrice. Beatrice was a Nurse who quickly became a Missionary Aide and Sunday School Teacher. Their son, Ryan, had been born while Reverend B. finished his Seminary training. Their second son, Leslie, was born while they served the Chippewas on Walpole Island and

Pelee Island. His flaming red hair earned him the nickname of Red.

The B.'s also served in Yellowknife, Northwest Territories, on Great Slave Lake, home of the Cree and Chipewayan Tribes. Then they were in Beaverlodge, Alberta, where their third son, Douglas was born. With three boys, the B's immigrated to Michigan to the railroad crossroads town of Durand. The three sons found themselves with typical family ranking. That is; Ryan was a wonderful little boy until Red came along, Red was serene, and Douglas observed the traumas of Ryan and Red and, therefore, never got in trouble himself. Raised by a Priest and a Nurse, they never heard a negative word about anyone.

After five years in Michigan, the railroad carried them west to Walla Walla, Washington. The family was temporarily placed in the 12 story tall Marcus Whitman Hotel, the tallest building for a hundred miles. Here Red saw a waffle for the first time. He also took the elevator to the top floor and climbed the stairs up to the roof. As he stepped out onto the roof, the door swung closed and locked. Red didn't know what to do. He looked down from the parapets on all four sides and thought about yelling at someone on the street. But he didn't want to be embarrassed. Then he realized that the fire escape started on the roof. He looked it over and made his decision. He climbed down the fire escape to the second floor, where it ended. But there was a really clever slide that could be pulled down to touch the street, which he drew down, and completed his escape.

With Walla Walla's many waters, the boys needed a dog for exploring the nearby woods and all the little streams cutting through town. The B.'s bought Dusty, a blonde Cocker Spaniel, for the family. Red got a bee-bee gun. His best friend, Wally Matson, lived beside him across Garrison Creek. They waded for crawdads and eels, floated down creeks and built bridges over the creek. They played ball every day on a sandlot near his house. When they weren't playing baseball, they were chewing bubble gum. They had started buying whole cases of bubblegum baseball cards. This was so effective that Red ended up being the only kid in town with Pee Wee Reese. He had three of them and traded one for the complete Cleveland Indians starting lineup. Red carried his cards and his gum in a suitcase In 1955 Reverend B. left his position with the Episcopal Church in Walla Walla and took a new assignment at the Church of the Redeemer on the Wind River Indian Reservation, home of the Shoshone and Arapaho Indians. The family's belongings were packed and loaded on a truck. The family started the drive east in their yellow 1952 Hudson Commodore.

They left with gentle tunes on the radio - "How Much Is That Doggy In The Window?" and "Que Sera".

The boys were too young to appreciate the trip. They would miss their friends. Red would especially miss his baseball buddies. Ryan wouldn't miss playing baseball, because he pitched a ball on the field at Pioneer Junior High and the batter drove a line drive right into his eyeball. Red thought the big black eye looked tough, but Ryan retired from baseball anyways.

As they drove across the wide-open sagebrush flats of Idaho, they felt lonely. Mrs. B. tried to keep them occupied with games, like looking for the A, B, C's in correct order on the road signs they were passing. Red remembered seeing flood irrigation for the first time, where arid land came to life with a flood of water. When they got to the trees and mountains of Teton Pass, they lost their lonely.

Teton Pass on Wyoming Highway 22 was a formidable grade on a hot summer day for a heavily loaded 1952 Hudson. By the summit at elevation 8,431 feet, Reverend B. found the car struggling. The three boys were not aware of the problem. Cars were of no interest to them at that time. In the near future, when they found that all ages drove free on the Reservation, their interests changed.

The boys would always remember their first view of the Teton Mountains, Jackson, Jackson Lake and Togwotee Pass. Red didn't know then that in the future he would encounter a moose mother and calf on a stream at the base of Mount Moran. He didn't know that he would be hunting Elk with three Sioux in the Gros Ventre Range. He did remember the yellow Hudson parked in the Dubois gas station and hearing the words, "burnt valves".

Red remembered the good news that Hal Gee, from Lander, was in Dubois that day picking up old tires to recap. He would take them to Wind River. Mrs. B. filled one suitcase with what they needed. Hal rearranged the old tires in the back of his pickup truck. Ryan and Red jumped up on the pickup bed, with Dusty, and sat up against the back of the cab. Reverend B., Mrs. B. and Douglas, rode in the narrow cab with Hal. They dropped out of the mountains and passed sites that would become familiar in the future – Big Wind River, Gannett Peak, Crowheart Butte, Diversion Dam, Bull Lake, Sage Creek.

Then, they crossed the Little Wind River and passed through Ft. Washakie. Hal turned at a Conoco Gas Station where a sign pointed to the

Wind River Agency and Grave of Sacajawea. A mile closer to the looming Wind River Mountains, they saw the circle of stone and adobe buildings of the original government fort. Hal turned left off the gravel Trout Creek Road onto a dirt road – the Old Wind River Highway. In a few hundred feet they entered a cool oasis of cottonwood trees and brush that defined Trout Creek. They arrived at a little white wood Church and an adobe house. Hal drove up to the house on the barren patch of ground between the Church of the Redeemer and the adobe rectory. A lady was waiting to greet them, Mrs. Mary Barker, of the Church Womens' Auxiliary. She and her husband, Cecil, farmed near Ray Lake. White Farmers on the Indian Reservation.

Mrs. Barker's 1950 Oldsmobile was parked in front of the kitchen door, and Hal parked beside it. The cramped family climbed out of the cab and off the tires. Dusty's nose was in heaven and he disappeared for the rest of the day. The B's didn't fully appreciate at the time the full meaning of having no lawn. This was the country. No lawnmowers needed here. You parked right at your door. Red, who had dutifully run a push mower around millions of acres of church lawns, was impressed. Unfortunately, Reverend B.'s sowing of good works included the sowing of abundant grass seed. In the future a parking area was designated adjacent to the dirt road from Wind River and green grass was created in the wilderness. Red would get to mow the expanse of lawn between the Church of the Redeemer and their new old adobe house.

Hal drove away and Mrs. Barker unlocked the kitchen door and gave the B.'s a tour of their new house. She told them the virtues of adobe construction – warm in winter and cool in summer. She took them through a porch into the kitchen. Then through the living room, warmed by a 4 feet square floor furnace, a novelty to the B's. "Don't step on this furnace with bare feet when it's running," warned Mrs. Barker.

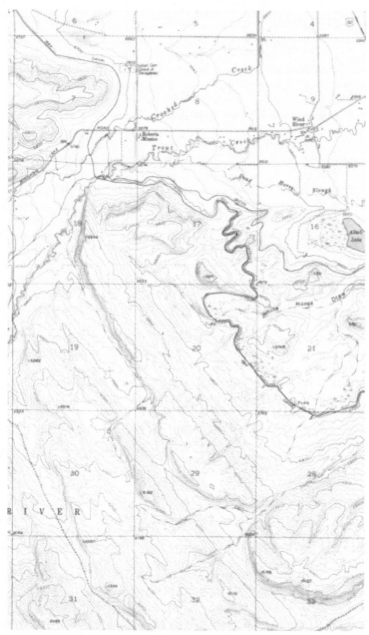

Wind River Quadrangle, USGS, 1952

Ryan and Red looked down at this black metal grate and delicately stepped on it. It was strong and just another part of the floor. Red looked down in the darkness within the furnace. It was pitch black and he wondered what was down there.

Their new old home had a long wing running to the east. It contained three bedrooms and the bathroom. Another floor furnace near the end of this wing was pointed out. Outside, near the rear of the house was an old, sun darkened wood garage that hadn't been used in many years. It was draped with cottonwood branches and willows.

Less than 100 feet away was the Church of the Redeemer. Willows and Buffalo Berry bushes choked the north side of the Church and extended east and west along Trout Creek. A giant dead cottonwood tree was midway between Church and house. A barbed wire fence separated the Churchyard from open fields lying fallow. A line of Buffalo Berry bushes defined both sides of the old dirt road that connected the Wind River Agency with U.S. Highway 287 to Lander.

Mrs. Barker told them that Ryan and Red would be going to the little white 7th and 8th grade schoolhouse where they had turned off Trout Creek Road. It was an easy walk. Douglas would catch the bus where Trout Creek Road wiggled around the schoolyard at the Wind River Agency. He would ride the bus several miles on the Ethete Road to the big Government School campus where the 1st through 6th grades were taught. Mrs. Barker said goodbye to them after her gracious welcome and tour. Then they were left alone for the first night in their new home. They had no bedding, no pots, no food, no car. They had no vices. Ryan and Red didn't even smoke when they arrived on the Reservation.

Late that first night, Dusty scratched on the door. He was let in covered with wet cow flop. He ran all over the house, excitedly jumping on them. "Phewww!" they all yelled and waved their hands back and forth under their noses.

The next day the truck carrying all their things arrived at Wind River. Several Church Members helped the family unload and carry things inside the long, army fort style adobe building. When the B.'s had settled in to this Rectory they were given a tour around the Reservation by Coach Wilson, the Priest of St. Michael's at Ethete. He also coached the Arapaho Boys' basketball team. He smiled with delight as he described how his Indian boys matured earlier than the white boys and how they ran circles around Lander and Riverton boys on the basketball court.

On a hot August day, the B.'s got in Coach's 1955 Ford, and he began racing around the dirt roads of the Reservation, oblivious to mud puddles and speed limits. The windows were all down. The tires sounded a chorus under the fenders, alternately slinging gravel or mud. A big dust cloud billowed behind them. Coach yelled out the points of interest to them. When they turned onto the paved highway to Lander, they all relaxed a little bit and spoke in normal voices. The radio played the new hits, "Blue Suede Shoes", "Heartbreak Hotel" and "Don't Be Cruel".

Ryan and Red watched the speedometer needle twisting upward. Ryan was in the back seat directly behind Coach, with the 70 mile per hour blast of hot dry air in his face. His hair streamed straight backwards. Suddenly, there was a loud "smack!" and Ryan grabbed his face, yelled, and jumped over on Red's lap. A giant Wyoming grasshopper, having escaped death on the grill and the windshield, had smashed his yellow life juices out upon Ryan's forehead.

Red held the carcass up for everyone to see and then threw it out the window.

"Can you roll up your window?" Ryan asked Coach.

"I don't think it'll happen again," laughed Coach, and he pushed further down on the gas pedal.

Fort Washakie and The Little Wind River

CHAPTER 4 How the Preacher's Kid became 7th Grade Janitor and Basketball Team Manager

When Red attended the seventh grade, the old white wooden schoolhouse at the Wind River Agency was within walking distance. It was only 1/8 mile from the adobe Rectory at The Church of the Redeemer. Red made friends with Mitchell "Freckles" Contado on the first day of school. Freckles had an oversized out of round leather basketball that he dribbled everywhere he went. The ownership of a ball made him very popular.

This ball had seen action in all the Tribal basketball games for some time. The leather slowly stretched and it was retired to the outside courts. Freckles acquired it after it had been kicked out of round by young athletes using it like a football. Being used outside, it got repeatedly wet on the dirt playgrounds of the Reservation. It continued to grow in size, weight and lopsidedness.

On Red's first September morning at the Wind River School, a group of 7th and 8th grade boys were gathered around the outdoor basketball hoop, waiting for Freckles. Red stood alone in the weed covered dirt playground as the sound of Freckles coming to school was heard. Thump – thump – thump. Freckles casually crossed Trout Creek Road, entered the schoolyard, and dribbled to the backboard. Two 8th graders, Sherman Wheeler and Layman Smart, chose their teams and they began to wear off the weeds grown up on the playground over the summer. The players occasionally glanced at the stranger standing alone by the barbwire fence.

He was dressed in a brandnew shirt, new Levis, and new black Engineer's boots. The Indian Boys wore colorful snap button cowboy shirts and Levis, with black shoes. A couple had cowboy boots. Red observed that the Shoshone Boys were very, very good at basketball.

After a few minutes of play, Sherman stopped playing. He held the ball against his leg and looked at Red. "Wanna play?"

Red walked over to the boys while they inspected his strange manner of dress, pink skin and wild shock of red hair sticking straight up in a crewcut. "Sure."

"You're on their side," said Sherman, pointing at Freckles. The game resumed.

They passed to Red a lot. As he dribbled Freckles' lopsided ball toward the basket, every bounce came back off the ground in a different direction. Red lost the ball and all the Indian Boys smiled. Soon, Red modified his dribble so that he could control the random bouncing. But, as he gained that ability and dribbled over the rough ground, he found the ball would hit a rock, root or weed stob protruding out of the ground, and go bouncing off with a mind of its own. The Indian boys smiled.

Red decided it was better to pass than to dribble. With this wisdom he found his teammates eager to pass to him for a shot. He caught a pass and everyone yelled, "Shoot, shoot!"

Red wondered if this big old ball would even go through an official size basketball hoop. He became aware of the huge weight and size of the ball he was holding and he tried to quickly evaluate the shape and angle of the backboard and the hoop. He tried a backboard shot and the ball wobbled off the board just as erratically as it dribbled. The other team laughed, and so did his own team.

Red didn't quit. He decided on a swisher. On the next pass to him, he launched the basketball right at the hoop. It wibbled towards the hoop, hit the far edge, boinged – and – went wild. Everyone smiled.

The two teams, led by Sherman and Layman, flashed around the court, dribbling expertly around each other and scoring basket after basket. Red decided to clump around in his boots a distance back from the basket and the rising dust cloud. A whistle sounded and all the children filed into Mrs. Keys 7th grade classroom and Mrs. Blooms's 8th grade classroom.

Mrs. Keys assigned desks alphabetically. Red, being a B, was far right and number 2, behind Arthur Amboy. This allowed Mrs. Keys to identify his pink face and red hair in the crowd of brown faces and black hair. At age 11, when Red started the

37

7th grade, he saw his classmates as no different than himself.

For indoor recreation, there was a tube of Pick-Up-Sticks, a board game called Dig, and some of Mrs. Keys own 45 rpm records, including Eddy Arnold singing Cattle Call. "Oooooh, oooooh, ooooh-upp-de-doo."

Mrs. Keys arranged all the desks facing away from the windows. The students saw real stone blackboards on their left, on their right and in front. Behind them sat Mrs. Keys. Pull down maps of America and the World hung above the blackboards. The students' art work was pinned near the ceiling. An American flag and a world globe stood in a corner.

The school had hardwood floors, shining with oil. A gas stove stood at the front of the room and had to be manually adjusted. It meant the room was usually too hot or too cold.

There was a third room in the schoolhouse, filled with folding chairs and used as a movie room. The films showed health information and health tips. Mrs. Keys appointed Red to be the Projectionist. He threaded the reels of tape through the machine and monitored its tension, sitting beside the machine and occasionally reaching out to increase the loop in the film. "Tick, tick, tick, tick" clicked in his ear.

Everyone was happy with the respite from the classroom. Red felt very important. The only thing he remembered from all the movies was the warning to watch out for a scar that wouldn't heal. He had no idea what that meant.

Dave Peters, the Head Custodian at the Government School, would clean the schoolhouse after driving a school bus up and down Trout Creek Road. The Government School Campus, two miles east, was 100 times the size of the little Wind River Agency schoolhouse and included housing for the single Teachers. Dave was stretched too thin with all his duties, so he asked Red to stay after school one afternoon and help with the cleaning. He showed him how to sweep the hardwood floors with oil soaked sweeping compound.

The wide red mop slid down the aisles of desks and along the walls. In the corner of each room and hallway was a large metal fire extinguisher. It was a big, heavy, brass and copper bottle with a round handle on the top. A little red hose came out from the bottom and had a little brass nozzle on the end. A metal tag riveted to the big extinguisher warned, "KEEP UPRIGHT!"

"Don't knock this over!" warned Dave, "Tipping it starts the chemical reaction that blows foam out the hose."

Dave showed Red how to erase all the blackboards and when to give them an occasional cleaning with water. The trash was taken outside to a barrel and a fire started. The desks and books were placed in proper order. Dave proposed that Red be the Official 7th Grade Janitor. Did he know anyone who would like to do the 8th grade room? Yes, he did – Freckles Contado, who lived only one minute away in one of the old adobe military houses.

Red and Freckles became Janitors at the agreed upon sum of $1.00 per day each. They went to school together, worked together, and on weekends took long hunting trips and fishing trips up and down Trout Creek and out to Ray Lake. Between their houses was a headgate damming up Trout Creek. To get to it required a zigzag course through a tangle of spiny Buffalo Berries, cottonwood trees and willows. They could swim in the deep hole made by the headgate. Freckles could borrow Lucky Strikes and Pall Malls from his Mother or Sister and the two boys could smoke them there in safety.

When Fall came, basketball season arrived. The boys were driven by old Mr. Dewey in a 1946 Ford school bus, with no heater, to the Community Hall Gym at Ft. Washakie. Basketball Coach, Bud Hand, gave every boy, including Red, a chance to make the School Basketball Team. As a little 11 year old 7th grader, he was assigned with other beginners to the coaching of Mr. Dewey. The sharpshooting Indian boys were at one end of the Gym with Mr. Hand, while Red and the other scrubs were at the other basket.

The first drill Red's group was given was shooting buckets underhand from the free throw line. How embarrassing! They dutifully lobbed shots from low between their legs and then turned to see if anyone had seen them. At the other end of the floor they were taking jump shots and floating through the air, calling out "Michaletti" the name of the big star at the University of Wyoming. If Mr. Dewey caught one of his scrubs shooting overhead, he would yell, "What'd I say?" which sounded like "Wod I say!" The boys borrowed the phrase from Mr. Dewey and would interject any argument with the final ultimatum, "Wod I say!"

"But, but, but . . . ."

"WOD I SAY!"

Some of the scrubs may have dropped from basketball due to sheer embarrassment. Red stuck with it even though he saw his skills as being at the bottom of the group. The starting five floated to the top after several practices – Sherman Wheeler, the big star who dated Becky Wagner, the head cheerleader; Ronnie Beauclair, the toughest guy in

Red's class; Jay Pat, the dribbling expert who could get around anyone; Layman Smart, who could out jump everyone; and Hank Contado, Freckles' Cousin.

The Indian Boys did run circles around the White Boys in the surrounding schools at Riverton and Lander. When the first game of the season came, the Community Hall Gym was packed with Shoshones eager to watch the sport - Riverton versus Fort Washakie. Little Grannies in shawls sat on folding chairs and lit up Camel Cigarettes with the sulphurous flash of a farmers's match. Coach Hand even suited up Red in one of the nice white and red uniforms.

The game progressed as expected. By the second quarter, Fort Washakie had won a commanding lead. Coach Hand decided he now had a safe enough margin that he could experiment with some of his unknowns – like Red. Red was sent to the scorekeeper to report in and the beeper paused the game so that he could replace Jay. The white team seemed surprised to see a white boy on the other side. The crowd of Indian Parents were surprised, maybe alarmed. The Referee, Joe Charbonneau, was surprised too. He recognized the kid he had been watching hunting and fishing around Trout Creek.

But no one needed to worry, as Red soon showed his true stuff.

The game resumed with a blast from Joe's whistle. The opposing Riverton team shot and Layman got the rebound. He passed it off to Red, who was only 10 feet away from Riverton's basket. Sherman yelled at him.

Now Sherman was the Big Shot in the School. He was the best athlete. He dated the prettiest girl. He was a natural leader, so when he said something, everyone obeyed. He was King of the Eighth Grade. Now, when he yelled at Red, Red believed him.

Even though Red was under the Riverton basket, Sherman yelled, "Shoot!" Red didn't hesitate, nor did he do a lob ball like old Dewey had instructed. He was surprised to find no defenders around him, so, with cool composure, he took a set shot at the wrong basket. And – he made it! A big gasp escaped the spectators and the scoreboard jumped up another two points for Riverton, the supposed opponent. Red found himself back on the bench for the rest of the game. Fort Washakie eventually won the game and everyone was happy. No one said a single bad word to Red.

The next day at practice, Coach Hand looked along his bench. He called Red over and made an attractive offer to Red to become the Manager of the team. He would be able to take care of the equipment, run the scoreboard, help the coaches, and travel to the away games with the Team. Red took the offer.

Sticking with the team as Manager helped him become better friends with his classmates. In the winter he got to ride in buses without heaters. He helped run the scoreboard and tally the fouls. Coach Hand appeared one day with a new basketball cleaner that he had ordered from an Athletic Supply Catalog. Red started scrubbing down one of the Voit rubber balls that they used. Red gave special effort to this assignment and he heavily slathered the ball with the chemical and buffed it down with a towel. He was going to remove every spot and make it shine. Riverton appeared at the Community Gym for a rematch. The Home Team supplies the game ball.

Red was still proudly grinding a towel on the ball when the game was ready to start. It was positively glowing as he rolled it around between his legs and buffed it. Coach held his hands out and Red flipped him the ball. Coach Hand gave it to Referee Joe Charbonneau and the game began. Riverton took the jump and passed the ball down court. The ball slipped through the player's hands and went out of bounds. Fort Washakie took possession and Jay Pat did his dribbling magic all the way in for a basket, but with a worried expression on his face.

Riverton threw the ball in and it slipped out of the player's hands. He recovered it and passed it away. It slipped out of bounds. The players began to be aware that there might be something wrong with that basketball. They rubbed their hands on their shorts. They couldn't hold on to it. Coach Hand stepped over to Red and asked to see his bottle of ball cleaner. Red, starting to feel guilty, handed it to him. The coach read the label. "Okay, I guess."

Maybe it was just cold hands. Each side was losing the ball, but not quite enough to easily determine what the problem was. This went on a little while longer, many players appearing strangely clumsy. They cupped their hands and blew into them. They wiped them off on their shirts and shorts. Finally, Referee Joe blew his whistle and asked for the ball. He felt it all over and walked over to Coach Hand. Coach felt the ball. They nodded and whispered. Then they looked at Red.

"Rub this stuff off," said Coach. Red scrubbed hard with a towel while Coach and Joe watched. Then he flipped it to Joe. It slipped out of his hands. He gave Red a look.

"Give me another ball," said Joe, flipping the shiny one to Red.

Basketball

The slickum on the ball contacted the slickum on Red's hands. It slipped right on past and bounced off David Weba's head. Red jumped after it and leapt around the floor trying to get a firm grip. The harder he grabbed the further the ball squirted away. He finally jumped on it like a football at the freethrow line.

Coach asked Red to keep scrubbing the ball. While normal basketball resumed on the court, Red wiped and wiped with a towel. He couldn't make any progress. The ball had been polished beyond perfection.

Naturally, Fort Washakie won again. No one said anything bad to Red.

The next week, at the Lander game, David Weba played the whole game, as Jay Pat wasn't there. "Where's Jay?" asked Red.

"He turned 18 and lost his eligibility," explained Coach Hand. Jay had been in the two years of Beginners Classes where students were taught English. He also repeated some years.

The next day was snowy. Red put Cattle Call on the phonograph at full volume while he swept the floor. He opened a window so that he could hear the music when he took the trash out. From the back of the schoolyard he heard the whole schoolhouse rocking with the sound, "Oooooh, oooooh, ooooh-upp-de-doo, Singin' his cattle call."

He came back in with muddy feet, holding an empty trashcan. "He's brown as a berry from riding the prairie". As he passed by the stove, he slipped and put his hand on the burning hot stovetop. "Oooooh, oooooh, ooooh-upp-de-doo!"

He looked at his hand and saw a perfect pattern of pink squares – just like the top of the stove. "Singin' his cattle call."

The following day he had to operate the movie projector with only one hand. They were watching another health film warning them not to drink too much when they were retired and went fishing. A White Man was shown, with a six-pack of beer, rowing away in a little boat from a wooden dock. A cigarette hung from his lips.

In the darkened room, the Indian Kids were bored and restless. The two Princesses, Becky and Laura, slipped out into the hall. As they left, the eyes of the older boys followed them. Red sat dutifully beside the Projector, monitoring the film loop and the whirring click of the gears.

Some other clicking caught his attention. The girls must be playing around in the other room. Then there was a loud scream. Mrs. Keys stood and went towards the door, but Red and the other boys were soon ahead of her. They burst open the door while both Laura and Becky increased their screaming. The girls had completely panicked and were shrieking and hopping about.

Red was alarmed by the shreiking. His eyes had to adjust to the light of the room before he could figure out what horrors the two girls must be experiencing. When he could see clearly, he saw that Becky was holding a fire extinguisher between her legs and both she and Laura were trying to grab the hose nozzle as it slithered about like a rattlesnake and spewed white foam all over everything. Foam covered the floor. Foam covered the girls and ran down their legs.

But, obviously, no one was hurt, nor could they get hurt. The Spectators just stood and watched while the Girls tried to control the big jets of foam. The girls finally realized that they couldn't get hurt. They stopped screaming. They looked at their audience. They looked at the foam rising in the room. They started to giggle.

Red wondered whether they had accidentally knocked the extinguisher over or if they had been experimenting. While he wondered this, Becky aimed at him and the audience and started foaming them.

CHAPTER 5 The Beer and Wine Garage at the Rectory ceases operations

Before Nicky Wheeler force traded his cowboy hat for the Preacher Kid's bicycle, the old black balloon tire one speed bike was Red's only transportation, besides his feet. No one else had a bike, so Red had to ride alone until Beazel got a 100 pound luxury bike one year for Christmas. Beazel's bike had chrome fenders, a tank with a horn and battery inside, knee-action front springs, a mirror, a headlight, mudflaps, a sidestand, whitewall tires, and a parcel rack in back. Red's bike had no fenders, no chain guard, no lights, no sidestand, and a handbrushed coat of black paint. In the winter he wrapped wire clothesline cable around the rear tire so that he could ride on ice and snow. The first time Red and Beazel went riding together was on a rainy day. They rode on Highway 287 to the Old Wind River Highway and there turned west toward Red's house. The road was muddy and soon Beazel's bike was packing mud between the tires and fenders. Beazel couldn't make it go any further, so Red, who was twice the size of Beazel, traded bikes with him. He was able to stand up on Beazel's bike and make it go a couple of hundred feet further. Then it locked up again. They tried cleaning the clayey mud out with sticks - an impossible job. Red pushed the bike over into the grass beside the road. He rolled and dragged it along until the grass mixed with the clay to make glue. The tires looked ten times their original size, with grass sticking out in all directions. They abandoned the monster and it stood up all by itself.

As they traveled along the muddy road they came to the Abandoned House. It stood completely empty along with outbuildings, a root cellar, and huge apple trees clearly planted long ago. They went to the windows and peered in. Nothing. They went into the root cellar where the door was ajar. In the cool darkness they saw a skull on the floor. Red kicked it and noticed the big front teeth. "Must be a rat."

The fields surrounding the farmhouse were overgrown but had obviously been cultivated at one time. They walked to the adobe Rectory at Wind River and called Beazel's Dad. When he arrived to rescue them in his pickup truck, the boys asked him what the story was on the old empty farmhouse. John explained that this one of the old Homesteads that predated the forming of the Reservation. The Whitemen living there went through bank panics, blizzards, droughts, world wars, and the Great Depression. Some simply walked away from their farms with only the clothes on their backs. John and Beazel slid away on the Buffalo Berry lined trail, leaving Red to ponder the rewards of farming and to smoke a corncob pipe behind the Church.

He usually smoked only in safe spots like the Trout Creek woods and the old garage behind their house. Red thought the garage would be a good clubhouse, so he painted "Beer and Wine" in large letters above the door and fashioned a crude table and four boxes to sit on. The large swinging back doors were permanently nailed shut long ago when the last Model A had backed out, probably with another Reverend in it going about his visits to the sick and the elderly. Red got a candle and put it in the center of the table. Candle stubs were readily available from the nearby Church of the Redeemer. Then he nailed up a wooden box with hinges and a padlock to keep his cigarettes in. He recruited Ryan, Freckles, and Robbie Beauclair for the club. He made a two by four barrier bar to hook across the small door so that they couldn't be bothered during meetings. With all that security he convinced the club members to also keep their cigarettes in his lockbox. Red had the only key.

A meeting at the Beer and Wine Garage behind the B.'s adobe house was called by the President/Treasurer. The President got there a little late. He knocked, the bar was lifted from the inside of the door, and Vice President Robbie Beauclair's eye peeked out at him. "What's the secret password?"

"What do you mean, I'm the President?"

"Just following regulation."

"Loose Straps, er, uh, I mean L.S.M.F.T."

"Enter," and the door swung open. Red saw Ryan and Freckles sitting in the dim candlelight. They were all smoking, even though Red had the only key to the smoke box.

Red checked the padlock on the box. It was still locked. "Where did you get those cigarettes?" he asked them.

They didn't answer, just leaned back, took long deep, satisfying drags on their cigarettes, and blew the smoke at him.

"Where'd ya' get 'em?" repeated Red. "I'm the Club President and Treasurer!"

Robbie reached out dramatically and flicked his ash into the can holding the candle. He folded his arms together and looked up at the ceiling. Ryan and Freckles made exactly the same motions while Red picked up the box and examined it. Everything looked okay.

Robbie broke first. He was too goodhearted to hold a joke too long. He laughed, "We unscrewed the hinges on back."

"Oh," said Red. He picked the box up again and looked at the hinges. Each one was held by wood screws, easily taken out with a screwdriver.

Someone made a motion that they no longer lock up all their cigarettes in the Treasurer's box and the motion was carried by a majority vote.

A knock was heard on the door. "Who's that?" whispered Ryan.

Robbie went to the door and asked, "What's the password?"

A voice outside said, "Open Sesame."

"No."

Pause. "Yogo horse."

"No."

Longer pause. Ryan whispered, "How can he know the password, all the Members are in here?"

"I think it's my cousins," said Freckles, "Hank and Harold."

The door started to rattle. It obviously wouldn't be able to withstand any kind of serious effort to open it.

"Ask them an easy question," suggested Red.

Robbie whispered loudly through the shaking door, "What's the Capital of Wyoming?"

"Fort Washakie," came the immediate reply.

"Wrong," said Robbie, and he leaned to brace the rattling door.

Red had an idea. He joined Robbie in bracing the door and whispered loudly, "You ask us a question."

The shaking stopped. There was a long pause. Then someone said, "What's pi to the 5th place?"

"Oh, that's my cousin, Harold, for sure," said Freckles.

Everyone looked at Ryan. "Er, uh, 3.141 – uh – uh – 3.141 – uh something."

"Close enough," said the voice outside, "open up!"

"Okay," said Red. He lifted the bar and opened the door. Freckles' two cousins slipped into the garage. When their eyes became accustomed to the candlelight, they looked all around like a pair of crows on patrol.

Freckles introduced them and they flipped up a couple of stumps to sit on. To break the ice, Harold reached out and bent their tin candleholder flat. Hank did all the talking. "What you guys doing?"

Freckles explained to his two older cousins about their club. His explanations were met with mild sneers. Everyone was uncomfortable. The Club

Treasurer offered to smoke the Peace-Cigarette with them, but it turned out that they were the only Indians on the Reservation that didn't smoke.

"Harold has to stay in shape for swimming," said Freckles. This warmed the visitors up a little bit and they started talking about Harold's experiences as the Life Guard at the Hot Springs. Then they talked about swimming in Trout Creek.

"You've got the only swimming hole on Trout Creek, at the Headgate," said Hank, "It's right behind the Church. "Want to go tomorrow?"

"Yes," said Ryan, who loved swimming.

"Nope, too far for me," said Robbie, who lived way down Highway 287.

"Okay with me," said Red, "if I can bring my fishing pole."

"There's no fish over there," said Harold.

"That's alright," said Freckles, "I'll fish with you, Red."

The older boys left. The Club Members moved for adjournment and then walked Robbie half way home down the Old Wind River Highway.

The next day Freckles was at the Rectory early, with his fishing pole. They fought through the brush to the Headgate on Trout Creek. The muddy water was made deep here by a big wooden dam 10 feet high and 20 feet across. The outflow below could be adjusted by turning a big iron wheel on top of the dam. It was padlocked. Red gave the usual check to the wheel, twisting it back and forth as far as the slack in the chain allowed. The two boys leaned over the center of the Headgate and looked down at the muddy water. They spat.

"A worm would work here," said Red. He glopped a big worm on his hook and cast it into the deep water. Freckles cast halfheartedly.

They heard rustling in the willows. Harold and Hank appeared on the other side of the creek. Hank said hello. Harold kept his mouth clenched. They stripped down to their underwear. Hank leaned on the Headgate and Harold climbed up into a big Cottonwood Tree leaning out over the water. Thanks to the government's intervention, Trout Creek was deeper in this area - actually a ditch.

Red watched with interest as Harold inched out over the water from a great height. Harold squatted on a branch and began deep breathing. He seemed to be meditating.

He was taking a long time, so Red spoke through Freckles as though he was an Interpretor, "Ask him when he's going to jump."

"When you goin' to jump?" Freckles asked.

"When you get those damn fishhooks out of the water," yelled Harold.

Freckles turned and yelled at Red, "When you get those damn fishhooks out of the water!"

"I know, I know, I heard him," said Red, winding in his hook.

"There's no fish down there anyway," sneered Hank, "if there were they couldn't see your worms in all that muddy water."

Harold suddenly slipped off the branch and into the water. He landed right at the deepest spot above the Headgate. The muddy water completely hid him, but not for long. He curved up under water and burst above the surface. It was amazing!

Red looked down at the muddy water and up at the Cottonwood. He decided he would rather fish instead. With Freckles in tow, he left the bigger boys and pushed through the willows, fishing up to where Trout Creek went under the Wind River road. Then they fished back down stream.

Freckles was a good sport and stayed right by his side. They worked the creek up and down. They used worms, flies, cheese, fish eggs, and spinners. They beat that creek into a froth. Every time they reached the Headgate again, they were laughed at, "How's the fishing?"

"Let's go upstream," suggested Freckles.

They crossed the road, walked by the borrow pit pond, and followed the creek beside the old ½ empty Government Agency with the stone buildings and abandoned parade grounds. Skookie Track lived there in one of the houses that had escaped the big fire in 1906. As they passed the last building and the Old Blockhouse, Trout Creek started to look more like a creek and less like a ditch. The water became clear. There were meanders with trees throwing shade over deep holes. The impassable brush of the ditch area gave way to native trees, grass, and bushes.

They started to catch little Rainbows. They caught them with worms. They caught them with flies. They tiptoed up just close enough to the stream to cast, so that their footsteps didn't scare the trout. Pretty soon they had a couple of dozen fish and were ready to go home. They sat on the creek bank and lit up cigarettes. Red had his Luckies but Freckles had a Salem because the menthol would cure his cold.

"You want to be Blood Brothers?"

"Yah."

They both took out their pocketknives. They wiped them on their Levis to clean any fish guts and blood left on the blades. Then they had a discussion on what they should cut.

"Can't be your wrists."

"No way!"

"Thumb?"

"Finger?"

"Yah, your first finger, your most important finger."

"Okay." The two touched the tips of their blades to the pads of their forefingers. Neither wanted to go first, but neither wanted to appear to be chicken. They made little tiny cuts, saw blood, and were happy. They held their fingertips together.

"Blood Brother!"

"Blood Brother!"

They stood and ambled downstream through the grass. As they walked past the old gray stone office building at the Agency, they met Hank and Harold coming out of the bushes. Red and Freckles each held up the willow forks holding their fish. In return they got dirty looks that said, "kid stuff".

A few days later, Game Warden Joe Charbonneau found a note under the windshield wiper of his big green Game Warden pickup. It read, "Too hume it mite concern. I seen the new preachers kid walking down trout crik with a fishin pole and a big stick full of Indian trout that he had cot! A frend, Anonymous."

Joe laughed at it and showed it to Tallboy and Millman at the jail. They laughed too, so the three prisoners sleeping off their wine wanted to read it. "What's so funny about that?" one asked.

"Because the author can't spell 'caught' right but he has spelled 'Anonymous' right. Joe decided to drive by Wind River. As he passed the Church of the Redeemer, he heard the sharp "craaack!" of a .22 rifle. He saw the red headed kid shooting at a target stuck on the big dead cottonwood tree beside the Church. "Hay Zeus Christo!" he muttered, and automatically crossed himself.

The Beer and Wine Club was disbanded. It really had no purpose or mission. All they did was smoke, and they could do that anywhere. Mrs. B. noticed the closure of the Beer and Wine Garage and decided to enter and do some cleaning. She later told Red she had found a can of foul smelling liquid and had thrown it away.

"Oh, no," wailed Red, "that was our spit can. We were seeing how much we could save up."

"What was in the matchbox?"

"That was our bellybutton lint."

"Oh."

Trout Creek Blockhouse, built 1871

CHAPTER 6 Sacajawea's Grave

In Durand, Michigan, Red had checked out a library book, "Red Cloud, Chief of the Sioux. He told Brother Ryan he was reading about the Sigh-Ox Indians and was quickly corrected. "It's not SIGH-OX, it's SUE!"

When the B's left Michigan for Walla Walla, Washington, Red's classmates gave him a copy of "Tom Sawyer" which they had all signed. Red wore that book out. He liked everything in it except the delightfully dreadful cemetery scene. The first time a long gray coffin was carried into the Wind River Church, Red was scared. He asked Mrs. B. about it and she reassured him, "You don't need to worry about that." So he didn't worry.

Freckles' cousins, Hank and Howard, based on their Beer and Wine Garage experience, saw an opportunity to help welcome the New Preacher's Kid to the reservation. They waited for a night with a full moon and then managed to bump into Red and Freckles shooting baskets under the yard light at the Wind River Schoolhouse.

After a few games of Horse, they played a half court game to 10. Trying to catch and dribble Freckle's oblong basketball in the halfdark gave them lots of laughs. All four were warmed up by the game and feeling pretty good.

"Red, have you seen Sacajawea's Grave yet?"

"No," answered Red as his mind raced through thoughts of Lewis and Clark, Indian Princesses, and deerskin clothing.

"Want to go?" Howard put his arm on Freckles' shoulder.

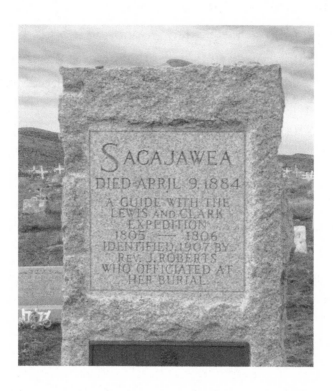

Red looked up at the moon and then pulled his pocket watch out. 8:30. He thought about the gray coffin. He thought about dead Indians.

"Unless you're scared," said Hank.

The Indian Boys watched him while he thought. "Okay, let's go."

Freckles hid his basketball in the ditch and they started walking up Trout Creek Road. They passed the houses of Bileaux, Bear, Cantado, and Mares. The Roberts Mission came into sight and then, when the clouds parted around the moon, they saw the little cottonwood trees that grew at the cemetery.

"Do you know how many dead people are out there?" asked Hank.

"100s, I guess," said Red.

"They're all dead."

"Holy Shit!" said Freckles.

Red thought about that as they came to the barbwire gate on the graveyard road. A stile beside the gate allowed them to cross the fence. Red touched down on a well worn path through the weeds. He looked around. In the moonlight he could see rusty old bedframes marking the graves. Further away were plain white crosses, and, at the edge were some granite headstones.

"Beds?" asked Red, thinking of the sleeping Indians below.

"Sure, they used to bury them in the trees."

Red thought about a skeleton lashed in a tree. "Did the birds eat the bodies?"

"Holy shit!" said Freckles.

"When they started White Man burials they took the bed they died in and marked the grave with it."

The moon came full out and Red could see "1918" on a cross at the head of a bed. Just then he heard a squeaking sound like someone sitting up on a bedspring. "What's that?"

"They say the moon makes them restless," said Howard, "the Ghost Dancers. Some people have heard harness bells and willow flutes."

"Who – who? Where's Sacajawea?"

"Hoo-hoo, yourself. She's down there," laughed Hank, pointing along the path. He led the way to the largest monument in the graveyard.

Red saw the inscription, SACAJAWEA, and strained in the moonlight to read the praise of her work for Lewis and Clark. Howard grabbed his arm and he jumped.

"That's her son, Jean Baptiste, beside her."

Red saw another oversized monument to Jean Baptiste. Moonlight reflected off the shiny angles of the monument.

"Squawk-squawk-squawk," sounded behind them like someone jumping up and down on a bed.

"What's that?" jumped Red.

"Prob'ly just the wind. Let's go see."

Hesitantly, Red and Freckles followed Hank and Harold toward the sound. They wove around through the crosses. Red realized he was walking right on top of some graves but couldn't help it. He heard harness bells tinkling.

In the newest part of the cemetery they came to an open grave with a pile of dirt beside it. A shovel was stuck in the pile. Red and Freckles stopped while Hank and Howard went right to the edge of the grave.

"Scared?" asked Hank.

"Shee-it, no," said Red. He stepped up to the grave. He heard some loose dirt fall in. It was pitch black at the bottom of the grave.

"Got your lighter?" asked Hank.

"Sure," Red reached into his Levis' pocket, pulled out his Zippo, and handed it to Hank.

Hank thumbed the lighter, got a flame, and they all peered down into the dark while their eyes adjusted.

"Holy shit!" yelled Freckles, "Is there somebody down there?"

Red tried not to jump, but his legs tightened and he automatically shot backwards into Freckles. They spun around and shot downhill towards the exit.

The two Guides began to laugh. Red heard them laughing and increased his speed. It actually sounded like three or four people laughing.

Freckles was already running ahead of Red on the Trout Creek Road but Red soon galloped past him and for the very first time outran a Shoshone.

That night, in bed, Red thought about death. He had the cold horrors. He decided to be good from now on and to quit smoking. To protect himself he repeated the Lord's Prayer over and over.

Our Father, who art in heaven, hallowed be thy name. Thy kingdom come, thy will be done, on earth as it is in heaven. Give us this day our daily bread and forgive us our trespasses as we forgive those who trespass against us. Lead us not into temptation but deliver us from evil, for thine is the kingdom, the power and the glory, for ever and ever, world without end. Amen.

Shoshone grave

CHAPTER 7 Red outruns another Indian

One morning, Red woke up to a perfect silence. He sensed something was different so he went to the window and peeked out. But the glass was covered with snow. He slid up the window and found the screen also snow covered. A few flicks on the screen cleared a peephole. Everything was white.

He quickly dressed and rushed outside to see this big snow. The flakes had been big and soft so they stuck to everything. The barb wire fences even held the snow and it clung to buildings and trees. Everything was white and the thick snow blanket damped out all sound. No cars could drive on the smothered roads. No birds flew.

He quickly got his .22 Stevens rifle and marched down the Old Lander Highway headed toward Alkali Lake. He had to step high to trudge through the deep snow. Looking behind him he saw the very satisfying trail he had forced through the snow. He remembered the warning about getting lost and walking in circles. Apparently, many lost and starved Hunters had been found lying near their earlier tracks. They had been walking in circles.

Red trained himself by occasionally looking backwards and evaluating the straightness of his footsteps.With practice he had become what he considered to be the straightest walker in the County. Sometimes, of course, he would purposely meander to switchback up a slope or avoid a cliff, mudhole, or dead cow. When he hunted with Freckles, Honch, or Beazel he waged a silent competition with them, comparing the straightness of his path to theirs.

Just a month before, Red had suffered from just the opposite kind of storm - golfball hail. He had been caught out in the open in the hail near the Wind River School. The hail started instantly and really hurt Red's head and ears. He covered his ears and tried to run for cover. However, a fence was in his way and he had to use his hands to slip through the wires. In that short time he realized how hail could drive sheep crazily into a fence where they piled up and could smother.

Now the sun came out, shining through crystal clear air and reflected by total snow cover. It blinded Red. His eyes hurt and he had to squint mightily to continue his hunt. Maybe now he would flush out a pheasant or a rabbit, but they weren't dumb enough to venture out in such deep snow.

His hunt took him across an electric fenceline. He had heard the lore about these and gave them the highest respect. The first time that he dipped under one he learned that a rifle barrel conducts electricity. Guns needed to be planned for at fences.

The Code of the West requires you to leave every gate like you found it. Don't close an open gate and possibly cut off cows' access to water. Don't leave open a closed gate and let all the Rancher's horses escape. Red avoided gates. They were the lazy way to cross a fence.

When Red approached a fence he first checked the type of post. Wood or steel? Condition? Were the wires tight or loose? A nice fat corner post could be climbed just like a ladder, but climbing a steel fencepost could cut your hands. There was also the danger of a staple pulling out and making your wire rung fail, dropping you onto the wires or top of the post. The scream "EEE-YUD-AR-ROOO!" then echoed through the hills.

If a barbwire fence wasn't new, sharp, and impossibly tight, the standard approach was to select the appropriate wire, push down with your hand, dip, and sidestep through. If hunting with a Buddy, you would put your foot on #2 wire and lift #3 wire as he dipped and pirouetted through. The Assistant also helped free snared bits of clothing

71

from the barbs. As Red got tall, he found he could straddle some top wires on tiptoes.

He first learned this trick when he approached a cow and newborn calf and learned that a cow can and will chase you.

Beazel, on the other hand, was very short. This difference was emphasized one day when Red was 1/2 way through over #3 wire and Beazel jerked it upward in a misguided attempt to help. "EEE-YUD-AR-ROOO!"

Red forgave him, of course, there being not a single revengeful fiber in his being. He did share with Beazel the ancient fables about electric fences. Could they kill you? Could they kill a cow? Where does the electricity come from? Last, but not least - what would happen if you peed on one?

Beazel thought you would get electrocuted very quickly because the spark had access to your internal organs, but Red said that was impossible because only metal was an electrical conductor.

That discussion came up every time they crossed an electric fence. On a snowy hunt one day they arrived at Beloy's electric fence on Trout Creek Road. They needed to pee so decided to use the nice deep snow to practice writing their names. Cursive writing was still taught in the 1950s in snow country. This turned into a competition to see who could pee the farthest. They were always amused to see that Indian and Whiteman Noyos looked alike. They aimed their weapons toward the electric fence.

"I think I'll do it, just to show you," said Red.

"I bet you won't," laughed Beazel.

"I'm not Chicken! What would you pay?"

"5 gums. I'd give you 5 gums to pee on this fence right now."

"Bazooka or Fleers?"

"Fleers with the cartoon."

Red thought a while, then shook his head, "No!"

"Ten gums then, or maybe you <u>are</u> Chicken".

Red was offended and showed it. "If <u>you're</u> not Chicken, <u>you</u> do it and I"ll pay <u>you</u> 20 gums."

"Okay," said Beazel, "I'll show you! EEEE-YUD-AR-ROOOOO!!"

Red started running in the deep snow and beat Beazel to the Church of the Redeemer where he sought Sanctuary. When he felt safe he snuck over to the Wind River Agency and watched Beazel mincing back to the electric fence to retrieve his boots.

Wind River Roads Building

CHAPTER 8 How Red swam free at the Hot Springs Pool and became a long distance swimmer

Because Mitchell "Freckles" Contado was Red's first best friend in seventh grade, he spent a lot of time at his house. It was an old army fort adobe with the same long layout as Red's house. Nearby were several decaying old stone government buildings. Freckles lived with his Mother - Norma, his little sister, little brother, Aunt Judy, Uncle Jaz, Grandpa and Grandma Robbins. Grandpa was the Manager of "The Plunge" - the Shoshones' Hot Springs Swimming Pool.

Every one in Freckles' family smoked. The house was always full of smoke. Their new '55 Chevy was always full of smoke, almost overpowering the new car smell. Red was soon smoking, too, whether he knew it or not. He settled on Lucky Strike as his brand of choice. He carried them in his Levi pockets until they got crushed. He carried them in his socks, until they got soggy. He carried them rolled up in the sleeve of his t-shirt, until he went home. It wasn't polite for 7th graders to be seen smoking in public. A pack cost 20 cents if you could outbluff a shopkeeper. Vending machines were discrete but scarce. When they had only a little money, they bought a sack of Bull Durham for 5 cents and rolled their own. This took a lot of skill, patience, and manual dexterity. Honch once rolled a Bull Durham so thin, that when he lit it with a great big old farmer match, it burnt all the way down in one puff, and burnt his lip.

One Saturday, Red walked along the Wind River Road, crossed Trout Creek Bridge, and knocked on Freckles' front door. Well, it looked to Red like a front door, but it really was a back door. The kitchen was in the back. All the cars parked in the back. Judy stood ironing all day long in the back. Grandma and Grandpa sat in the back and smoked all day.

Freckles let him in the door and they sat and talked in the dark living room. Freckles' Mom called him from far down the hall. He went to talk with her and was gone a little while. Red started wondering if maybe he could take a quick smoke and not get caught. The house already smelled like smoke, anyway. He took out a Lucky and lit up. Then, he rolled his levis up into a cuff to use as an ash tray – a trick he had seen someone in high society do. He puffed merrily along and flicked the ashes out of sight into his cuff.

This was all well and good until Red heard someone coming down the hall. He quickly stuck the cigarette into his cuff and pinched it repeatedly to put it out. Just in time, as Freckles' Mother walked into the room. "Hello, Red".

"Hello, Mrs. Robbins."

While she looked for some magazines in the room, Red suddenly noticed that there was smoke coming from his pants. He uncrossed his ashtray leg and pressed it against the other one. Still, a telltale line of smoke curled up and departed Red's leg at his knee. He tried to remain calm.

76

Freckles' Mom found what she had been looking for and started back for the kitchen. As she passed Red she said, "you better put that cigarette in your pant cuff out."

Red was mortified. He slithered out of the chair and slithered out the door. Then he slithered down the ditch along the dirt road home. He saw Ryan practicing sitting in the Hudson. He jumped in and practiced riding. They saw a brand new 1956 Ford approaching. There wasn't anyone in the car. When the car got closer they saw the brim of a cowboy hat on the passenger side. When the Ford arrived and stopped, they saw a tiny little Granny in the back and a little boy at the steering wheel. Granny introduced herself as Burtie, the driver as Jimmy, and the cowboy hat as Durward. Durward looked like Tyrone Power when he was 11 years old. Burtie asked Jimmy for her cane. Then Durward helped her out and she walked to the back door of the Church of the Redeemer Rectory.

"How old are you?" Ryan asked Jimmy.

"Eight," said Jimmy.

Ryan stuck his nose in the driver's window and looked down at Jimmy's feet. "How do you reach the pedals?"

Jimmy fluffed up a big pillow behind his back, scooched way forward, and held himself from

77

falling on the floor by mashing his left foot against the firewall.

Ryan looked at the three speed shifter on the column. He looked at the gas pedal, brake pedal, and clutch pedal. He looked at Timmy's one free foot. "How do you push down the clutch?"

"I use Granny's cane."

Durward nodded, pushed his hat back on his head and offered them all a Camel. He and Jimmy both smoked Camels because that was what Granny smoked. They all lit up with a farmer match. Durward pointed at the Hudson beside them, "You guys drive that?"

"Not yet," answered Ryan, "I won't be 16 for three more years."

"So what?" laughed Durward. "You can drive anytime you want here. Look at this empty dirt road you have. Just stay off 287."

This perked up Ryan's ears a little bit. They all walked over to the yellow Commodore and looked it over. Ryan opened the driver's door and slipped behind the wheel. Then they all got in. Durward and Jimmy were surprised when they had to step down into the car. They had never seen a Hudson before. Everyone on the Reservation bought either a Ford or a Chevrolet. Pickups were good for the muddy roads. They often passed by with a bright blanketed Granny sitting in back against the cab.

Ryan showed them how you could twist a knob above the rearview mirror and the outside antenna would spin down and park across the windshield. He showed them the automatic transmission lever and how there was no clutch pedal. "You could drive this easy," said Red to Jimmy.

The screen door spring squawked on the porch and the four boys quickly jumped out, stepped on their Camels and ground them beyond recognition into the dirt. They spun, twirled, and kicked away the remains as Granny walked to her car. Durward helped her into the back seat, and Jimmy took the wheel. Granny handed him her cane over the seat. Ryan and Red waved at them as they backed out and drove away on the dirt road toward the Trout Creek Bridge. Durward had his cowboy hat tilted back high so that everyone would know at least one person was in the car.

Ryan was so excited about driving that he approached his Father and asked if he could drive the Hudson. "Yes, you can back it up in the parking space."

So, Ryan started learning how to drive. He would carefully start the car, shift into reverse, put his right arm on the back of the seat, swivel his neck, look through the rear window, and press down on the gas. He would back up the 20 feet to the road. He had interpreted his permission to include driving forward to return to his starting point, so he learned how to drive forward as well as backward.

Red showed no interest in this operation. He was only interested in wading in creeks, catching fish, and shooting slingshots. He hardly noticed that Ryan had got really good at backing up and Reverend B. had started teaching him how to drive up and down the dirt roads of the Reservation.

Driving being available to anyone for free on the Reservation, it wasn't long before Ryan was ready for his first solo flight. At least for a flight without a parent present. Freckles Contado provided the solution. He reminded everyone that his Grandfather ran the Hot Springs where all the Indians swam for free. Grandpa sold tickets to the White People who came from Lander or Riverton to swim. He managed the bathhouses, the grounds, and regulated the pool temperature. Freckles told Ryan and Red that Grandpa said they could swim for free. That was exciting news, and the cooler Fall temperatures had increased their interest in swimming in the hot springs.

Reverend B. gave Ryan permission to drive the few miles to The Plunge on the gravel Ethete Road.

Freckles and Red, with their swimsuits rolled inside a towel, rode with him. The radio played Fats Domino singing, "Blueberry Hill."

Red brought his white rubber facemask with a yellow lens that he had bought in Walla Walla. Ryan drove very slowly and carefully over the gravel and made it uneventfully to the fog covered parking lot at the hot springs. Freckles led them past Grandpa at the ticket window and into the pool area. They could hardly see in the fog. They went into the mens' dressing room, put on their swimsuits, and put their clothes in a locker. Then they went to the pool and slowly stepped in.

Ryan and Red had done lots of coldwater swimming in the past. They had frozen in Lake Michigan and Lake Superior. Red had almost drowned in Peace River when someone had borrowed his inner tube in deep water. Several swimming pools in Walla Walla kept kids cool and busy in the summer. Red now tried his facemask at the hot springs. A big yellow lens covered his eyes and nose. It allowed him to see under water without any eyestrain. Freckles admired it very much but the other Indian Boys looked at it with disdain.

Two older Indian boys, Chuck Barris and Willy Bowen, gave Ryan and Red welcoming dunkings.

"Just relax," Chuck told Red, as he advanced toward him in the fog. Red relaxed. Chuck grabbed him and held him under water for a while.

Once those ceremonies were over, the two brothers swam around and explored the pool. The hot springs bubbled up from an unmeasurable depth and filled a circular lake several hundred feet across. The Tribes' swimming pool and bathhouses were built on the south edge of this lake. It was in the shape of a horseshoe and had concrete sides and bottom just like any swimming pool. One side was open to the lake and had a mossboard floating across the gap to keep the moss from floating in from the natural part of the hot springs. Lots of mineral welled up from the springs. It bubbled, steamed, and was at its hottest right in the middle of the lake. Brownish orange minerals coated the muddy lake bottom and built up a six feet high stalagmite on the north side of the lake, called "The Rock". It stuck two feet above the steaming water.

The Public was not allowed to swim outside the mossboard. The bottom of the lake had never been reached. It was dangerous. Freckles took Ryan and Red, under cover of fog, under the mossboard and out to the center. It was bubbling and very hot. Their imaginations ran wild thinking about the unknown depth of the chasm below them. They swam further to the Rock. Here they were able to touch bottom and rest. Some people would only sneak out into the natural hot springs if they had an inner tube. Ryan and Red were soon crossing the depths freestyle, although they were always super alert when they crossed the hot and bubbling center in the fog and in the dark.

The Plunge had a low diving board and a high diving board. When it was cold out and a lot of fog was coming off the water, you could not see where you were diving. One day someone jumped off the high board and landed on Freckles' Cousin, Harold. They had to fish him out unconscious. Everyone thought that he was smart before. Now they thought he was a Genius. After that he only swam underwater. Red saw him squatting at the edge of the pool in the mist like a Buddha.

"What's he doing?" Red asked Freckles.

"He's deep breathing to totally fill up his body with oxygen. Then he can swim back and forth under water without coming up."

Sure enough, Harold slipped into the water and Red never saw him again. Freckles said that Harold was the best swimmer on the Reservation. Red had seen him dive into shallow water in such a way as to not hit the bottom. No sooner did he enter the water than he curved right up and hit the surface.

On freezing winter days, the Hot Springs was especially fun. The fog was thick. They tried to sneak up on ducks that landed in the warm water. They snuck up on each other. Their hair froze instantly as they came out of the water. Then they could instantly thaw it by bobbing under water. At the end of their swims they were exhausted. Perhaps that is why the B.'s were happy to have Ryan drive the Hudson to the Plunge.

The next time Ryan drove the friends to the Plunge in the Hudson, Alan Beauclair was with them. As the rocks ticked and clicked under the car's fenders and a plume of dust billowed behind them, Alan leaned over the back of the front seat behind Ryan's ear. He looked at the speedometer and said, "30 miles an hour?"

Ryan sped up a little bit.

"35 miles an hour?" laughed Alan, "you can do better than that. Give it some gas!"

Ryan sped up some more. The other boys started to pay attention. Everyone watched the needle of the speedometer.

"Come on, Ryan," said Alan, "Faster!"

Ryan kept pressing down on the accelerator. The gravel was drumming loudly under the car. The gray cloud behind them rose high in the sky.

"Faster, faster, faster!" urged Alan.

Everyone felt the excitement of speed.

They sped along faster than they ever had. Only the sight of the Plunge in front of them made Ryan back off on the gas pedal. They turned on the entry road, parked, and the thrill seekers entered the hot springs.

The two White Boys nodded at Mr. Robbins in the ticket office. When they entered the pool, they found that Chuck Barris was there again, with his little brother, Dane. Chuck suggested that they swim under the wall of the pool buildings where you could get trapped and never find your way out. Access to this area under the floors was strictly forbidden, but a little tiny window at the bottom of the concrete pool was necessary to equalize the water pressure under the building and private baths. Chuck was going to lead them through this hole and show them the forbidden labyrinths.

Red wasn't interested in this at all. He stayed in the main pool while everyone else slipped under water and through the hole. They never came back. Red wondered what they could be doing so long. He thought he might be missing out on something. He wondered if he should go in and look around. What if there was no air in there? What if he tried to come up for air under the floor but was unable to fight through a bunch of bobbing dead bodies? What if skeletons of previous idiots littered the bottom and ensnared him as he tried to find air to breathe? But, his brother and the Indian Boys finally came back.

"Red's chicken, enit?"

"Yah, you could tell, enit?"

"You could tell real easy, enit Pard?"

Some White People from Lander were swimming there that night. Among the group were the two Lyons sisters. 11 year old Red didn't notice them at all, but some of the older boys did. When the girls stepped up the stairs out of the pool and entered the Womens Dressing Room, Chuck made another suggestion. "You guys want to go look through the hole in the girls' shower room wall?"

Red had a vague thought that this was illegal. He showed just as much interest in this as he did in swimming under the buildings in the dark, unknown corners. Several others seemed interested, though, and Red watched as they did a strange tiptoeing through the fog around the building corner and into the storage room. They never came back.

Red amused himself in the proper public pool area. He wondered what they could be doing so long. Red thought he might be missing something. He wondered if he should go in and look around. What could they be looking at? What if they made noise fighting for a peek and got caught? But, his brother and the other older boys finally came back.

"Red's chicken, enit?"

"Yah, you could tell, enit?"

"You could tell real easy, enit Pard?"

Red thought that the outer pool was where the most fun was. No one seemed to care that so many swimmers were out of sight in the muck beyond the mossboard. One of the competitions they had was to see who could swim to the Rock and back the most times. Ryan was a strong swimmer and won for some time. However, as the winter continued, and the boys sometimes swam every night, Red became stronger and stronger. He found that he could swim full speed until he tired and then tread water over the deep spots while he rested. Eventually, he could swim forever. Many nights he crossed the bubbling deep hot spot, back and forth, alone, in the steamy mists.

The big Hudson Commodore made a lot of trips to the Hot Springs that winter. They arrived quicker and quicker with every trip. Ryan learned to drive sideways on ice, snow, and gravel. At the Wind River Tribal Police Station, Officer Tallboy Taylor and Game Warden Joe Charbonneau spent all winter discussing the judicial aspects of illegal driving by White Boys on the Reservation.

Fact 1 – said Drivers were under age.

Fact 2 - said driving was on Indian Land under their jurisdiction.

Fact 3 – said driving was sometimes at extra-legal speeds.

Problem 1 – an Indian was in the car with them at the time.

Problem 2 – what if the Indian wasn't a Shoshone?

Problem 3 – what if the Indian was less than ¼ Shoshone?

Problem 4 – what if the driver was a Preacher's Kid?

"Should we go to the Tribal Council for a decision on all this?" asked Tallboy.

Joe looked down and shook his head, "Nah, then we would have to call a General Council meeting and you know what that could mean."

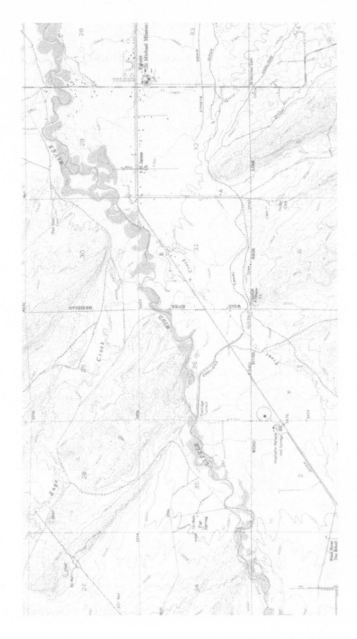

Ethete Quadrangle, USGS, 1959

CHAPTER 9 The Preacher's Kid almost makes a fortune in the Magpie business but loses all

Contados had a brand new 1955 Chevrolet. When you got inside you were overwhelmed by new car smell. Then, when everyone had lit up his cigarette with the automatic popout cigarette lighter, the crisp smell of Camels, Luckies, and Pall Malls took over. Freckles' Uncle Jaz was a Senior in High School and always jumped in the driver's seat when Freckles' family went to Lander. The first time Red rode with them, Jaz had a little fun with the Preacher's Kid. The first trick was passing on a hill. Red was sitting in the back seat behind Jaz. On a hill near Ray Lake, Jaz came up behind a slow moving car and then passed it over the double yellow line. Jaz's sister, Norma, said, "What are you doing passing on a hill?"

Jaz looked in the rearview mirror to see Red's reaction. But Red was so open to new adventure that he sat still and just watched. When he started driving himself he remembered Jaz's trick. You could see so far ahead before you got to this hill that you knew you could pass safely going up it. Good luck if a parked car or Farmer pulled out. The next trick Jaz had was making it appear like he was going to sleep at the wheel. He closed his right eye and drove with his left eye open. Then he started to nod his head as if he was going to sleep. Every once in a while, he would jerk a little bit as if he had waked up. Freckles bumped Red and pointed at Jaz.

But Red noticed that no one seemed concerned about it, so he didn't react. When he made no response and no one else said anything, Jaz "woke up" completely and drove sanely the rest of the way into Lander. On the way back home to Wind River, Jaz saw a Magpie standing by a dead rabbit on the road. He pushed his foot to the floor and the Chevy hurtled down the narrow Highway 287. Even though Jaz got the car going over 100 miles per hour, the Magpie flew safely away.

"That was dumb," said Freckles' Mom, "magpies never get hit by cars."

"I know," said Jaz, watching Red in his rearview mirror. "Hey, Freckles, it's just about Magpie Season, you know. You should take Red with you."

"Want to make some money getting magpies?" asked Freckles.

"How much do you get?"

"10 cents bounty each. They sit on the cows backs and peck, so the Government wants to get rid of them."

"You shoot 'em?"

"No, we take them out of their nests. You'll see."

Red calculated how much 10 cents per bird would be worth. You could buy a Snickers or 3 Musketeers or Mars Bar or Hershey Bar for 5 cents. You could buy a Coke, Pepsi, 7Up, or Hires Root Beer for 10 cents. You could buy a box of 50 .22 short bullets for 45 cents or 65 cents for long rifle bullets. A hamburger in a restaurant was 35 cents and a new pair of Levis cost $3.00. A sack of Bull Durham cost 5 cents and a pack of Camels was 20 cents. "How many do you think we'ld get?"

"Hundreds!"

The next morning, Red went over to Freckles' house to go on a Magpie hunt at the prearranged time. Freckles had his .22 rifle. Hank was there holding a burlap sack. "Jaz gave us a sack."

"Where is Jaz?" asked Red.

"Oh, he's not going with us," said Freckles. "He can help us sell 'em down at the Agency though, if we want. Let's go down by Amboy's."

The three boys walked along the Buffalo Berry Bushes that lined the Old Wind River Road. The Magpie nests could be seen a long way away because they were as big as an Eagle's nest. Why, Red wondered, would such a smart and wary bird build such a conspicuous nest? They walked up to the first bush that had a nest in it, about 8 feet above the ground. Three boys with a .22 guaranteed that no big Magpie would come anywhere near them while they robbed the nest. A magpie even knew exactly how long it took a person to aim. They sat still to tease you and then flew off in a floppety up and down zigzag that made them impossible to shoot. They were smarter than a crow, wore nicer clothes, and were better at public relations because they didn't caw-caw-caw and wake you up in the morning.

"You're the tallest 7th Grader and have long arms, Red," said Hank, "climb up and see if there's anything in there."

Red was proud to make his first climb up to a Magpie nest, so he looked for a way to get started on the Buffalo Berry Bush. The bush was about the size of a small two-story garage. Red pushed into the branches and found out right away why the Magpie built his nest in the Buffalo Berry Bush – thorns! Lots of them. And spiky branches! Lots of them. The branches bent with his weight and forced him to zig and zag his way higher.

"Just weave around the stickers," prompted Freckles.

Magpie

Buffalo Berry, *Shepherdia argentea*

"Climb up the big branches," said Hank.

Red's T-shirt gave him no protection from the thorns. They drew blood. When he had crushed through the Buffalo Berry Bush for a couple of feet he realized there really wasn't much of any kind of trunk that you could climb. It was all just a big crunchy mess of stickers and stabbers. He looked up at the big nest of dry branches and twigs.

"Kinda lay on the branches and roll upwards," coached Hank.

"Remember, it's 10 cents each," encouraged Freckles.

Red got at an angle and used his arms and legs to kind of spider walk up to the nest. Every move clawed and stabbed him. The old dust from the road sifted into his eyes, ears, nose, and down his back. He got to the nest and looked in – "three chicks!"

"Toss em out," said Hank. Red reached in the nest and plucked the chicks out one at a time and threw them clear of the Buffalo Berry Bush. Red knew he was doing the right thing because the Government was paying a bounty on the birds. Hank slipped them into the burlap sack. "Come on out."

So Red happily fell crashing down from the nest and bulldozed his way out, a chore that was almost as bloody and as difficult as going in. He dusted himself off and they marched further along the road.

"You're real good at that!" gushed Hank, the bag holder.

"Great!" said Freckles, the .22 holder, slapping Red on the back.

"Thanks," puffed Red, the Buffalo Berry Bush Climber for the day. He realized there was a lot he could learn from his Shoshone friends.

When they reached the end of the bushes along the Old Wind River Highway, they walked back towards Trout Creek. Just past the corner at Amboy's, they saw a big green Game Warden Truck coming their way. Joe Charbonneau slowed and stopped. He saw the gunnysack, the .22 and the lacerated Preacher's Kid. "Whatcha got in the bag?"

Hank stepped close to Joe's door and opened the bag so that he could see inside.

"Magpies," said Joe. He looked at Red. "You got your Reservation Magpie License?"

"Er, uh, no," stammered Red. He looked at Freckles and Hank, who were smiling.

"You're just climbin' I guess?"

"Yes, Sir," said Red.

"Will you two vouch for this guy?" asked Joe, pointing his thumb at Red.

"Yes, sir," chorused Freckles and Hank.

96

"Well, okay, if you're just climbing." Joe slipped the truck into gear and drove away. The three magpie hunters continued toward Trout Creek.

They zigzagged up the creek, going from nest to nest. Red was getting pretty thrashed as the day grew late. Hank said they had about 30 birds. Wow, that was $3.00 worth! They called it quits and walked back down the creek towards home. At the bridge the boys split up and Freckles took the gunnysack home with him.

Red was a mess. He healed over the next few days and forgot about the birds for about a week. When he dropped in on Freckles he asked about their magpies. Freckles said, "Oh, Jaz said they started to rot and he had to throw them away."

"Oh," said Red with a suspicious look. Red later went to a Round Dance at the old wood Community Hall. They served a Buffalo Berry stew to everyone there. Red was still White back then but they gave him a bowl without anyone having to vouch for him. Jaz was there all dressed up in a brand new pair of Levis.

*   *   *

One fall day, the floor furnace in the B.'s adobe house came on. Red jumped out of his bed and walked into the living room. He smelled burning dust at the same time that he stepped on the hot

97

grate and burnt a bunch of little square marks on the bottom of his foot. "Ouch, ouch, ouch!" he yelled as he sat down and rubbed his foot. He looked down into the floor grate. The hot, dusty smelling air blasted his face and dried his eyes out. He couldn't see anything down there in the dark and he wondered if all that dust could start a fire. He hopped into breakfast with the family.

"Good Morning, Red," said Mrs. Barker, who was sitting at their table.

"Hello." Red sat down, put a little butter on his plate and then rubbed it on the bottom of his burnt foot. Big Brother Ryan and Little Brother Douglas watched him out of the corners of their eyes.

Mrs. B. told Red that Mrs. Barker was going to show them how to make Buffalo Berry Jam. "The bushes are all around here."

"I know," said Red.

"And the first freeze sweetened them up," said Mrs. Barker, "want to go with us?"

"Of course," sighed Red. He finished eating, hopped to his shoes, and joined the two Ladies, Ryan, and Douglas outside. Mrs. Barker had brought a canvas tarp, two pails, and a long stick. They walked down the road to the first Buffalo Berry Bush. A magpie perched in it saw Red and flew away. Red approached the bush and started to apply his expertise at thrashing into it to reach the berries.

"Whoa, whoa!" said Mrs. Barker when she saw Red's technique. "Watch this." She laid the canvas tarp out on the ground underneath the bush. Then she used the stick to whack the branches. The berries popped off and fell on the canvas.

"Oh." They picked them up and put them in the bucket. There might be something Red could learn from White People too.

Later that day he walked over the Trout Creek Bridge to visit Freckles. Jaz was there still wearing his brand new pair of Levis.

Ft. Washakie Quadrangle, USGS, 1951

Ft. Washakie, 1883

CHAPTER 10 Red makes a little money and wears an Indian Necklace

When Freckles and Beazel taught Red to shoot a .22 rifle, they unleashed an obsession. They would roam Trout Creek shooting rabbits, pheasants, and anything else that moved. They walked out to the desolate Alkali Lake, shot at curlews, and went home with big white mud balls on their feet. The

101

alkali there had risen to the surface as a result of the government's irrigation program. Whites who had bought Indian Allotment parcels were using flood irrigation with Indian water to raise hay. Now, they were having their turn suffering. However, the alkali bog at Dead Horse Slough saved Jay Mundy's life when he rolled his new Chevy at 100 miles per hour in the slough with four of his buddies in the car. They had been drinking in Lander. It was common knowledge that a drunk would always survive a car wreck because he is relaxed and doesn't go all stiff during the crash. Red tried to remind himself to be always ready to relax if he saw he was getting in a wreck.

.22 bullets would sing when they ricocheted off the water at Alkali Lake. Red spent a lot of time worrying about where they might go. He occasionally heard bullets flying overhead and smacking into the tops of the cottonwood trees. Red asked his parents for a rifle, but they said no. Red saved his money. When the family went in to Lander to shop on Saturdays, he would go to the Lander Sporting Goods store and stare at guns. They were on display on every wall from floor to ceiling. In glass cases were pistols, holsters, bullets, elk calls, knives and all the equipment a Hunter might need. With elbows on the glass, Red circled and circled the store. He saved his money until he had the $14.00 necessary to buy a single shot Stevens .22. He bought it for himself for Christmas and wrapped it up. When he opened it up on Christmas morning, his parents couldn't deny him. He had also received a box of .22 short bullets from himself, so he immediately went out in the snow and began practicing.

Besides worrying about ricochets, Red was extremely careful about fire. He made sure his cigarette butt was completely out and he doused water on a campfire until his buddies yelled at him "Hurry up and come on!" He opened his rifle bolt to cross a fence and unloaded the bullets when he was in a car or inside a house. He decided to use the big dead cottonwood in the back yard for a safe target backstop. Some other kid in the past had attempted to chop it down and had made a few cuts about three feet high. This was the type of mark every tree around a campsite in Yellowstone Park had. Millions of boys chopped for a while on millions of trees until they found out it was hard work or got a blister. Red used this hole in the tree to set his targets.

The gift of a single shot rifle showed great wisdom. Red had to make every shot count. If he missed a rabbit, he couldn't just pull the bolt and shoot again. He had to painstakingly take a single shell from his pocket and put it in the chamber. If his fingers were cold it took even longer. He practiced with .22 shorts that cost 45 cents for a box of 50. If he wanted big power for hunting he might buy Long Rifles for 65 cents a box.

Red had paced off 100 feet from the cottonwood. His shooting position was between the back door of the adobe Rectory and the Church. The huge old cottonwood made an excellent backstop. Even if a bullet could get past it, there was nothing to hit in the big empty field beyond.

Red was plinking at a target one day when Russ Crosman, the old Carpenter who built all the houses at Hunt's Corner, came by. He and his wife, Betty, were church members.

Red paused his shooting as a courtesy while Russ walked from his blue 1955 Ford pickup to the Rectory, "Hello, young man," he said to Red. He was wearing a billed watch cap, bib overalls with a carpenter's pencil in the pocket, and lace up work boots. His face and hands were weathered and wrinkled. Honch later told Red that Russ had cut off just about all his fingers and thumbs at one time or another at his lumber mill or on his table saw.

"Hi," smiled Red, "want to take a shot?"

Russ stopped in midstride on his way to the Rectory door. He thought a while, "Yes, I'd like that." He walked over to where Red stood marking the official firing line. Red carefully handed him the Stevens single shot, with barrel down, and showed him the cocking pin on the back of the bolt. Then he pointed at the target, "There's a flashbulb sitting in that tree."

Russ cocked the gun and drew a sight, showing the smoothness of many years of experience hunting in the Wind River Mountains for deer and elk. He shot. He hit the bulb. They both smiled. Russ handed the rifle carefully back to Red. He continued shooting while Russ visited Reverend B. When he walked out the door to leave, Red offered him another shot, which was declined with a smile and a flick of a grisled hand. Red paused shooting until Russ had driven out of sight.

Russ Crosman had delivered an invitation for dinner to the new Preacher. On Saturday night the B.'s went to the Crosman house and had a feast prepared by Betty. All her vegetables came from her own garden. She took them into the back yard and showed it to them. Red was given a carrot fresh from the ground. He wiped off most of the dirt. It was the best carrot he ever ate. They walked through the tall corn. The whole yard was one big garden. A big waterbird sprinkler circled around making big and little sprays of water and made the area cool.

Everything in the Crosman home was made of wood. The furniture was hand made by Russ. He showed them his woodworking shop in their garage. Before they left, Russ asked Red if he would be interested in making a little money helping with some carpentry work?

"Yes!" said Red. He was eager to learn and eager to continue the regular cash flow he had received as Janitor of the 7th Grade.

In a few days, Russ called him about the job he was currently doing down at the big Government School. He was remodeling the Unmarried Teacher Apartments and needed help with the sheetrock. Red agreed to help. Every morning Russ would pick Red up at Wind River and they would drive Russ' Ford pickup to the school. Russ always wore Red Wing boots, bib overalls and a cap. Red knew bald men often wore caps full time. Red's Mother said, "Hats will make you bald."

Red helped Russ unload the sheetrock and stack it inside the apartments. Then, the hard part started. The sheetrock had to go up on the ceiling. They had to muscle the heavy 4 feet by 8 feet sheets up on ladders, hold them up with their heads, and start nailing. When they had enough nails in a board, they

106

could relax their heads and necks and finish nailing the entire edge of the board. The trick was for each of them to smash their heads upward at the balance points. Russ pressed with his cap, Red with his full mop of red hair. It was clear why Russ needed help for this job.

The days went by. Russ' hat never left his head. Red's head started to get sore. He rolled it around to fresh scalp and made more sore spots. He figured Russ had built up a big callous under his cap after many years of sheet rocking. Red wasn't going to complain.

One apartment after another got a new ceiling. Russ was doing all the ceilings first. Red's skull got rawer. He wanted to ask how many more apartments they had to do. He checked to see if any of his hair was being torn out. He checked to see if he was bleeding.

Then, one day at lunch, Russ took off his hat for the first time. They were sitting on the floor and had just opened their lunch pails. He set the cap upside down on the floor. Red looked at it. Inside the cap was sewn a big spongy chunk of foam rubber. Red looked at Russ' bald head. He looked back at the cap. Red smiled and stayed on the job.

When the apartments had been gutted, some lead sheets were taken out that had wrapped the

107

electrical wiring. Red asked if he could take some of these to make fishing weights. Russ agreed, as the lead was simply going to be thrown away. When Red got the lead home he realized that the sheets were just about the same thickness as a quarter. Hmmm? He wondered what that could mean? Hmmm. He took a quarter out of his pocket. Hmmm, it was the same. Hmmm.

Red wondered if he could cut out a circle of lead the same size as a quarter. Hmmm. He tried it. Yes, he could. A knife could cut it and a file could dress it to the right size and shape. Hmmm. He cut out another one. Hmmm. He wondered what he could do with them. Hmmm.

He showed his coins to Beazel. Beazel also started to wonder what they could do with them. Hmmm. The boys took some into Lander with them one Saturday and looked around town for a while until they found that the cigarette machine in the Fremont Hotel had recently increased its price to 25 cents. Hmmm. Red and Beazel, with guilty hearts, slipped a lead coin into the machine and pulled the button. Out popped a pack of Luckies. Hmmm!

Red thought that maybe that was illegal. But, they had more coins. Maybe they were just lucky that the coin had worked. They tried again. It worked again.

The boys felt guilty. They thought about police. They thought about prison. Hmmm. They walked along Main Street. The guilt was growing stronger and stronger in their hearts. They went into Hallam Chevrolet. There was a candy machine by the doorway into the garage. Hmmm. They looked at each other and selected their choice. Clunk, clunk, the lead coin fell through and came out the reject hole. They tried again. No good. They looked around to see if anyone was looking. They put the coin in again. Clunk, clunk, it made a lot of noise, it seemed. Then, a Mechanic in the back room yelled as loudly as he could, "Hey, you kids stop trying to slug that machine!"

Red and Beazel nearly shit their pants. They were already full up to their necks with guilt and ready to pop. They levitated sideways 10 feet and scurried out the front door with their heads down and their hands in their pockets. They didn't speak for a long time while they beat their retreat with their tails between their legs. They wondered if the police would be called. Red and Beazel were so scared they couldn't even talk to each other for a couple of days. That was the end of Red's career as a counterfeiter, his only punishment being his exposure to lead, which, happily, wasn't a hazardous material back then.

The .22 bullets Red handled so much were also lead. He had amazed Ryan with his thoughtful gift selections that Christmas. Ryan had gotten a pair of speed skates that he had always wanted. The blades were 2 miles long, it seemed to Red. He didn't know how they could navigate the crunchy rippled ice of Ray Lake or the Little Wind River. Ryan had also gotten a gift from Layman Smart, his 8th grade Indian Wrestling Partner. Layman was a great Artist as well as a great athlete. He drew horses, elk, and deer. He made his own Dance costume with beads, feathers, and bells. He worked in leather and silver. His gift to Ryan was a metal shield on a leather thong. It had the initials R.J.B. on it against a silvery background. A "Y" crossed the shield and on it was engraved FORT WASHAKIE, OYW. On the back it was signed, "By Layman Smart".

*　　*　　*

Honch was a Boy Scout and his big brothers, Will and Larry, had both become Eagle Scouts. Honch went to the Scout Summer Camp at Cody every summer. During the Christmas Holiday, Honch invited Red to a Boy Scout Meeting at the Fort Washakie Grade School. Honch and Red walked to the school for the meeting and went into the kitchen in the rear of the building. Several other boys were already there. The Scoutmaster, Willard Perry, came

110

in and asked them to all follow him into the front room for the meeting. Honch and several others left. As Red started to move, a little Indian boy jumped up on him and grabbed him in a neck hold. The move caught Red totally by surprise as he had never seen this boy before and had no idea why he would jump him. In addition, the boy was so much shorter than Red that his feet couldn't reach the ground while he maintained a neck lock on Red. Red didn't feel in any hurry to fall down with this little kid trying to crush his neck, so he grabbed him and held him up. Everyone else had left the room. Red appraised the situation. The kid's arm lock hurt, but it couldn't go anywhere. Red wondered what the heck he was doing. He wasn't punching or kicking, just locked into a neck hold. Red didn't know what to do.

Red held the kid in his arms and waited. His neck hurt. Finally, Honch came back into the room and said, "What the heck are you doing?"

"This kid's got me in a neck lock and he won't let go," answered Red.

Honch came close and looked the situation over. It didn't take him long to come to a solution, "Punch him."

Red thought about that, but it wasn't logical. Why would he punch a Stranger? Why would he punch

111

someone he didn't even know? On the other hand, this kid had been trying to crush his neck for about 5 minutes now and gave no sign of tiring out. Red got an idea. He simply carried the kid with him. Honch followed and they went into the room where the Scoutmaster was telling them about his plans for the year. Red and his necklace got lots of strange looks during the meeting. He stood there holding the kid. The kid crushed Red's neck furiously. Red thought that everyone else in the room thought that they were just playing. They weren't – this kid was trying to hurt him. Red held him and waited.

The point of absurdity arrived. Red wondered if he would have to carry the kid home and eat dinner with him while being choked. But, finally, the kid let go. Red set him down gently. The meeting ended. Honch and Red went home. Red never joined the Boy Scouts, even though he had worked his way up to Bear Badge and two arrowheads in the Cub Scouts in Michigan.

Agency Building at Ft. Washakie

CHAPTER 11 How Red and Honch escaped a car full of drunks and sat in for Tribal Elders

When Robbie Beauclair and Red walked around the triangle formed by Hunt's Corner, Fort Washakie, and Wind River, they carried their slingshots. As they walked they kept an eye out for the best sized rocks to shoot and loaded up their pockets with quality ammo as they went. At any telephone pole, one of them might declare a contest. Each would take a turn shooting at the pole to see who was the most accurate. The telephone and power lines followed the old dirt Wind River Highway, not the newer Wyoming State Highway 287. Robbie said that Dude Sawyer used to shoot at the glass wire insulators and break them. This sounded illegal to Red.

Robbie taught Red how to make a good slingshot. They had walked into the cottonwood trees around Trout Creek and selected good Y shaped branches. They cut them out of the tree with their pocketknives. Then they whittled a little circular notch just below the two fork ends. These would help secure the rubber bands. They rubbed the fresh cottonwood juice off their knife blades.

"Wanna be Blood Brothers?"

"Yah."

They looked at their fingers, trying to see where they could make a cut and do the least damage. "Little finger?"

"Nah, too little."

"Thumb?"

"Nah, we'll need it for shooting."

"Big finger?"

"Yah." The boys couldn't show fear by hesitating, so they both managed to get a drop of blood showing on their big fingers. Then they held them together for a minute.

114

"Blood Brother."

"Blood Brother."

The Brothers struck out walking crosscountry past the Headgate and the apple trees. They waded Trout Creek and struck the Trout Creek Road near Kicks' House. They continued to Hunt's Corner and went to the Sacajawea Service Station where Conoco gas was sold. Chuck Chipman was working that day and Robbie asked him if he had any old inner tubes.

Chuck knew exactly what Robbie was looking for. He went to the tire changing machine and picked up a couple of old tubes that had been damaged beyond repair. He gave them, one black, one red, to Robbie.

"Thanks," said Robbie, and motioned Red to follow him outside. They set up a workshop on a junk car behind the station.

Robbie handed the black tube to Red and then used the red tube to cut two 10 inch long strips about ½ an inch wide. "This red tube is real rubber, so it stretches more. The black tubes are synthetic rubber. They aren't as good as the natural ones, but they last longer."

Red copied every move that Robbie made. The long rubber strips were tied with the knot kept out of the line of sight through the forks. Robbie pulled

115

a piece of old, worn leather out of his pocket. It looked like part of an old shoe. He cut out two little rectangles and handed one to Red. Then he showed him how to knife little holes through each end of the leather strip. The rubber bands went through the holes and tied tightly. They now had complete slingshots.

They picked up some rocks and loaded. They aimed at a telephone pole. "Whack!" Robbie hit it. "Ouch!" Red hit his thumb. Robbie reached over and bent Red's thumb down out of the line of fire. "Try again and aim high."

Red shot again. He missed his thumb and the pole. He kept practicing. Cans and bottles in the ditch were set on the top of fence posts as targets. All the boys were armed as they walked up and down the dirt roads in the summer. Red noticed the different preferences in slingshot design. Some liked big cottonwood forks, some liked small willow forks. Some had short rubber bands, some long. Everyone preferred red real rubber bands, but often had to do with black ones which could suddenly rip or come untied and smack you in the face when they broke. When not in use, the bands were twirled around on the fork and the weapon stuck in the back pocket of their Levis.

No magpies would come close to them. Red knew from his previous experience in the Magpie Business that the Magpies knew that the Government had a bounty of 10 cents on their heads. Officials were still convinced that Magpies sat on the backs of horses and cattle and pecked them to death. Red thought maybe they were just eating bugs and worms or keeping their feet warm. He admired the Magpies' tuxedoes and the fact that they never got hit by a car.

After a day of walking and shooting in late summer, Honch suggested to Red that they go to the Annual Sundance. "Oh, yah!" said Red, thinking about all the Adventure that lay ahead. They left their slingshots at the Wind River Rectory and started walking down the Old Wind River Highway toward Fort Washakie. They passed their Schoolhouse and Brickmans' house. They saw Vernon's Motel over to their right. They were within earshot of the Sundance Grounds and they could hear the booming of the big drum and the singing.

Then they heard a car driving up behind them. It was the green 1949 Ford Tudor belonging to Willy Bowen. He and his friends were three years older than Red. Honch and Red stepped aside to let him pass. Willy slammed on his brakes and skidded to a stop beside them. He slung open his door and a blast of smoke poured out of the car. He leaned forward against the steering wheel and grabbed the back of his seat. He flipped it forward, making room to jump into the back seat. "Yoush guys wandsh ya ride? Ch-yump in."

Willy slurred his words, his eyes rolled and his head bobbed loosely. Red looked at the other boys in the car and at the narrow passage to the dark and dangerous rear seat. His imagination raced ahead completing a variety of scenarios that might be played out if he and Honch got into that car.

"Shawl right, shump in!" slurred Willy.

The two white boys weren't moving. Honch spoke first, "No, thanks, we're just going a little ways."

"Shokay, wheel take you to the Shundance."

"No thanks," said Red.

Then Willy straightened up and said, perfectly clearly, "We're not drunk, just fooling you. Come on, jump in." And – Willy really was sober and clear eyed.

Chuck Barris and Chester Beauclair leaned over and smiled out of the car. They were obviously stone cold sober also. But Red and Honch stuck with their decision, standing well clear of the car. Willy gave up, closed his door and drove off, "Okay".

Red and Honch continued walking to the Sundance Grounds. Soon they could hear the tooting of the Dancers' whistles in the Sundance Lodge. They walked through a sea of cars, filled with Shoshone families. They passed some concession stands and said hello to some of their school friends. Several joined them. They saw Ryan, Alan, Chester and Layman there. They joined the group.

The round Sundance Lodge was newly built every year out of freshly cut Cottonwoods. One big trunk was at the center. Smaller trees radiated out from it to form a roof. The outer circle was supported by smaller cottonwood trees and the entire outer wall was filled in with freshly cut saplings, branches, and leaves. The smell of the fresh cottonwoods was powerful. Near the one East facing opening was a big fire. Next to it was a giant drum with five or six old Shoshone Men pounding on it and singing, "Waah, yaah, yaah, aaaah, aaaah, yaaah-ah, waaah-ah, yaa-aah!"

About 20 young men danced to the music, a basic two feet hop timed with the beat of the powerful drum. They started near the wall of the Lodge, where their sleeping blankets for the three days and nights were laying. They danced toward the central Lodge pole as they blew their whistles. "Tweet, tweet, tweet." When they reached the center, they danced backwards to their starting point at the outside wall.

Red was fascinated. He slipped all around the Sundance Lodge, forcing aside the branches and leaves to look inside. He listened to the repetitious beating of the big drum and wondered what the wailing words of the Singers meant. He breathed in the smoke from the big fire. He smoked a couple of Lucky Strikes. The Dancers and the Drummers took a break. Red joined up with Ryan, Freckles, and the pack of 7th and 8th graders strolling around the Sundance Grounds. There were pairs of young girls walking around, and young men talking quietly. The older Shoshones sat in their cars. Little kids ran to buy soda pops and candy. Joe Charbonneau was in his '57 Chevy but didn't wave at Red when he walked by. Red saw lots of Indians he had never seen before. Some may have been from other Tribes and other States. Sundance was the high point of the year and everyone was there.

Through an open car window, a radio played Johnny Preston singing "Running Bear."

As groups watched, and walked, and smoked, and talked, and spun off into new groups, the hour grew late. The families with little children drove away, then the Romeos finally retired. Past midnight, the Elders who chanted and played the drum left. The

Dancers got under their blankets and went to sleep. But, the B. Brothers' Pack was still high on Cottonwood and Tobacco smoke. They were unsatisfied with the silence.

So-uh, someone got the bright idea that maybe they should go into the Sundance Lodge and play the giant drum themselves. Why not? They looked all around. The Dancers were asleep. The Drummers were gone. Only a few cars sat empty looking at the far edges of the field. Led by the big 8th graders, everyone followed Ryan and Layman into the Lodge. They sat down on the stump seats. They picked up the drumsticks. They tapped the huge drum. "BOOOM!" It was good! They burst into song, "Waah, yaah, yaah, aaaah, aaaah, yaaah-ah, waaah-ah, yaa-aah!"

They gained confidence and volume very quickly. Red looked around. This looked wrong somehow. No one seemed to mind. The Dancers lying about them didn't throw rocks at them. There were no dirty looks. They pounded harder. They chanted, "Waah, yaah, yaah, aaaah, aaaah, yaaah-ah, waaah-ah, yaa-aah!"

They thought they sounded pretty good. They howled plaintively. They soared from basso to falsetto. Their voices cracked. They pounded harder. Red looked around but no one tried to stop

121

them, perhaps because most of the young drummers were Shoshone. Technically they were part Shoshone. Both African American Soldiers and White Soldiers had been stationed at Fort Washakie, so the drummers ranged from 1% to 100% Shoshone, Arapaho, Sioux, African American, Mexican, White, Irish, and Episcopal. Many with 1950s style haircuts were obviously Flatheads. Chief Washakie's father was allegedly Flathead.

There wasn't a single person outside the drum circle moving. Red knew that the Dancers were now all awake, but they lay still. "Waah, yaah, yaah, aaaah, aaaah, yaaah-ah, waaah-ah, yaa-aah!" The Pack pounded and wailed until they grew tired. They finally set down the drumsticks. It was in the wee hours and getting cold. With hands in pockets, they walked out of the Lodge and headed for their homes. Not a single complaint was ever made about their performance.

On the third and last day of the Sundance, a Tourist car with out of state license plates pulled up beside Honch and Red as they walked along Highway 287. "Is this the road to Lander?"

"Yes, it is," said Honch, "it's about 15 miles."

"Is this the Reservation?"

"Yes," said Red, "The Wind River Indian Reservation. Shoshones and Arapaho."

"Are there lots of Indians around here?"

"Oh, yes, and we expect an attack tonight." The Tourists thanked them and drove off quickly.

"You didn't tell them about our night time Grizzly Bear Hunts," said Red.

"I know. They just didn't look that dude."

Sundance, 1966

CHAPTER 12 Red punches a cow and gets attacked by Wild Trout

Red and Ryan rode horses at Camp Willapa on the Pacific Ocean. They got a deal where they could work for two hours and then ride for one hour. They cut blackberries in the Washington rain and then galloped the Camp's horses across the only clearing of trees within two states. When they got done with their ride, the blackberries had already grown back. Red helped Ned, the Camp Caretaker. They rode around in a wooden cart picking up horse pucks. A giant Shire, with hairy feet, named Queenie, pulled the wagon. Whenever Queenie made a pile, they would stop and Red would shovel the manure into the back of the wagon. One day Red found Queenie all alone in her stall. He walked in behind her and went up to her front shoulder. He was about ½ her height. He stood in the tight space between Queenie and the barn wall. Queenie shifted her weight and put her right front foot on top of Red's left toes. Red couldn't move. He waited a while. He wondered if Shires really do weigh 2000 pounds. He divided 2000 pounds by 4 feet. He got 500. He tried to twiggle his toes. He couldn't. He looked at Queenie's eye way up there and wondered if she was stepping on his toes on purpose. He wondered if Ned would come by and rescue him. He stood still and waited. Eventually, Queenie shifted her weight and let Red go. His toes were okay and he thought that Queenie had just been joking around with him.

The two brothers next rode horses with their Shoshone friends at Fort Washakie. Robbie Beauclair had a huge horse named Chocolate. Red rode on Chocolate behind Robbie. With every step Chocolate's hips made a loud grinding sound. Robbie said it was old age. Freckles Contado and Alan Beauclair rode two of Beauclair's horses, all saddled up. But, Robbie gave Ryan a black pony to ride bareback, asking him if he thought he could hold on. Ryan insisted that he could. The boys took off riding, with everyone keeping an eye on Ryan. There was lots of open space in Wyoming and they soon got to break into a gallop. They kicked the horses to get into the mad fun of galloping at full speed. Ryan slipped off the side of the Black and tumbled through the sagebrush. It looked pretty bad, so they couldn't laugh. Ryan got up and jumped right back on the Black's back. He clenched his teeth and off they went at full gallop with his fingers in the horse's mane and his legs clamping its sides. He never fell off again.

125

Layman Smart had a horse. Red sometimes saw him riding around on it wearing a big black cowboy hat shaped like a cloud. There were a few other horses scattered around the fields near Wind River, but the Shoshones rarely rode them.

One day Jerold Wheeler came riding his mare behind the Church of the Redeemer and ran into Red and Freckles walking back from the Trout Creek Headgate. He jumped off his horse and told them in an excited voice, "watch this!" He took off his saddle and blanket and held the mare by the reins.

"What are you doing?" asked Freckles.

"Just watch!" whispered Jerold.

Then they heard a horse whinny and saw a big stud come running through the brush of Trout Creek. The snorting and bellowing stud saw that Jerold's mare was corralled between the brush and the barbwire fence. Jerold slipped off the bridle and stepped back.

"Is that George Darrow's stud?" asked Freckles.

Red recognized the stud that he always saw contained by an electric fence along Trout Creek Road. He had been told that a stud would go right through a barbwire fence if he smelled a mare in heat. He looked for wire cuts on the stud, while it mounted the mare in front of them. He didn't see

126

any. He wondered if a stud could jump a fence. When the stud finished, Jerold smiled and told them that he was going to get a free colt. Then he added that he wouldn't know for a while. The stud, now aware of the three boys watching him in the confined space, walked out of the brush and disappeared. Jerold saddled up the mare and walked away with her. Red never heard anything about a colt. He hadn't known that Jerold even owned a horse.

Cecil and Mary Barker had horses. They had some irrigated acres, chickens and some dairy cows, but Cecil was basically a Cowboy. He had over 100 head of Herefords. Red helped their son, Norris, irrigate, milk cows, haul hay, and collect eggs. Cecil showed Red how to flood irrigate by laying a canvas nailed to a 2x4 across a ditch and weighting it down with chunks of sod. The farm was once a Shoshone Indian's Allotment. The water was Indian water. No one was getting rich around here, no matter how much water they had. In fact the water carried alkaline salts to the surface where it evaporated leaving salt behind. The result was a sterilized alkali mud bog, devoid of vegetation. Alkali Lake was on the north. Dead Horse Slough was on the east.

The Barker farm had their house, scattered barns, sheds, silos, and a collection of rusting old tractors, trucks, and farm equipment. There was a moss ringed pond where the Boys could raft around and catch mudpuppies and frogs. The whole farm was circled by tall cottonwoods and Russian Olives so that it was an oasis in the hot Wyoming sun.

Cecil asked Red and Ryan to come out and ride horses with Norris. He wanted the horses to start getting in condition for their summer cattle drive. That was great fun for the two B. boys. Ryan was assigned Seabiscuit, a roan. Norris rode his black horse, Whirlaway. Red got Dean, a tall gray. They learned to bridal and saddle a horse and how to lace up and tighten a cinch. They got used to their horse and their horse got used to them.

When the snow had melted enough in the Wind River Mountains, Cecil prepared to push his cows up into Sanford Park where he had secured a Forest Service Grazing Lease for the summer. Mr. Barker assured Red that Dean was an excellent cow horse and would be easy to ride. Cecil gave each horse a new set of shoes. Red watched him as he tied up each foot, cut out the old shoe and then rasped down the hoof. Cecil forged the new shoe and blacksmithed it into the right shape. He hammered the horseshoe nails through the hoof, bent them over, and cut them off flush. When Cecil shoed his own horse, Citation, the big gelding reached back, grabbed the cigarette out of Cecil's mouth, and ate it. All the time that he did this work, the middle finger of his right hand stuck straight out. He told Red that he got it caught in a plow and it had broken and frozen up all the joints. With this finger sticking out, Cecil rolled his own cigarettes out of Prince Albert canned tobacco. He made it look so good that Red started smoking it, too. Red rode with Cecil to get tank loads of drinking water for the farm from a water hydrant in Fort Washakie. As Cecil drove, his broken finger stuck up in the air to greet passing cars.

The hardest part of the big drive was getting up at 4:00 in the morning. Mrs. Barker gave Cecil, Norris, Ryan and Red a big breakfast. She packed up their 1950 Oldsmobile with food and water. She would be the Chuck Wagon during the push. The four riders saddled up and started to move the cows out of Barker's pasture and cross country towards the Wind River High Country. Cecil yelled, "Hike!" at his biggest Bull to get him to lead the herd. Red watched Cecil's moves for chasing down stragglers and copied his yells. A cow turned out of the herd and ran for home. Red kicked Dean into full gallop, flanked her, and brought her back to the herd. Cecil gave him a worried look.

The herd had to cross several fences before they got on the Dickinson Park Road. Barkers had permission to cut them when necessary. Cecil forced the Bulls through the fences first and the boys pushed the cows after them. After a while the cattle quit balking and got used to the idea of continually moving. When they reached the road, the path was clearer to them. Now the Cowboys could just push the animals along the road and only worry about an occasional car causing a temporary bottleneck. The locals were all used to cattle being moved down the roads, so they sat patiently in their cars while the herd was driven past them. At the end of the first day they camped at the base of the mountains. Mary Parker fed them like kings and they went to sleep immediately.

The next day began the big climb up the mountains. They followed the dirt road, switchbacking up the steep grades. The cattle were tiring now and that helped to keep them grouped. The Cowboys were handed big sandwiches to eat in the saddle. They whistled and "hiked" the cows up the mountain. When they were on Old Baldy, they could see the pine trees ahead and they felt the cooler air. At the steepest part of the last switchback, a cow jumped out of the herd and ran out to the face of the mountain. Red flicked Dean's reins and chased the animal. He got around the cow and sent her flying back to the herd. But now, Red realized that Dean had got himself out on a cliff and couldn't turn around. Red was leaning way, way back in the saddle to keep from falling off the horse and down the cliff. Dean didn't move. Red didn't move. Red wondered if he could get off the horse and walk it back to safety. Dean stood unmoving. Red thought maybe he was frozen in fear. Finally, Dean started to move. He spun around on the cliff and trotted back to the road. When Red got to Cecil he asked him if he had seen Dean get in trouble back on the cliff. "Oh, that's nothin' for a horse," said Cecil, "they know what they're doing. He was just funnin' with ya."

They worked a long day to get the cows up to Dickinson Park and water. Mary Barker again fed them a huge feast and they slept in their bags near the creek. The next morning, they planned to complete the trip, so Mrs. Barker fed them and then left for home. Cecil, Norris, Ryan, and Red had to push the herd through the trees into Sanford Park. They tried to move out. The cattle didn't want to leave the water and the long grass of Dickinson Park. Cecil picked up a boulder from the ditch, mounted up, and carried it on his saddle over to his lead bull. Then he lined himself up over the bull's head and dropped the boulder on one of his horns. That put some sense in the leader, and Cecil convinced him to take to the trail.

The Cowboys were all saddle sore. Red had a world class sunburn. The most pain was yet to come. When they got into the trees, the trail narrowed and became rocky. Cows would try to get away by running out through the trees. The boys had to go get them and when they did, the horses had to break through a lot of pine branches. Armored and protected by the saddles and by their riders' legs, the horses could crash through some pretty heavy pine branches and sticks without getting hurt. The riders got pretty beat up by the trees. The going was pretty tough until they started downhill into Sanford Park. Downhill was easier for the herd and, at some point, they smelled water and moved a little faster. When they reached the open grass of the park, Cecil just got the lead bull and a few cows over the creek and into the grass. The herd followed. He stopped and got off his horse. Red rode across the creek and got off too, but quickly laid down to get a long, cold drink of water. As his mouth touched the water, he saw a bunch of Brook Trout shoot toward him and one bit his lip. "YI-DEECHY!" he shouted and knocked the fish off his lip. "What the hell."

"They've never seen a whiteman before," laughed Cecil. He scooped water up in his palm and drank.

The other two Cowboys joined them. "Aren't you worried that your cows won't all be here when you come back for them?" asked Ryan.

"Nope," said Cecil, "there's no place for them to go. They won't leave the grass and water."

The Cowboys relaxed for a while at Sanford Park. They cooled down and started to realize how beat up, sunburned, dirty, and sore they were. Red thought that his tailbone was paralyzed. They filled their canteens and then filed out on the trail back to Dickinson Park. The once a year cow horses were just as tired and beat up as their once a year Riders. When they realized they were headed back home, they started to pick up the pace. First, they started walking fast, then, in silent agreement, they broke into a trot. The horses didn't care that their favorite gait, the trot, was a Cowboy's least favorite. Cecil started Posting to offset the jerks. He raised in the saddle on the horse's downstep to smooth out the ride. Red tried to reduce the beating by reining Dean in. He saw the other Riders trying to hold back their bolting horses. Nothing could hold them. The horses won and got the Cowboys back to Dickinson Park pronto. The saddles came off and the horses drank their fill. Then they walked them up the loading ramp into Barker's stock truck. They drove the horses down off the mountain. They hadn't lost a single cow, horse, or Cowboy.

A month later in the summer, Cecil asked Red to help him pack some salt in to Sanford Park. "Bring your fishing pole this time."

They trucked the horses up to Dickinson Park and spent the night in Crosman's log cabin. Cecil cooked their dinner on the old iron stove and they talked a while with only a kerosene lantern for light. When they got in their sleeping bags, Mr. Barker said, "Well, might as well lay down and wait 'til morning." Red didn't know what he meant and was soon sound asleep in the fresh mountain air.

The next morning, they laced the salt blocks up on the horses' panniers and started down the trail into Sanford Park. The ride was a pleasure when you didn't have to crash through sharp tree branches to chase down cattle. Red noticed that Cecil used his saddle for an ashtray to make sure that his sparks went out on the leather and didn't start a forest fire. He decided to light up too. He smoked a while and waited for Mr. Barker to say something. But Cecil saw how careful Red was and didn't say anything. When they reached Sanford Park, the Barker herd was all there grazing on the abundant mountain grass. They set the salt blocks out around the park.

Then they untied their fly poles from their saddles and started fishing. Red cast in the hole where the fish had thought his lip was a worm. He caught a Brookie on the first cast. Cecil caught one on his first cast also. These fish were completely fearless. Each cast would bring in a fish unless they muffed it by jerking too soon or not keeping tension on their lines. They soon had their limit. They put away their poles and cleaned the fish. Then they rode back with Red smoking happily along the trail.

Cecil drove the big truck down off the mountain with his middle finger sticking up above the steering wheel. Oncoming cars waved back. When he deposited Red in front of the Rectory at St. David's, he got out and walked around to where Red was unloading his sleeping bag. He handed Red a $5.00 bill. Red looked at it and said, "Thanks, but I can't take it. It was too much fun." Cecil put the bill back in his pocket and drove away. Red went into his house and showed Mrs. B. all the fish he had caught.

CHAPTER 13 Red appears with the Ft. Washakie Redskins and his first taste of firewater

When Red started the 7th grade at the little white schoolhouse at Wind River, he was 11 years old. He loved baseball. His collection of bubblegum baseball cards included every player in the American League and in the National League. He even had two PeeWee Reese cards and no one else had a single one. In addition to the suitcase full of baseball bubblegum cards he had brought from Walla Walla, he had a first baseman's glove, a baseball, and a pair of cleats. One day he brought his ball and glove to school. Only one classmate, Johnny Rodda, was interested. He played catch with Red at recess and asked if he had another mitt. Yes, Red said he would bring brother Ryan's glove the next day. It was also a first baseman's glove. Ryan agreed to this, saying that he had, "...outgrown the game of baseball."

At the Wind River Agency Schoolhouse, Red and Johnny lobbed the baseball back and forth while the nearby basketball players fought the spring mud on their court. Red began to leave the gloves and ball overnight at the school.

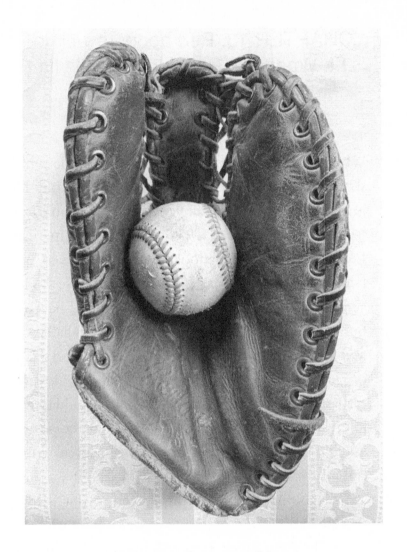

1955 First Baseman Glove

Sherman Wheeler, Basketball Star and King of the Eighth Grade, took an interest one day at the

137

morning recess. He asked Johnny for the glove and took over playing catch with Red. Sherman was standing between the basketball court and the front door of the 7th grade classroom. Red was north of him, with the barbwire fence behind him that separated the school playground from Vernon's overgrown hay field. Sherman tossed the ball too hard. It soared far over Red's head, over the fence, and out into the weeds.

Red slithered between the top and middle wires and searched around in the brush until he found the ball. He returned to the fence, slipped through, and walked back to an appropriate distance from Sherman. He tossed the ball.

Sherman uncorked a similar overshot, sending the ball far out into the field again. Red slipped through the fence again, found the ball, returned to the schoolyard, and tossed it back to Sherman.

Sherman did the same thing again. And again. And again. He did it every single time that he threw the ball. And – every time, Red marched through the fence, into the field, searched for the ball, climbed back through the fence, and threw the ball from his original position. Everyone on the playground watched out of the corners of their eyes. This continued until the bell rang to end recess.

Red didn't think there was much fun in that game. He was glad that Sherman didn't seem interested in baseball the next day. Johnny Rodda and Red seemed to be the only baseball enthusiasts in school.

But, one day, Johnny told Red that there was a Reservation Little League Team that played Lander, Riverton, and the other area teams. Coach Rick Beauclair wanted to know if Red would like to play?

"Yes," was Red's answer. He joined the team for practice in the weed field in front of Rick's house. Red wore his baseball cleats, but they were getting too small and they hurt his toes. After playing an hour in his favorite position at first base, his toes were all crushed and his toenails loose. Then he stepped on his own big toe with his sharp cleats. "OOOuuucchh!" he yelled.

Red was suffering from a growing spell. He retired the cleats. He was "big for his age" among the small Shoshone boys, but he didn't know it. He was getting The Clumsy. Luckily, the Bureau of Indian Affairs (B.I.A.) was there.

The B.I.A. would fix them. All the 7th and 8th Graders were lined up and given inoculations for Rocky Mountain Spotted Tick Fever. Three times their right arms were delivered a shot that would knock a horse to its knees. Then a traveling squad of Dental Hygienists strapped them to Dentist's

Chairs and jackhammered all the rock deposits off their teeth. Pebbles could be heard hitting the walls. Blood was everywhere. The Hygienists were all Trainees and this was their first job.

The Reservation School Nurse gave them all eye tests. "You have 20/30 in your left eye," she told Red, "Do you think you'd like to wear glasses?"

No, Red would hate wearing glasses and didn't know what 20/30 meant, although, it sounded pretty bad. Reverend B. and Mrs. B. hauled him off to Dr. Sunshine in Lander. He was prescribed with a pair of eyeglasses and they were ordered. When he picked them up two weeks later, he hid them in his shirt and snuck across the street to the bathroom in the Noble Hotel. Nobody was around. He looked in the mirror and put on the glasses. "Holy shit," he thought, "I look like shit!" He put them in his pocket and left.

Over the next weeks he tried putting the glasses on now and then. He was pleasantly surprised to find that Ronnie Beauclair, the King of the 7th Grade and Basketball Star, also had a new pair of glasses. They compared their experiences. The glasses went on and off, on and off. Ronnie tried playing basketball with his glasses strapped to his head and with them off. Some of Ronnie's shots started missing the basket.

Finally, Coach Hand told Ronnie, "Either wear them all the time or leave them off all the time."

Red noticed that he was having trouble judging a pop fly ball hit his way. He noticed that he could no longer see the blackboard clearly from the back of the classroom. The glasses went on and off. Only Nicky Wheeler called him Four Eyes.

Nothing seemed to bother Red. One day, his good friend, Honch, was walking with him, arms over shoulders, down Lander's Main Street, in front of the NuWay Café and the A.G. Grocery Store. Lyle Rupe, the Lander Football Coach and Little League Coach walked by them and said, "Do you guys sleep together too?"

Before Red got too clumsy and blind, the Little League Season started. Coach Beauclair loaded his car's trunk with all their uniforms, bats, gloves, and balls. Some of the baseball players' older brothers who owned cars made up a caravan for the trip. Riding with them was more comfortable for smoking. They headed for a sunburned country field between Ft. Washakie and Riverton. On a little gravel side road, they stopped and put on their uniforms. They continued to the field where the Shoshones and one White Boy would play the all white Riverton Little League Team.

The game didn't go very well. The Indian Boys' great skills at basketball weren't carried over into baseball. It was slow and didn't require speed and cleverness like basketball.

They still had fun. Chuck Barris, Dane Barris' big brother, told a story about Little Leaguer, Darin Sun. Years before, during a very busy inning, Darin felt such a sharp stab in his groin that he yelled out and jumped 10 feet in the air. Everybody paused and stared at him until the Umpire said, "Play Ball!"

Darin settled down and hoped the attack wouldn't happen again. But, he felt something stabbing him down there and he barely held on until the end of the inning. He ran into the dugout and pulled off his pants, his shorts, and his jock strap. He looked around and under. Sure enough – there was a great big old sheep tick sticking in his crotch. His teammates watched and laughed as he pulled it out, threw it down, and stepped on it.

"Yep," repeated Chuck, "that tick bit him right in the crotch right in the middle of the game! He jumped 10 feet high!"

"He jumped 10 feet high!" confirmed Nicky.

Coach tried Red out at Shortstop. Seeing the White Boy towering above his Indian teammates, the Riverton Players started to yell, "Hit it to Shorty!"

Red got a pretty good workout for a while. He was finally sent back to his beloved first base and Robbie Beauclair went to Shortstop. The older Indian Boys watching the game performed as informal base coaches and raconteurs. When Red got a hit and got on base -

"That Red is Greased Lightning."

"No, let's call him Flash."

"You call that running?"

Then, in the fifth inning, Red was playing a few feet off first base and intently watching the batter while Hank went through his windup. As the pitch reached the batter, Red took a quick sidestep over to the base. A piercing pain shot up from his crotch and he jumped 10 feet in the air.

"Yih Deetchy!" It felt like someone had stuck him with a needle right under the under there. What the heck could that be? He recovered his composure and kept his feet wide apart. He felt something down there pinching him. He was determined not to let anything show. He controlled his hopping, gritted his teeth, and held on.

Sheep Tick, *Ixodes Ricinus*

Red made it to the end of the game. He was coping with the constant pain of a needle sticking in his under there. He ran to an empty dugout on the adjacent field, jumped down in it and tore down his pants. He searched his under there and found a great big sheep tick, the size of a dime, stuck under the skin. It was several times the size of a Spotted Tick. He grabbed it between thumb and forefinger and began to worry it out. It came free and he had some relief. He couldn't tell for sure if he had got the whole head out. He buttoned up and went back to Coach Beauclair's car where the Players were loading up to go home. He looked around the trunk. He thought maybe Coach had been shearing sheep

144

and left some wool in his trunk. No – it didn't look like it. He didn't see any sheep shears or wool sacks. He wondered how the tick had got into his uniform.

Riverton won, 5 runs to 3, revenging themselves for some of the many basketball games they had lost to Ft. Washakie. Chuck Barris kept smiling and repeating, "He jumped 10 feet high!"

They started back to Ft. Washakie. Red rode in the back seat of Coach Beauclair's Mercury. All the windows were down and they smelled the new cut hay in the fields. The narrow little blacktop road wound through the sagebrush covered hills and over little cottonwood tree lined creeks. Coach Beauclair had to drive around dropping off the boys at their homes.

It was dark as they neared Beauclair's house on the way to Red's house. Coach said he was running out of gas. He pulled into his yard and drove up next to a little Ford tractor parked in front of his house, "We'll have to siphon some gas."

Parking gas tank to gas tank, with a cigarette dangling from his lips, Coach pulled out the necessary siphoning equipment – a hose. They twisted off the gas caps of the tractor and the Mercury. Coach put his end in the tractor and handed the other end to Red. Red bent over and started sucking. No gas came out. He tried again, with more suck. Nothing. He paused a little while and decided to give it full power. He sucked the end of that hose as hard as he could. Luckily, he had his throat closed. The gas surged out and filled his mouth. It blew out his nose. He dropped the hose, blowing more gasoline out his nose and mouth. Coach Beauclair managed to hold the hose and direct the now flowing gasoline. Red crouched over and spit repeatedly on the ground and rubbed his face off with his shirt. He reeked of gas. His nose and throat burned.

The big Mercury then went to Red's house. He jumped out of the car, went into the house and explained to his Mother why he smelled like gasoline.

"That's logical," she nodded, waving her hand back and forth under her nose.

He ate a cold dinner, which he couldn't taste. Then he was afraid to smoke for the rest of the night, and went to bed feeling unsatisfied. He slipped on his crystal set headphones and listened to Elvis sing "Don't Be Cruel."

In bed, Red wondered if that had been Farmer Jim Hurst's tractor temporarily parked in Coach's yard.

CHAPTER 14 The life of a dog on the Reservation

Dusty, the B.'s Cocker Spaniel, had found heaven in the wideopen country around Wind River. He was no longer a City Dog. He sniffed out trails in the jungles around Trout Creek. His bird dog instincts were satisfied by flushing out pheasants in the grasslands and Sage Chickens in the sagebrush. He walked beside Red on their long Saturday and Sunday hunts. A cottontail or jackrabbit sent him flying. Ducks in the ponds teased him from the water. He wasn't very tall and his long curls picked up lots of foxtails and cockleburs. He would get some grooming help from Red until he started being a shit roller dog. He would often come home streaked, stained, and stinking of fresh cow flop.

"They do that to disguise their scent," said Reverend B. He had just ordered Dusty's sleeping quarters moved outside. "They can sneak up on animals better and bigger predators can't smell them."

"Oh," said Red. He relocated Dusty under the back porch. However, the cat, Statinius, that Gwen Roberts had given them, was also living under the porch. Sometimes you shouldn't force different creatures to share the same territory.

"SSSSSzzzRAAR!" Dusty went arr-arr-arring out from under the porch and disappeared behind the Church. He found his own place to sleep and became an outdoor dog and a country dog.

Statinius produced a litter of 7 kittens. This must have been a mystery to Dusty. One morning, Red looked out the kitchen window and saw Dusty walking with a guilty look along the side of the Church of the Redeemer. He was holding a kitten with its head in his mouth. Red grabbed the nearest weapon, a big raw potato, and walked out the back door. "Duh-uh-usty," he yelled in an accusatory voice. Dusty lowered his head and tried to look innocent. He kept walking. Red lobbed the potato across the yard and hit him right in the side. Dusty dropped the kitten with a loud, "Arh!"

Red walked across the yard and picked up the kitten. No broken neck, no blood. It was okay, just a little wet with spit. Red put it back under the porch with the rest of the kittens.

Dusty disappeared. It took a while for them to realize he was gone for good. Red had heard about Dog Eater Tribes, but everyone had eaten dogs. Lewis and Clark ate fat dogs they traded for in the barren Montana crossing. Arctic explorers liked the meat of their sled dogs.

"Coyote probably got him," said Beazel's Dad. Hardins didn't have a dog. Red looked around. No one had a dog at Wind River. The Fort Washakie Jailer, Dean Millman, had a bloodhound named Scout. He said it was good for the prisoners to see him napping outside their cell while they sobered up.

A year later when the B's had moved from Wind River and into the new house, Honch drove up in his Ford pickup truck. He brought into the Rectory with him a big tan Boxer. Mrs. B., Ryan, Red, and Douglas gathered in the living room while Honch explained how he had found the dog way up in the Wind River Mountains. It had a collar and it had professionally clipped ears and tail. It was obviously someone's pet but was running loose up at Dickinson Park. They looked all around. No people were seen in the area. What could such a valuable pet be doing in the high country? Honch had brought him home, called the Police, the Forest Service, and Joe Charbonneau. Honch put up a "Found" sign at the trading post. A week went by and no one claimed the dog. "Do you guys want him?" asked Honch.

This was a beautiful and very big dog. He was barrel chested and big even for a Boxer. While they thought about this interesting offer, Reverend B. walked into the room. When the dog saw him he went into the kind of ecstatic dance that a dog does when he first sees his Master after a very long absence. It was just like they were long lost friends. The dog jumped all over and licked Reverend B.'s hands. He whined and squeaked with joy. He jumped on Reverend B. and forced him to hold him. His whole body wiggled and his tail wagged non-stop. The lost dog could not contain his joy. It was contagious. They saw that this showering of affection upon the Reverend had closed the sale. They named him Duke, as he was clearly of royal blood.

Duke accompanied Red on his long hunting loops around Wind River and Fort Washakie. He got in pretty good shape. Joe Charbonneau noticed and named him Poachin' Pooch.

Duke also had a lot to learn about the country. The first time they took him camping he tried to bite a porcupine. He came back to camp with dozens of quills sticking out of his face. Red had never grabbed a porcupine, yet. But, he knew from his reading of Field & Stream, Argosy, and True magazines, how to handle this. He clipped the end of the hollow

150

quills off. That was supposed to release the pressure inside the quill. Then, while Ryan and Douglas held Duke down, he grabbed each quill with a pair of pliers and pulled them out. The surgery was more painful than the encounter. Duke never bit a porcupine again.

Red and Honch decided to take him camping with them up above the South Fork Falls. This was a raging whitewater creek crashing down cliffs and over huge boulders. Keith Boatman had discovered that Brookies had migrated down from the lakes above and could be caught in the whitewater. At the toe of the Wind River Mountains, the dam at Chief Washakie Reservoir had slowed the creek so much that it looked more like a flatland river than a mountain stream. The artificially wide river looked strange in the mountain canyon. Its temperature was higher and it produced only transplanted Bluegills and Sunfish. Most fishermen went up the canyon to where the natural stream held trout.

They parked at the end of the dirt road, slipped on their backpacks and grabbed their fly rods. They walked the trail up the canyon. Duke ran effortlessly ahead of them. On the switchbacks he would stop far above them and look down with a questioning look. He wasn't even panting. They began hearing the roar of the falls. The canyon was narrowing and the sides were becoming cliffs. At the base of the falls, the sound was almost deafening. It was eerie in the way the roar filled the rocky chasm and seemed to come from all directions. Red watched for Little People who might be watching them from behind the rocks and trees. The boys set their backpacks and sleeping bags down on a little flat spot near the creek. Then they started to climb the rock cliffs to get to the whitewater.

Honch and Red soon found that Duke needed some help getting up the cliffs. When they got to the big rock face at the top of the falls, they threw their fishing poles up on the ledge above them. They realized they would have to lift Duke up somehow. Honch grabbed Duke and started to push him up the cliff. Unfortunately, that filled up the one place where you could safely climb up over the foaming water and rocks below. Honch found himself in a predicament, with the big Boxer starting to slip away from him and towards the drop off into the falls. He yelled at Red, "Hurry up! Get on top!"

Red was alarmed. Without thinking, he leaped around Honch and scrambled around the dog. This put him on the steep wet cliff edge straight above the rocks far below. He hung from his outstretched arms from the ledge above but he didn't have the strength to pull himself straight up. Dragging yourself up a rock cliff is far different from doing a chin-up in gym class. Red's arms trembled with his straining.

"Hurry up!" yelled Honch.

Red looked at Honch and Duke and saw that one or both of them were going to go down the rocks into the waterfall. He looked down at the falls below and knew that he was in an even more dangerous situation. He was a goner if he couldn't get up on that ledge! His mind seemed to slow down a little. He found extra strength in his arms and found himself slowly rising. The lift got slightly easier once he got his head above his hands. His shoulders got up to the ledge. He reached out and clawed for a handhold in the rock. He had enough adrenalin running through him that he clawed his way up and stood. He reached down, grabbed Duke, and hauled him up. Then he gave a hand to Honch and he stepped up top. Red looked down at the cliff he had just climbed. He didn't know how he had made it. Honch seemed oblivious to Red's close call and cast a fly into the whitewater above the falls.

They caught a bunch of little Brookies as they worked themselves farther upstream. When they had enough they decided to climb off the cliffs and go back around the flatter slopes away from the creek. They found a place where they thought they

153

could climb down the rocks and then jump into a pine tree growing close to the rock. They reached as low as they could and dropped their fishing poles off the cliff. But they realized that Duke couldn't make that jump. They thought for a while. Duke was a big problem again.

They both wore military web belts with brass buckles. They were handy because you could also use them for straps. They took off their belts and put one belt end into the other's buckle. They locked it down, making a belt almost six feet long. Then they locked one end of the belt around Duke's chest. Pulling him over to the cliff's edge, they hung him out in the air and lowered him down toward the tree. Duke had a concerned look on his face. When he was a few feet above the tree they let go of the belt. He landed in the tree. As he fell, his scrambling legs caught at the branches and eased his fall. He ended up on the ground in pretty good shape. He dutifully stood there and waited while Honch and Red climbed down the rock and then jumped over to the tree for the last 10 feet to the ground. They inspected Duke and their fishing poles. They decided that they shouldn't take Duke on any more rock climbing trips.

Red might have worked Duke too hard. There were many miles of the Little Wind River to fish and swim in. There were miles of hills to hunt in summer heat and through winter snows. Duke got plenty of exercise but he played dumb when Red shot a pheasant or sage hen and then waved at the Boxer to retrieve the bird. He was not a Retriever but he was loyal, thought Red. During the school year Duke waited at the Churchyard for his Master to come home and for the adventures to begin.

Red and his first dog, 1949

But he didn't always just wait. Red ran into Millman the Jailer fishing on the Little Wind River below the trolley car. Millman was the greatest Fisherman there ever was, according to Beazel. The boys always tried to see what he was using for bait and where he cast. Millman didn't make it easy for them. Red suspected him of fishing barren spots when he was being watched.

Duke was with Red this particular day and Millman mentioned to Red that his dog was always coming over to the Jail.

"What does he do there?" Red asked.

"He comes for dinner. The prisoners always throw him stuff."

"When?"

"Every day."

Then, a few days later, Red was talking with Howard Perry at Fort Washakie. Duke stood beside him. Howard pointed at him and said, "Your dog stops by Beauclair's every day for lunch."

"Every day?"

Then, Red took a load of stuff up to the dump and found Norman Young up there. When Norman saw Duke, he said, "Your dog comes by our place to eat all the time."

"Every day?"

"Yep."

156

Red's feelings were hurt. He had accidentally learned that his Best Friend had been making the rounds of Fort Washakie getting meals. He wondered how many other places he was eating at. Red examined the delicious Purina Dog Chow that he served Duke with a bowl of water every night. Red tasted some of the Chow. "Shit!"

*   *   *

The next day, Ronnie Beauclair drove over to Red's house in his Jeep Station Wagon. He wanted to drive down to the big old barn behind the Government school but he was out of gas. Red suggested that they look for pop bottles and get some money for the deposits. Ronnie agreed. Red and Duke jumped in the Jeep and they began driving along Highway 287 looking for bottles.

The boys could always get a little pocket money from bottle deposits. They would walk along the borrow pits one bottle throw out from the road. Where, when, and why a driver threw out a bottle was a big topic of conversation. It was like fishing. They would cash the bottles in at the trading post or at a gas station. Most bottles had a one cent deposit but they occasionally found a quart bottle that had a 5 cents deposit. Gas cost 27.9 cents per gallon.

The job of finding bottles while driving turned out to be difficult. Ronnie kept an eye on the Fuel

Gage. It was on dead empty and never made a single bounce. Red spotted a bottle from his seat, ran for it and brought it back to the Jeep. He also spotted a bunch of no deposit/no return bottles and lost time running for them. After about half an hour, they had gathered about 25 cents worth of bottles.

Wallace-McCart Gas Station

Ronnie sighed, "I think we're burning gas at 2 cents a minute and finding bottles at 1 cent a minute."

Red volunteered to walk a while so he could see in the grass better. He jumped out with Duke and

158

they walked along the ditch. Ronnie drove at one mile per hour down the highway. Red found a freshly thrown case of beer bottles. He stuck four in his Levi pockets, two in his shirt pockets, and two in his boot tops. He put three under each armpit. Then he stuck his fingertips in eight more and grabbed one with each hand. He headed towards the Jeep while beer dregs spilled on his hands and clothes. He started unloading the bottles on the floor and beer dregs spilled out. "Phewww," said Ronnie, waving his hand back and forth under his nose, "they don't pay for beer bottles".

Red started slinging the beer bottles back into the ditch. Joe Charbonneau, in his big green Game Warden pickup, came up behind Red and Ronnie. He hit his brakes as he realized the Jeep was barely crawling. He flipped on his Red light. Ronnie froze at the steering wheel and Red froze holding the last two beer bottles.

Joe walked to the Jeep and looked in. "Phewww!" he yelled, waving his hand back and forth under his nose. He thought he had caught the Tribal Chief's young son driving without a license, drinking with the Preacher's Kid and littering. Joe looked around inside the Jeep and didn't see any Fish and Game violations, so he walked away. Back in his truck, he checked to see there were no oncoming cars. Then he drove up beside Ronnie and through the window yelled, "Get off the road, someone's going to hit your ass!"

Joe floored his truck and disappeared in the direction of Hunt's Corner. Ronnie and Red turned around and went to J. B. Challis's Chevron Station at Fort Washakie. J.B. was in the log office behind the candy counter talking to McCord about selling the business to McCord.

As Ronnie's Jeep ran over the bell, J.B. told McCord how profitable the gas sales were. The two walked outside and J.B. went to the Jeep's window. Ronnie told him, "25 cents of regular please."

"Phewww," said McCord, waving his hand back and forth under his nose, but J.B. didn't even notice just another reservation car smelling like Coors.

J.B. put the gas in the tank but didn't offer to wash the windshield. The boys followed him into the office carrying 25 cents worth of bottles. J.B. motioned to the empty pop case on the floor by the pop cooler and said, "Thanks a lot."

Ronnie, Red, and Duke drove off in the direction of the big barn. They looked at the gas gage. The needle still read flat empty and would not even flicker. The Jeep made it down the Ethete Road and into the big barn between the school and the Little Wind River. They sat in the Jeep, rolled Bull

Durham cigarettes, and lit them with farmer matches.

They talked about the movie they had seen at the Diane Drive-in, "Broken Arrow". Red pretended he was James Stewart and Ronnie pretended he was Jeff Chandler, as Cochise. They developed a secret handshake, slipping their hands over their friend's hand and grasping their forearm. "Brother," said Red. "Brother", said Ronnie.

"Hey, wanna become Blood Brothers?"

"Yah!"

Red and Ronnie each took out their pocketknives and unfolded a blade. Red wiped his blade with his beery fingers. Then they looked for a place to cut. Where should they cut themselves? How deep? They touched the tip of their blades to their thumbs, then their forefingers. They wondered if it would hurt. They wondered who should go first. They settled on the first fingers, gave each other a look and then made tiny little trial cuts. Both of them got a little blood and they realized that was enough. They lined up the cuts and pressed them together, joining White Boy, Shoshone, and beer. Their hands locked their fingers tightly for a minute.

The two Blood Brothers then went into the big barn and explored. It was completely empty except for a big rope the size of a ship's hauser hanging from the ceiling. They could swing on this all the way across the big open room. They could climb up to the hayloft and then slide down the rope to the floor below. It was great fun.

After some running around in the big barn, one of the boys felt the need to take a shit. He went down into the basement area of the giant building and found a dark corner. He squatted and took a dump. Then he returned to the upstairs and swung on the rope some more.

Duke had been exploring the barn while the two boys were swinging. Just as Red got ready to kick off from the hayloft, Ronnie yelled, "Hey, look at your dog!"

Red looked at Duke and saw that he was prancing with pride toward him. He had a big turd sticking out of his mouth just like he was smoking a cigar. "He's offering you the first bite," laughed Ronnie.

"Duke!" yelled Red in such a voice that poor Duke knew his Master was very, very mad at him. Apparently, his Master didn't want the gift so Duke flipped his head back and gulped down the cigar in one swallow. Then he ran out of sight.

Red was picturing in his mind what Duke did with that turd. He thought about how Dusty had been a shit roller dog. Red yelled out loud, "Now I've got a shit eating dog!"

162

Ronnie laughed and laughed at Red. "He'll lick your face tomorrow."

Red laughed too, and the Blood Brothers rope swung until they were tired. They called Duke from his hideout. He appeared with a sad hangdown look and jumped into the Jeep. They hoped there was enough left of their 25 cents worth of gas to get them home.

Red jumped out of the Jeep at the Rectory and went inside. As he walked past them, Reverend and Mrs. B. both yelled, "Phewww!" and waved their hands back and forth under their noses.

Red had to explain his day's adventures, minimizing the beer part and stretching out the big barn part and Duke's lunch selection.

"All dogs eat shit," Ryan told Red, "just like they all drink out of toilets." Everyone agreed. Red felt a little better. He wondered what he would eat if he was very hungry. He wondered what he would eat if he was starving.

Reverend B. came into Red's bedroom at the St. David's Rectory one night and told him that Duke was gone.

"Where's he gone?" asked Red.

"Gary Winchell came over today and told me that Duke had been chasing sheep. He said he did what he had to do."

Red's shit eating dog was gone. He told Beazel about it. "That means Scout is the only dog left on the Reservation." The two boys walked to the fence beside the jail. The old, overweight bloodhound was lying outside with his eyes pointed at the barred window from whence occasional scraps of food flew.

"He doesn't look like he hunts very much," said Red.

"Nah, he's just good P.R. Everyone in jail knows there's a hound dog outside that could sniff 'em out and run 'em down."

"Yah?"

"Yah, one time Millman was in a big hurry to go fishing. He set the prisoners' food inside the cell and then he forgot to lock the door when he left. No one cared, they just sat there. 'Cept Sky Acoma. He walked out and went back up to Ellshire's."

"Scout let him go?"

"Oh, sure, he's not a guard dog, he's a tracking dog."

"So, what happened?"

"When Millman got back, he couldn't find Scout. He went in to ask the Prisoners where he was and saw that Sky was gone. The other Prisoners ratted on Sky. Millman didn't call the police. He just walked up to Ellshire's and looked outside where everyone sits. He saw Sky sitting there with a can of Coors. Sitting beside him was Scout. On the ground was a dish. Scout was drinking beer out of it. The jukebox inside the bar was playing Jailhouse Rock."

"Isn't he supposed to bark or bellow or bay when he catches a criminal?"

"Yah, but Sky wasn't really a criminal. He was just sleeping off a two week drunk."

"That's logical."

CHAPTER 15 How Red hits a grand slam home run but makes a lifelong enemy

There was going to be a Little League Baseball game with the Lander Tigers. Red was going to ride in to Lander with Durward and Jimmy Burton. Red thought Durward drove really well for an eighth grader. With his first baseman's glove and his cap, he waited outside the new Rectory at St. David's Church. Across Highway 287 he could see his Coach, Rick Beauclair, loading up his '55 Mercury with their uniforms, bats, balls, and equipment.

165

Chuck Barris and Nicky Wheeler, too old to play Little League, were there. They had their own cars and were helping Coach Rick by chauffering some of the Fort Washakie Redskins.

Red saw the '55 Ford round the corner onto Highway 287 and then enter the driveway to the Catholic Church and cross the cattle guard. It drove along the loop between the two Churches and pulled into the B.' s driveway. Durward had his cowboy hat pushed back on his head, as usual, so that it looked like someone was sitting behind the steering wheel. When Red stepped closer he saw that Granny Burton and Jimmy Burton were sitting in the back seat. Red said "Hi," and slid into the front seat. The radio was playing "Peggy Sue" on Station KOVE.

"You going to drive on the Highway?" asked Red.

"Yah, I'll stay right behind Rick and we should be okay. Granny's with us".

"Does she have a license?"

"No, she doesn't drive."

Red glanced at Granny in the back seat and she nodded agreement. Her eyes twinkled in her majestically wrinkled brown face that was framed by a scarf. She took a big drag on her Camel. He wondered if he should light up a Lucky but noticed that Durward and Jimmy weren't smoking. They respected their Grandmother and wouldn't do just anything they wanted when Granny was around. They told Red that when they snuck off in the car at night they piled it full of pillows to help muffle any sounds and then rolled it a way down the road before starting the motor. That way they didn't wake up Granny.

The procession started southward toward Lander: Rick leading, then Chuck, then Nicky, then Durward. They passed Vernon's Motel, The Mormon Church, Sacajawea Gas Station, Hunt's Store, Braman's, Shipton's and then across Trout Creek. They passed Bybee's, McCarts, Parkers, Wilsons, Stagner's, and Ray Lake. Halfway through the 15 mile trip, they went around Aragon's Corner, the only place where Teenagers had to slow down when they raced each other. The road from Mill Creek and Ethete joined there and 287 continued across Boulder Flats. They passed Kniffin's, Murphy's and Clark's. They left the Reservation when they crossed the North Fork of the Little Popo Agie River. Crossing a ridge of sagebrush covered hills, they dropped into the Valley of the Little Popo Agie River and the Town of Lander.

In town they passed the new A&W Drive In and the Bowling Alley and turned left at the High School. They followed the six-team wagon wide

167

Main Street through town and turned on South
Second Street. Soon they were at Lander City Park

Lander, Wyoming 1950s

and the baseball fields - one full size and one Little
League size. A Little League game was in progress
so the three cars parked near the empty field and
everyone jumped out. Coach opened his trunk and
they took out their uniforms. They got dressed in an
empty dugout. Red examined the crotch of his pants
before putting them on. He picked out a big white
sheep tick hidden in the seam and crushed it. Coach
Beauclair told them to watch the end of the Little

168

League game just finishing up, but Red talked Wesley Noseep into warming up at the empty field. Everyone else carried the catcher's gear, balls, bat bag, and their gloves over to the ongoing Little League game.

At the empty ballfield, Wesley hit grounders to Red on First Base and Red warmed up darting all around catching the drives and throwing back to Wesley. He worked up a little sweat and was feeling really good by the time they heard the buzzer signal the end of the game on the other field. As Red left his warmup session he noticed that one person was sitting far up in the stands watching him. He couldn't recognize who it was.

Wesley and Red joined their Team, took their positions and started warming up on the Little League Field. Pitcher Hank batted flyballs to Left, Center and Right Fielders. Red stood near 1st base and threw grounders to Second, Third and Shortstop. Then the Lander Tigers, with Coach Rupe, warmed up.

The Umpire signaled for the game to start and the Redskins, as Away Team, went up to bat. Coach Rupe looked at the Redskins bench full of Indians and one White Boy, and said to his Players, "This ain't basketball."

Not much happened for a few innings. Hank Contado pitched for Fort Washakie. A few innings passed. Some substitutions were made. Coach Beauclair put Red in as Pitcher. Although one of the youngest Players, he was big for his age and had a natural curve ball which took a little wiggle right in the middle of the pitch. Unfortunately, it should have wiggled a little closer to the plate, and Lander scored two runs before Coach Beauclair put Red back on First Base.

The Team Big Brothers, Chuck and Nicky, made the most of this, yelling mock praise at Red, and showing great interest in his every play. "Hum in there, Red-Babes." "Good one, Red." "Way ta go, Flash!" Red heard Chuck tell his "Jumped 10 feet high story" again.

The last inning dragged around. Score: Lander 2, Fort Washakie 0. Freckles got a hit and got on base. Then Wesley hit and got on. Hank singled, making the bases full. Red was up. He brought to the plate all his Walla Walla sandlot baseball experience. He brought his Big for his Age. He wasn't completely blind and clumsy. The Indian Boys sat silently and stoically and the Lander Tigers went deadly quiet.

The two Game Announcers, Neal and Dave, made the most out of announcing, "Batten battin' - Noseep on deck, and Wadda in the hole."

Red chose a bat from the selection lying on the ground by their bench. He walked to the plate and took a few practice swings. The Pitcher wound up and pitched the ball. It sailed right in the strike zone to Red, and he took it. Red swung, hit the ball foul, and broke the bat. He grabbed another bat. Red swung on pitch two, hit it foul, and broke that bat also. Red figured that they must have been cracked to start with. Maybe Chester had driven over the bat bag at some time. Red picked up a third bat. The Lander Pitcher looked at his Coach, looked at the three Redskins on the three bases, and then went into his short windup. With two strikes already on him, Red swung. The bat met the ball with a satisfying "chunk!" and it went sailing far out towards left field. It sailed over the fence. It sailed over 4th Street. It sailed over Chuck Vargas' house. Home Run! The three base runners came home, driven around by Red.

The Redskins all clapped and cheered. But, at the Lander Bench, things looked mean. Coach Rupe walked out onto the field and picked up Red's bat. He looked for a size mark stamped on the end of the bat – there was none. He motioned for Coach Beauclair to come over. There was a discussion held among the two Coaches and the Umpire. The four points were given to Fort Washakie. They won the game.

The boys jumped into the cars still in uniform. Most of them lit up smokes as soon as they were out of sight of the baseball fields. Red would have to wait, in deference to Granny Burton. Some cars stopped at the A&W for root beer, but not Durward. He was afraid of getting caught driving without a license if he pushed his luck too far. He pushed his hat back on his head and they drove for the safety of the Reservation.

Red soon found out what the incident with his bat was all about. At the next practice session in the stubblefield at Beauclair's, Coach told him that you couldn't use a bat bigger than 32 inches in the Little Leagues. Lander's coach, Lyle Rupe, had accused Red of using an illegal 35. But the bat wasn't marked and the complaint had been denied by the Umpire.

A week passed. Red was out mowing the acres of weed stubblefield in front of St. David's Church and the Rectory. Dust and rocks were flying. Coach Rick Beauclair with Chester Beauclair drove into the St. David's road and parked. Red shut off the mower and walked over to them. They were both smoking Viceroys. Coach pushed his straw cowboy hat back on his head and said, "We need a copy of your birth certificate."

"Oh, okay," said a surprised Red, "I'll ask my Mom for it."

"Good," said Coach, "practice at 5:00 tomorrow."

They drove away and Red finished his mowing. He didn't know anything about birth certificates but he relayed the request to his Mother. She very efficiently handled everything. Red never did actually see his birth certificate or hear anything more about it from Coach.

A little later, though, he mentioned the incident to Beazel's Dad, John Hardin. He wasn't surprised at this news at all and immediately told Red, "Coach Rupe thinks you're a Ringer."

"What's that?"

"A professional player or superstar they sneak in to win against amateurs. In your case they mean an older boy they sneak in to play against younger kids and win illegally."

"Oh," Sighed Red. He had never heard of a Ringer.

You couldn't play Little League after you turned 13 years of age. Mrs. B. found the family's official documents. They had fortunately survived the fire that had burned down the old Rectory at Wind River. She gave the Certificate to Coach Beauclair. He drove it in to Lander to show Coach Rupe. The very fact that a Birth Certificate was being offered should have told him that Red was of legal age, but he still grabbed out for it. Imagine his surprise to see that Red not only wasn't over 13, but that he wouldn't turn 13 for four months.

Red told John Hardin about the birth certificate. "Where were you born?" asked John.

"Chatham, Ontario, Canada."

"You're a Foreigner," laughed John. "Wonder what old Rupe thinks about that?"

The Indian couple who helped tame Red. John and Penelope Hardin

CHAPTER 16 Red and Honch carry 100 fish past a White Game Warden

Honch, Red's current best friend one summer, was actually named Ron. His brother, Will, had started calling him Honch, and it stuck. Red suspected that it was a Shoshone word and suspected that it was either insulting or sexually suggestive. The only words he knew – yogo, noyo, dye, beechy dye – were all anatomical. Many of his Indian friends spoke English as a second language. They had been raised by a Shoshone speaking Grandmother. They were taught to not look their white teachers directly in the eye. A slower response to a question could give the false impression of failure.

Red heard Honch's Father, Paul, speak Shoshone to a customer at his Trading Post. White people owned most of the businesses on the Reservation. You could buy groceries, meat, and sporting goods at Hunt's Trading Post. Red thought it a wonderful thing for Honch to have available free .22 bullets, fishing lures, Milky Ways, Pepsi, and cigarettes. Whenever someone bummed a smoke and suggested Honch got his Lucky Strikes free, he very carefully corrected them and said, "No, we have to pay for them".

Honch introduced Red to Mary's Lake, high up in the Wind River Mountains and off the Reservation. It was bursting with Brook Trout. A one hour drive up the switchbacks was followed by a one hour climb from Moccasin Lake in to Mary's Lake. The hike was well worth it. The first time Red went, he caught 40 fish, and, that was a bad day.

Red bought a Wright and McGill fly fishing rod at Hunt's store. They loaded up with Toomey's Pancake mix, cans of mixed fruit and Dinty Moore Beef Stew. They bought two packs of Luckies at Vernon's Motel and four pockets full of bubble gum. They didn't carry canteens because there were lakes and streams all along the trail. Honch drove them up the mountains in the 1950 Ford Pickup they used at the store.

They parked above Moccasin Lake and walked in. When they got there they found Russ and Betty Crossman chumming on a big rock sticking out in the lake. It was the best fishing spot on the lake. For chum they used corn, throwing it out in the area they were casting into. They were catching fish on every cast. They greeted the boys and showed them a bucket full of fish. "There's nothing much over 10 inches in the lake, but there's lots of 'em."

Honch and Red began to circle the lake, hopping from rock to rock and catching lots of fish on flies.

The west and south sides of the lake were swampy grasslands, being flooded by the beaver dams below the lake's outlet. Red was willing to get wet wading through all that water, but Honch stayed on the dry side.

The beaver had cut down all the trees in the swampy area, so there was no shade for the fish. The sun hit the water longer during the day, making it warmer. Not surprisingly, the fishing wasn't very good. Red tried a few casts at the lake's edge but hurried to get back around to the shady side. He stopped in the middle of the small creek draining Mary's Lake. He let his fly float for a while on the water. Nothing happened – until – a sharp SMACK! right at his feet made him jump almost out of his boots. A beaver had come around the corner to exit the lake where Red was standing and had almost bumped into him. His tail slap was a warning to his family that a predator was in the area. The beaver disappeared. Everything had happened so quickly that Red just heard the SLAP! and saw a fur ball jump back into the lake. He realized that he had scared the beaver as much as the beaver had scared him.

Red continued circling the lake until he was back at the trail to Moccasin Lake. He started cleaning his 40 fish while waiting for Honch to come back. He knelt on his knees at the water's edge, gutting the fish and throwing the guts in the lake. After doing this work for 10 minutes or so, he focused on the water in front of him, where all the guts were sinking. There, snacking on these remains was the biggest Trout Red had ever seen. That exploded the myth that Mary's Lake only had small fish in it. He immediately stood up to get his fishing pole lying behind him. The giant trout instantly vanished and Red never saw or heard from him again. He tried a few casts using fish guts on his hook. He caught nothing.

When Honch got back, Red had finished cleaning all his fish. He told about the Giant Trout, but Honch just gave him a suspicious look. Honch cleaned his 58 fish. They packed up and started up the trail for home. Red's Red Wing Irish Setters squeaked and oozed water with every step. When they were well into the trees and high up on the mountain, they met a Wyoming State Game Warden hiking towards them. "Oh, shit!" they both thought at the same time.

The Warden, seeing their fishing poles asked, "Catch any fish?"

"A few."

"If you guys catch your limit and want to keep on fishing – go ahead. They're way overstocked and can't grow. Just lay them out on the shore and let them die."

"Oohh, yahh, thanks," said Honch. The two smiling boys left the Warden and continued their climb. When they were a little further along, Red smiled at Honch and said, "Whoooh!"

Honch smiled back and said, "Yiiih!" They scrambled around the boulders on the steep trail out of Mary's Lake.

*　　*　　*

One of the highlights of summer was firecracker season. A boy could buy a huge pack of Ladyfingers for $1.00. These had all their fuses twisted together so that you could light off a hundred at a time like you saw them do in the newsreels in foreign countries. Red pulled all of them apart so that he could light them one at a time. Some people bought a Sparkler to light them with, but, since everyone smoked at that time, Red used a cigarette.

Living in the country provided lots of opportunities to make a buck for firecracker money. They could mow lawns, wash cars, haul hay, drive cattle, paint, clean out septic tanks, and chop brush. The buck they got was a real buck – a Morgan Silver Dollar to clink around in Levi pockets. By the time they got four or more they began to feel the weight and had to get rid of some of them.

Honch, of course, was "rich" because his Dad owned the Trading Post. He had a regular work schedule as a stock boy. Red always maintained enough income with part time jobs for smokes and ordinance. This particular summer they started buying firecrackers in the days before the 4th of July and walked around Fort Washakie, the nearby hills, and the Little Wind River blowing stuff up. A good fuse would burn underwater, so they always allotted time for dropping depth charges in fishing holes. The results were disappointing. No fish in his right mind would sit around watching all the fizzing and bubbling that a firecracker fuse makes underwater.

Any prairie dog hole they passed would get a firecracker dropped in it. They threw it and then ducked clear. The results were negative. No prairie dog in his right mind would stand around watching flaming fuming firecrackers in his underground living room. Around the abandoned buildings of Fort Washakie they would drop firecrackers in metal fence posts, pipes, and culverts for a louder bang. Projectiles could be fired from pipes using firecrackers as powder.

Any can or bottle lying along Highway 287 got its appropriate charge, except for quart pop bottles, which were good for 5 cents cash at the store. 5 cents would buy a sack of Bull Durham or a Hershey

Bar. Residents of the area could chart Honch and Red's progress by the explosions.

The first experience with firecrackers finds beginners attempting to light them, observe the burning fuse, and then throw them away at the last moment so they will explode in mid-air. This is fun until they encounter "the fast fuse." Cherry bombs weren't available yet in Wyoming and they both still had 10 fingers.

Honch and Red were pretty darn good Demolition Men by July and they roamed far and wide looking for the bigger bang. One day, they wandered down the Ethete Road until they found themselves at their schoolyard, where they were bussed during the school year. The Government School had acres of yards, several generations of buildings, and housing for the single Teachers. This summer, a new Gymnasium was being built adjacent to the old original limestone schoolhouse. The nearby bus garage was also getting repairs and the underground gas tank was being replaced.

Basketball is the first love of many on the Reservation. Skills honed on muddy and bump filled back yards are refined in the Community Hall Gym and at school. This new gym was going to be the biggest and best ever. Red and Honch saw the Ironworkers up on the roof and heard all their clanking. They found the scaffolding stairs and climbed up to the roof. They approached a couple of roofers working in the hot sun.

"How much you guys get paid?" asked Honch.

"$2.00 an hour," one of the workers replied.

"Geeez," said Honch, "I'd work one hour and quit."

"Oh, yah," laughed a carpenter, "how old are you guys?"

"13", said Red.

"That sounds just like me when I was 13," smiled the carpenter.

The two looked around at all the interesting stuff lying about and then climbed down. They walked back up the Ethete Road for their dinners but made plans to meet up and revisit the construction site that night.

After dark they rendezvoused at the Russian Olive windbreak and walked together to the school. Honch and Red stayed out of sight of the Teacher's Houses looking for any opportunity to put a firecracker in an appropriate place. Imagine their delight in finding a mountain of construction material lying around. At the wall where the new gym met the old stone building they found an old 1,000 gallon underground gas tank lying up against a wooden crawlspace door. It had been replaced with a new tank. This old tank was about 20 feet long and 6 feet in diameter and looked like a good place to sit down for a rest. Red jumped up on it and lit a Lucky while Honch milled around a few feet away.

Studying the tank he was perched on, Red noticed a hole in it just a foot or two from where he was sitting. Instantly he recognized the perfect candidate for a firecracker. He pulled one out of his pocket, lit it with his cigarette and dropped it in the tank.

KAABOOOOM! The gas fumes in the tank exploded and shot Red off the tank and onto the ground. Flames leaped out of the end of the tank and started the wood door on fire. The explosion ricocheted off the stone building and woke up everyone on the Reservation. Honch just stared while Red examined himself to see if he was all still there.

Then they had to determine whether to flee or report. Too late! Dave Peters, the Head Custodian arrived. Red and Honch mumbled a few words to him and he left to call the Fire Department. The two Explosive Experts were surrounded by excited halfdressed Teachers asking what happened. People in shock cannot think fast, so, they told them the truth. Red and Honch were relieved to find the Police weren't called. In fact, they were allowed to walk off before the fire truck arrived. They skulked away, staying off the road, and hid in the Russian Olive windbreak. They saw many of the Volunteer Fire Department speeding to the school, including Joe Charbonneau in his great big green Game Warden truck with its red light flashing on the roof.

Joe arrived at the back of the school where the big flame was licking up the sides of the new gym. He was met by Dave Peters. "Who did it?"

"Red and Ron Hunt," answered Dave.

"Why am I not surprised?" sighed Joe.

After walking home in the dark, Red found the only damage was a ringing in his right ear. Red never heard anything more about the incident except for some silly gossip that the explosion had knocked the new gym over an inch and it was going to be completed that way. Honch might have heard more, because his Dad was President of the School Board. Their only punishment, besides Red's damaged hearing, was guilt. Red noticed that Honch had to work full time for the next month.

Red's remaining firecrackers sat safely in his wooden lock box. Finally, he couldn't stand it any longer. He took them out and started wandering around Ft. Washakie blowing up culverts, cans, and rabbit holes. His "pop, boom" progress was remarked upon by Joe and Tallboy from their location at the Jailhouse.

"Going to check it out?" asked Tallboy.

"Nope, I've learned to identify the sound of the Little Devil and the Lady's Finger especially when they seem to commence in the area of St. David's or The Church of the Redeemer."

Tallboy nodded. The explosions looped around and then returned. Red was walking down the ditch of US 287. Several cars were driving out from the Churchyard and turning onto the highway. He lobbed firecrackers at their tires. Last was a big old Chevy Carryall. He lit a Lady Finger from his cigarette and tossed it at the rear wheels of the truck. It popped right as it passed him.

Red tramped past the Catholic Church and over toward St. David's. He walked into the front door and saw Reverend B. in his collar in mid-day. "What's going on?"

"We just had Riding Chief's funeral. That was him going up to the cemetery in the Carryall."

CHAPTER 17 Beazel and Red survive bear attacks but were diagnosed with lung cancer

Beazel was Sioux, but he wasn't tall so he could pass for Shoshone. Most of the Sioux, like Tallboy Taylor, the Reservation Cop, were very tall and came from way up north in Montana. They worked for the Bureau of Indian Affairs – the B.I.A. In their spare time they won basketball games. Beazel's Mom was an Accountant at the B.I.A.'s Ft. Washakie Office. His Dad was a Brave, who taught Red hunting and fishing. Beazel was in 7th grade with Red and first came to public notice when he won a fistfight with Mary Huron. Beazel and Mary were both about the same size, but Mary didn't smoke and was considered a better athlete.

One summer day, Beazel walked over to Red's house carrying his fishing pole, backpack and sleeping bag. He told Red that Crosley was going up to Moccasin Lake to cut firewood. Moccasin Lake was at the end of the road for cars high up in the Wind River Mountains. Only foot and horse trails could take you the last few miles to the Continental Divide and the giant granite peaks. Beazel thought the two of them should catch a ride up with Crosley and pack in for some good fishing. They could camp over night and then hitch a ride back down with whomever came along.

Moccasin Lake

"Crosley?" asked Red.

"Yah, he's okay. He fishes the Little Wind from our house up to the cable car. He's really good. He knows we fish all the time and never says anything."

Red thought for a few moments, picturing Mary's Lake and all the Brookies jumping at the chance to get caught. "When's he leaving?"

"Ten minutes. He'll pick us up right here."

"Okay," said Red, and he began to gather his equipment. Fishing pole, sleeping bag, ancient army surplus backpack, matches, cigarettes, Levi Jacket. "Oh, you got anything to eat?"

"I got gum," said Beazel. He reached into his pocket and pulled out a handful of grape bubble gum balls. He opened his mouth and showed the wad he was chewing and his purple tongue.

"Is that all?"

"Yah, but I got a lot." He patted all his bulging pockets. "There's more rolled up in my bag." He patted his sleeping bag and smiled. Then he handed a warm one from his pocket to Red, and he popped it into his mouth after dusting off some lint.

Red grabbed his spinning pole but double checked his tackle to see that he had a clear bubble and flies. The high country lake fish were pretty dumb and you could make a big splash with a bubble and not offend them. Many had never seen a White Man before.

A toot from outside told them Crosley had arrived. They hauled their camping gear and poles out to his flatbed truck and set them up in the back against the cab. The ancient Ford was half green and half rust. Bald tires were hiding under drooping fenders and there were no license plates. Crosley wore Levis, a snap button cowboy shirt and cowboy boots. He grunted hello.

Red waited for Beazel to jump in first because he was short and etiquette demanded it. So Beazel looked around for a while like he was busy, giving time for Red to get in first. They milled around near the door until Crosley said, "Whoever's shortest, get in, so I have room to shift – or – you can shift".

Beazel gave in, jumped up into the truck, and straddled the big gearshift lever between his legs.

"Keep your feet away from the gas," warned Crosley.

Then Red got in and bounced off Beazel several times to make room for the three of them in the narrow cab. Red slammed the door and Crosley said, "Hold on to that door, sometimes it pops open by itself."

"Oh," acknowledged Red, and he squeezed the door between his chest and his right arm.

The truck headed along the road to Wind River and turned at Beloy's house onto Trout Creek Road. Crosley took the corner pretty briskly and both boys looked back through the cab's rear window to see if their bags and poles had made the corner with them.

They were visible under the dust. Lucky for Red, it was a right turn. In the distance they could see the switchbacks crisscrossing the bare foothills and Old Baldy. The first part of the long climb had steeper and steeper grades between the sharp, hairpin turns. Crosley had to do lots of fancy clutching and shifting. Occasional raps on the kneecaps from the lever kept Beazel attentive. He used his legs to push back into the seat to avoid a groin shift. Crosley got tired of finessing the gear knob and told Beazel to do the shifting. That gave Beazel lots of relief.

"First! Second! Third. That's not second, shitass!"

Red held tightly to the door. He could look straight down the cliffs as the truck made its northbound switches. If they went off here they wouldn't stop rolling for a long time. Before entering the timber the road narrowed and passing an oncoming vehicle would be tricky. They got into the rocky part of the steep climb and the ride got rougher. The truck's frame flexed and groaned causing Red and Beazel to hold on tighter and peek more often at the dusty freight behind them.

As Crosley topped Old Baldy with a nearly 360 degree hairpin curve, Red's door popped open and Red swung out over the cliff. His legs clawed in search of the running board while he hooked his neck over his arm and stared down at the rocky cliff below them.

Beazel was too busy holding on to the gear lever to help Red. But Crosley simply stepped on the gas, saying, "Shheeeee, that ain't nothing".

The speeding up of the truck on the steep hill allowed the door to close by gravity, just before Red hit the first trees.

"Crosley," said Red, "you need to get that door fixed!"

"Just don't hang on so tight," said Crosley, "Yur tweakin' the frame." He pried the distracted Beazel's hands off the shifter so that he could gear up again.

The heavy timber marked the easygoing part of the trip. The temperature seemed to have dropped about 20 degrees and the old truck seemed to run better. At the turnoff for Dickinson Park they saw Joe Charbonneau's big green game warden pickup. He waved at them as they passed and Crosley poked the air to wave back. Beazel and Red acted innocent and looked straight ahead.

At the Moccasin Lake Turnaround, Crosley stopped and let them out. They beat the dust off their sleeping bags and slipped on their packs. With poles in hand, they thanked Crosley and started down the trail to the lake.

"If I don't have a load by tomorrow, you might catch me in two days for a ride down," said Crosley, beaming at them.

"Thanks a lot!" they both answered. They waved their poles at him, accidentally in the pattern of an X.

Beazel and Red didn't talk. They popped fresh gumballs in their mouths and got serious about the trail. It was getting late as they reached Moccasin Lake and started across the stretch of sandy beach.

"I have never caught a fish in this lake," said Red, "have you?"

"Nope, I think you need a boat."

"Want to stay on the Reservation or go to Mary's Lake?"

"Doesn't matter, does it?"

"Except you can catch all you want on the Reservation."

"I'm Sioux, not Shoshone," frowned Beazel.

"I don't think Joe Charbonneau would say anything. We've never had any trouble before – fishin' or hunting."

"Nope, not yet. It's getting dark. We need to find a place to sleep."

The pair were well into the trail that climbs the back side of the big rock at Moccasin Lake. They decided to bushwack a little way off the trail and look for a cave to sleep in. They worked along the granite boulders until they found something like a cave.

"How do we know this isn't a bear's cave?" asked Beazel.

"If this was a bear's cave, we'd see bones and stuff. There's nothin' here."

"I thought bears ate bones and everything."

"Nah, they always leave the bones."

So, the two of them tried to drag out flat spots on the ground in the cave. They spread out their bags and then gathered a big supply of firewood for the night.

"If there's bears around, we'll need to keep the fire going all night, Red."

Red used a stick match to start the fire. "Mr. Wolcott said he shot a bear six times with a 30-30 and it just kept coming at him like nothing happened."

"I know," said Beazel. The smoke from the fire made him cough. "Remember last year that bear tore through a tent in Yellowstone Park and ate both the Man and his Wife."

"How'd he know they were married?" Red threw some more wood on the fire.

It was pitch black outside now and they lay on their sleeping bags and watched the eerie shadows

193

from the fire flicker on the dark rocks and trees. Nearby boulders and trees made giant shadows projected on the rocky hillside. They listened for sounds over the crackling of the fire. Beazel lit up a Lucky Strike and Red lit up a Kent to calm their nerves.

"What's that?" asked Beazel. He coughed again and pursed his lips at Red's cigarette.

"It's a Kent. I snuck them from my Dad." Red coughed. "I read in Readers Digest that smoking causes lung cancer, so I'm switching to filter tips. Cough."

"I saw something on T.V. about smoking causing lung cancer," said Beazel. A big flame shot up, made a big shadow jump on the rocks, and scared him.

"The Readers Digest said lung cancer has more than doubled because of smoking."

"How long have you been smoking those regular cigarettes?" asked Red, coughing. "They showed a black lung in a jar that they took out of a guy who smoked Camels all his life."

"Couple of years. Why, what's so great about Kents?"

"Well, these have a Micronite Filter made out of asbestos, so they filter out the stuff that gives you cancer."

"Orly Benson told me that his Dad smoked filter tips all his life and he died of lung cancer."

Both boys were alternately watching and listening for bears and picturing their own lungs looking all black in a jar. They took big gulps of air to make sure their lungs weren't black and leathery. They decided to turn in. They took off their boots, rolled their pants and shirts up for pillows, and slipped inside their sleeping bags. Now they found that there were lots of rocks sticking up from the ground and the floor of the cave was sloping both down and sideways. The smoke was backing up in the cave.

They were both coughing. "Have you ever noticed that cough you have?" nodded Beazel knowingly.

"Look who's talkin'."

"Want a gum," asked Beazel. "Cough."

"Yah, thanks. Cough."

They both chewed a while to calm their fears. Then Beazel coughed and said, "You know what?"

"Cough, what?"

"Cough, I'm going to quit smoking!"

Red coughed out his answer, "m – m – me, too!"

"Let's make a pact," said Beazel.

"Okay, what?"

"Let's swear to each other that we'll quit smoking and never smoke again."

195

Red thought about the black lung in the jar. He thought about the Readers Digest. He thought about the Bear eating the Man and his Wife. "Yah, I agree, let's swear."

They raised their hands up and made a solemn vow to quit smoking. Then they shook hands, both right and left. Then they took out their packs of cigarettes, shook them all out into their hands and crushed them up, letting the tobacco fall on the ground.

"We did it," said Beazel.

"We made it," said Red, "we're going to live after all!"

Then they chewed grape bubblegum a while and watched the fire and the eerie shadows outside. They were filled with the seriousness of their vows.

"Want to be my Blood Brother?"

"Sure."

The two solemn campers took out their pocket knives and pulled their blades out. They looked them over a little, spit on them, and rubbed the bubblegum and crud off on their pants. Then they had to decide where to cut themselves.

"We just need to prick a finger, don't we? In 'Geronimo' it looked like they slashed their wrists. I heard in the old days they used to find lots of blood brothers lying around dead from blood loss or Tularemia."

"Isn't Tularemia what rabbits get?" Red pushed the tip of his knifeblade around on his forefinger until he got a little hole. Then he squeezed it and made a little bubble of blood. Beazel did the same and they held their fingertips together to complete the ceremony.

"Blood Brother!"

"Blood Brother!"

The ceremony jogged Beazel's memory. "Wait a minute, we were already Blood Brothers! Remember that deer hunt when my Dad gave you the liver to eat?"

"Oh, yah, you're right. We're double Blood Brothers!"

Then they discussed the ramifications of being blood brothers. They would have to fight on the same side in the next war. They might have legal obligations and financial obligations. They didn't know for sure. Could you marry a blood brother's sister? Then the question was raised whether you automatically became blood brothers with everyone that your new blood brother was already a blood brother with. If someone had 5 blood brothers and each one of them had five blood brothers, then everyone would automatically have 24 blood brothers. If those 25 had 5 more blood brothers there would be 125, then 625, then 3,125, then 15,625, then 78,125, then 390,625, then 1,953,125.

"Hey that's two million. I bet everyone is our blood brother."

"Sure, two million, 10 million, 50 million, 250 million." They ran the math in their heads and had soon included everyone in the world. They thought about that for a while, but, eventually, the fears of the night started to return.

"You know," said Beazel, "you're not supposed to have any food in your tent when you're in bear country."

"We're not in a tent."

"Tent, cave, what's the difference?"

"Yah, I see what you mean." Red strained his eyes harder to see any bears illuminated by their campfire. "We don't have any food."

"Gum."

"Yah, we got gum," agreed Red.

"Well, we've got to get rid of the gum."

"Okay, throw it out."

So Beazel gathered up all the gumballs, tucked them into his shorts, and crawled out of the cave. He tried walking barefoot across the sharp rocks while keeping his eye out for bears. "Ouch, ooch, sheesh," he chirped. When he was as far from the

cave as he dared go, he started throwing the
gumballs into the woods. Red let out a big,
"ROOOOOAARRRRR" like he guessed a bear
might sound. Beazel dropped his balls and ran
painfullly back to the cave as fast as he could. "You
Yogo Horse, Red!"

"Okay, okay, I'll go get your shorts for you."

Beazel was so mad he couldn't go to sleep. The
ground was so rough and sloped and the thoughts
of bears so scary that Red couldn't go to sleep either.

"We need to keep the fire going all night," said
Red.

"We're going to run out of wood," said Beazel.

"Then you'll have to go out and get some more,"
said Red.

"Cough, I'm sick."

"Cough, cough, cough, I'm worse."

The night wore along. The friends' concentration
on the sounds and flickering shadows dimmed. The
firewood pile got lower. The bumpy ground seemed
bearable. They went to sleep. The cold mountain air
settled in and froze them through their thin bags
making them toss and turn while they dreamed.

Ahh, the glorious sleep of youth! The fire went
out. Through the dark and into the brightness of day
the two slept. No worries about bears, no worries
about black lungs. The sun drove out the cold and

199

began to scorch the air and the rocks around the cave. The two sweltered in the safety of daylight as long as they could stand it.

"I have to pee!" Beazel jumped up and ran out of the cave.

His yell wakened the bursting Red and he joined Beazel outside the cave. Everything looked so different, so safe, in the light. The two relieved themselves. Scattered all around them they saw purple gumballs.

"Hey," said Red, pointing at a gumball, "wouldn't these be all gone if there were bears around here?" He picked one up, looked it over curiously, dried it off, and put it in his mouth.

"Yah," said Beazel, joining Red in breakfast. They started to feel a little bolder.

They went back to their beds. Chewing and thinking for a while, another craving started to hit them. They looked at each other. Both of them were thinking about how good a smoke would be right then. Neither one of them wanted to speak first.

Some time went by. Finally, Red accidentally found a bunch of tobacco lying on the cave floor. "Hey, look, our cigarettes."

"Yah?" asked Beazel.

"Yah, there's a bunch of tobacco here," sighed Red.

LSMFT

"What are you thinking?" asked Beazel.

"I'm thinking we could roll up this tobacco and smoke it!" Red reached into his pocket and pulled out some folds of toilet paper he had brought for the trip.

Beazel put his nose down on the ground and began picking up little strings of tobacco. They rolled it in toilet paper just like a Bull Durham.

"You know, Beazel," said Red, "I don't think there are any bears in these parts."

"Nope, and my lungs are feeling a lot better too!"

CHAPTER 18 How Beazel elects to capture a mild-mannered Cottontail Rabbit, *Lepus timidus*

Red ambled along Highway 287 carrying his fishing pole hidden alongside his leg. At the jailhouse, close to Beazel Hardin's house, he saw one police car but no game warden pickup. At Hardin's he saw several legs sticking out from under the Dodge Convertible that Red's Brother, Ryan, had blown up by racing foot to the floor into Lander every day. He leaned over the open engine compartment and saw three faces looking up at him and clanking wrenches. Beazel's Dad, John, was instructing Ryan and Beazel on the replacement of the Dodge flathead six cylinder engine.

"Ahh, just in time," said John, "can you hand me that 3 in 1 oil up there?"

Red grabbed the oilcan sitting on the radiator. He slipped it downward along the engine block, knocking grease clods down on the faces of the workers below. They sputtered, yelled and slid out from under the car. Red leaned deep over the motor and feigned interest in the car.

"Ever seen a flathead Engine before?" John asked.

Red frowned but quickly recovered, "Yah," he puffed, "I saw some from Montana at the Sundance. What's wrong with Ryan's car?"

"Just like all Flatheads, it's got a loose rod. It's got to get a bore job and its crank ground, or else a new crank." John was proud to be able to deliver his diagnosis and to display his mechanical knowledge. Noticing Red's fishing pole, he said, "Looks like you need a crew for a fishin' trip?"

Everyone looked at Ryan since it was his car that was being fixed. Ryan shrugged. He didn't need his little brother getting in the way and he didn't want to go fishing himself. He didn't understand what fun Red and Beazel got out of going fishing and getting cold and wet. When he got a new motor in his car he would go back to cruising Main Street in Lander. The heck with the Country.

"Go ahead," waved John. Beazel ran into his house and reappeared with his fishing pole.

Red and Beazel didn't understand cars yet. They were happy walking along 287 toward the Little Wind River Bridge. Beazel was chomping loudly on a big wad of gum, so Red asked, "You got gum?"

Beazel stuck out the pink blob and said, "I don't have any more but you can have some of this." He estimated the 1/2 way point on the gum wad, bit with his teeth and stretched the rest out until it broke. He handed it to Red who quickly popped it in his mouth and tested how much good was left in it.

Red carried his pole openly now, even with a flourish, even though Beazel was only a Sioux. If he was a Shoshone or an Arapaho, they could catch all the fish they wanted. No limit. If Joe caught them with fish they would say that Red hadn't caught anything. So far, Beazel and Red had never been challenged by a Game Warden.

They broke out their Luckies when they were out of sight on the bridge and lit up with big farmer matches. Red cracked his match alight with his thumbnail, but a big chunk of sulphur broke off under his nail, flared, and burnt him. "Ookey dah," yelled Red, waving his hand in the air.

Beazel laughed that sweet laugh you laugh when a Buddy screws up. He lifted his leg up and proudly struck his match along his Levis on the underside of his thigh. He dragged it too long, though, and it flamed up on his pants and burnt his leg. "Shit, shit," he yelled.

Red laughed a longer and louder laugh. "Beazel did you know you have sulphur and burn marks all up and down the butt and legs of your Levis? Guess your folks sure don't know you smoke."

Beazel plunked down on the bridge railing to cover up his butt. Red sat beside him and tried to work the sulphur out from his thumbnail. "I never catch anything off this bridge," said Red.

"Me neither," nodded Beazel. They both got up and spit in the river.

They continued a couple of hundred feet further to where the woods gave way to open sagebrush flats. They slipped through the barbwire fence, leaving the highway. Now they were headed downstream between the River and Signal Hill. On the west end of Signal Hill was a notch where the old water tank for Fort Washakie used to be. Mr.

Barker, who farmed out by Ray Lake, told them that an old Tim McCoy cowboy movie was filmed on Signal Hill. A bunch of Indian Boys had been hired to ride their ponies at full speed down the hill.

When they walked clear of the Buffalo Berry bushes near the Highway, they dodged through the cottonwood trees over to the River. They cast for a while but didn't catch anything.

"Want to go to Chalk Butte?" asked Red.

"Yep," said Beazel.

So, they started back toward the open sagebrush hills and the trail to Chalk Butte, where the River was blocked by a big red and white rock cliff. A deep fishing and swimming hole was scoured out where the water turned hard right and cleared the rock. Before they left the Cottonwoods, however, they were stopped by a skunk family sauntering along at an unhurried pace.

Signal Hill and The Little Wind River Bridge

The two froze instantly and let the skunks pass. There was a Mother skunk and four little babies. Both boys knew not to mess with either a mother grizzly with cubs or a mother skunk with kits. "Mmmm, tempting, though," thought Beazel. He looked at Red. He had heard Red's stories of wildlife grabs and was envious of the resultant fame. Red looked at him and shook his head no.

The skunks safely passed and the boys continued their trip, bobbing back and forth off the trail to check local points of interest. There was the swimming hole with the big boulder firepit they had built. There was the old riverbank hole where they had found some puppies one spring. A pack of wild dogs that they would occasionally see from a great distance hunted this area. It was composed of an outrageous mix of breeds, sizes, and colors. Their sounds when in full hunt were indescribable and a little scary.

As they topped the last big sagebrush covered ridge, they tensed, ducked low, and snuck over the ridge. One day when they were out hunting, they had discovered a Sage Chicken Booming Ground on this slope. There were thousands of birds there that day, and they always crossed that slope with great expectations of seeing that same sight. They didn't, as it was the wrong time of year.

But, now they could see the top of the cliff at Chalk Butte. Their path would take them beside a tar seep and an old oil well that had been drilled and abandoned a long time ago. Scattered about were barrels, cables, pipes, and rusty drill casing. Powdery white drilling mud lay about and lots of gooey black oil and tar floated in the mud pit. The junk piles always demanded a little inspection in passing.

As they arrived at the old well, a Cottontail Rabbit jumped out from the sagebrush in front of them and ran for cover. Its choice of cover was an old pipe strewn with others on the ground. Red and Beazel looked knowingly at each other. Beazel saw his chance and whispered, "I'm going to grab him!"

"Okay," agreed his friend.

They approached the stack of pipes, each about 30 feet long. Red motioned for Beazel to go to the other end of the pile to head off the rabbit if he tried to escape. Then they knelt down and looked through the top pipe. They both looked through the same pipe at the same time, making it dark. Red moved over to another pipe and so did Beazel. It was still dark. They did this a couple more times. Red observed Beazel's style of looking down pipes. Then he pretended to look at the next pipe. When Beazel looked at his end, Red jumped back to the last pipe and looked through it. It was empty. Red started thinking that maybe a rabbit could be rabid and behave in an unusual way, like jumpin' out of a pipe onto your face and biting off your nose. "Beazel, I'm blocking off your light. You check all these pipes and tell me when you find him."

Cottontail Rabbit, *Lepus timidus*

"Okay," smiled Beazel, appreciating his friend giving him this opportunity. He worked along the ground on all fours, with his butt up in the air, eyeballin' every pipe. He soon found the Cottontail and pointed to the pipe he was hiding in.

"I'll throw some rocks in," whispered Red.

"Okay," whispered back Beazel.

Red grabbed a rock, bent over sideways, and flung it with a sidearm pitch at the hole in the end of the pipe. He missed the hole and the rock skittered off the pipe and ricocheted along until it whacked Beazel in the side. "Ouch," he yelled.

"You should a ducked," whispered Red. He looked around the piles of junk and found a long iron rod that he could push down the pipe. He dragged it back and stuck it in the hole, "Ready?"

"Ready," whispered Beazel. He knelt down tucked up to the end of the pipe and placed his hands on each side of the opening.

Red started pushing. He looked at Beazel and saw that he looked poised, ready, and confident. He pushed the rod further.

Beazel was grinning broadly as the rod, along with the rabbit, neared his end of the pipe. Red saw only a flash of fur as it burst out of the pipe and hit Beazel in the crotch, knocking him down by the surprise of its attack. Red laughed. Beazel's hands automatically closed on the ball of furry fury, much to his regret. He jumped up and tried to hold on to the claws-out Bunny, who was trying to run up Beazel's body and was ripping up his sleeves and flipping open the snap buttons on his shirt. Red laughed harder.

Beazel was learning that a rabbit is really a ball of solid muscle with sharp claws attached. In normal life, that is, the Beazel-free life, it doesn't realize that it could use its massive rear legs to claw to shreds any predator that grabbed it. It can jump 10 times

211

its own height whereas Beazel's personal best, assisted by a Prairie Rattler, was only half his own height. This gave a factor of 20:1 to the Cottontail.

Beazel crouched over and attempted to pin the exploding rabbit against his legs. This allowed *Lepus timidus* to find support for his back and he ripped Beazel's arms with his claws. Bleeding only made Beazel more determined. He threw himself on the ground on top of the rabbit, but the spot he landed in was the tar pit. He mucked and splashed around with his fierce foe until both were covered with black tar. Fortunately for Beazel, the violence of the struggle was now partly cushioned by the tarry goop, and he staggered to his feet in slow motion and yelled, "I'm blind!"

Now Red just couldn't believe that little ol' Bunny Rabbit could be giving Beazel such a fight. He figured Beazel was hamming it up for a joke. Therefore, he continued laughing when Beazel jumped up all black with tar. "You look like . . . " - but Red didn't get his sentence all out before Beazel tripped backwards and fell into a big puff of powdered white drilling clay. When he got up he was all white.

"Ohhh, Beazel," whooped Red, "now you're white! Oh, ha, ha, ha, ha!" Red wiped his tears with his sleeve. He fell to his knees.

Beazel, meanwhile, was changing his mind about the character of rabbits and the desirability of gaining experience in the ways of Nature's creatures, great and small. Especially small, come to think of it.

He had also reached that point in a fight where the ego must come to and accept the fact that you are getting the shit beat out of you. He decided to end this fight and fling this vicious killer away. He gave it a fling, but it wouldn't away. The tar and the clay had cemented the Rabbit to his hands and created a black and white jackhammer pounding and slashing up and down on his body.

This unleashed even more screams of laughter and tears from Red. His bubble gum fell out of his mouth, saving him from choking. He lay down on the ground and held his stomach.

Beazel ran all the way to the river and jumped in. This parted the contestants very effectively and they went their separate ways. When Red quit laughing he couldn't see his friend anywhere. He picked up his gum and put it in his mouth. On the riverbank he found oily footprints aimed homeward. Red picked up both fishing poles and headed back home. "That Beazel sure is funny."

He started singing, "You ain't never caught a rabbit and you ain't no friend of mine." Beazel had to listen to this all the way along the Little Wind River as he rushed for the first aid kit at home. When Red got to Highway 287 he realized the sand in his gum was scratching his teeth. There was still some sweet left in it but he spit it out anyways. He thought he should stash the fishing poles in the woods or under the bridge, but he didn't. While he was walking across the bridge with a pole in each hand, he heard a vehicle coming up behind him. Joe Charbonneau's big green Game Warden pickup passed him, slowed, and tapped its brake lights on. Red's heart skipped a beat, but Joe didn't stop. The truck turned on the road that led to Hardin's house and the Jailhouse. Red kept on walking right through Fort Washakie, into the Catholic Church driveway, and over to his own house – St. David's Rectory.

In the following days Red repeatedly called the Hardin household to see when he could return Beazel's fishing pole. But someone had instructed all the Hardins to answer the same way – "I'm sorry, Mr. Hardin is out of the office, may I take a message?" Sometimes Red recognized Beazel's own voice saying this, but he didn't say anything, just played along, and said, "I'll call back later."

CHAPTER 19 A New Chief is chosen and leads a Raiding Party

The Indian School had been given a complete wood shop. It was coated in Army Surplus cosmoline as it had been intended for shipping overseas. All the saws, lathes, and hand tools had to be tediously rubbed clean by the boys. The cosmoline cleanup was the hardest part of building the wood shop. The machines were set up in the basement of the administration building. Workbenches were placed around the walls. Every hand tool was hung on the wall and its shape was painted on the wall so that you knew exactly where to return it.

Red unpacked a micrometer. It was in its own little wood box with padded interior. Red was fascinated by its weight and its metallic perfection. He showed it to Beazel. They spun the handle and measured several things. It was great. They decided to take it home and measure more stuff, like .22 shells, rifle barrels, bolts and bicycle axles.

Then Mr. Walton assembled all the boys in the middle of the wood shop. He told them that the micrometer was missing.

"If it's returned, no questions will be asked."

Later, Red and Beazel discussed those strange words. What did they mean? "It sounds like he thinks the micrometer has been stolen." They felt bad. "I wonder what kind of questions he wouldn't ask." They felt guilty. They agreed they had to put the tool back. Then they worked out a plan to return the tool and put it in its little box. When would no one be around? Who would carry it? When was the wood shop unlocked? They managed to replace it and learned that it's sometimes harder to undo something than to do it. No questions were asked.

The first assignment in Wood Shop Class was to turn a lamp on the wood lathe. Each boy was given a chunk of wood. It was clamped in the lathe and spun while a chisel was held against it. Long fresh curls of wood fell on the floor as the boy moved the chisel further into the wood. Eventually, every student had a voluptuous rounded lamp to take home and show off. These lay around their homes for years unless someone mistook them for firewood.

While the boys were taking their shop class, the girls had Home Economics Class. Miss Marshall taught them to knit, sew, and cook. By Christmas they had made lots of potholders. The girls were also going to have a Fashion Show in which they would model their own handiwork and and get the opportunity to dress up.

When the date of the Fashion Show approached, the girls posted notices around the school directing students to the old original stone school building. It had a half gym with hardwood floors and an elevated stage with big theater curtains. It was the only time of the year the old building was used.

On the day of the Fashion Show, the 7th and 8th Graders filed outside the new school building and over to the old schoolhouse. They had to stand jammed up in the half gym. Miss Marshall slipped through the curtains and explained that the girls were going to model their clothes.

The curtains then parted and the girls paraded around the stage showing their Home Economics creations. Miss Marshall explained each girl's work and everyone got a nice round of applause when prompted to clap. They were seeing children turned into women.

Set playing in Red's head was Sonny James singing "Young Love."

The 60 year old stone building they were in didn't have modern heating or cooling. No fresh air was coming in. 100 bodies could heat up a room pretty fast and wear out all the oxygen. By the climax of the Fashion Show, everyone was sweltering. The worst off were the Home Economics girls lined up for the Grand Finale in skirts, blouses, jackets, girdles, nylons, and high heels. They were toasting.

All the elastic, straps, and cinches of this wardrobe were new to these girls. They squirmed around and wobbled in their high heels. The boys in the audience noticed that Verdette Antelope was especially uncomfortable in her new clothing. She squirmed, made adjustments, then pulled and twisted around to jack everything into place. This was naturally pointed out by everyone in the audience and they smiled at her contortions. Verdette noticed their noticing from up on the stage. Her blazing eyes picked out Red.

The Fashion Show ended and everyone was sent outside to the playground to fill the remaining time until lunch. Red was milling around near the basketball court with Freckles and Honch when Verdette walked up to him looking stunning in her new suit. He was quite surprised when she walked right up in front of him and looked him straight in the eyes with her big brown eyes.

Red waited for her to say something. Verdette swung her arm as hard as she could and slapped Red across the cheek. His eyes watered. Verdette turned in her high heels and wobbled away, without saying a word.

A giggling crowd gathered around Red. They stared at him as their smiles grew bigger. They finally blurted out with laughter. A perfectly shaped red handprint was appearing on Red's left cheek.

"What? What?" asked the embarrassed Red.

"A hand, a hand," yelled Tony Knight, "a red hand!"

"It's Chief Red Hand!" yelled Dean Stockman, "Chief Red Hand!"

"Chief Red Hand, Chief Red Hand!" everyone cheered. The confused White Boy touched his hand to his cheek and then wobbled off to lunch with a band of gigglers following him. He darted into the Mens Room after lunch and saw the still bright hand print on his cheek. He went to class and all the girls took glances at him, whispered, and giggled with their hands over their mouths.

At recess the boys were restless. Someone said they should take off and go down to the Little Wind River. "Cut classes?"

That idea excited them and perhaps Chief Red Hand promoted the idea because he had been laughed at so much that day. The Fashion Show had already made it seem like a holiday – why not take off the rest of the day? The idea was spread around the basketball court and the playground. They would play hooky and skip Miss Mitchell's Math

Class. A plan to run for the old barn and then the river was agreed to by –

Chief Red Hand

Honch

Beazel

Robbie

Freckles

Ronnie

Layman

Who would make the first break from the schoolground? Honch declared that he was held back because his Father was President of the School Board. Ronnie then claimed his need for discretion because his Father was Tribal Chief. "You go first, Chief Red Hand", someone said. They all looked at his cheek, so he sighed and then ran to the east end of the school building where no one could see him. The others followed him one by one when they thought no one was looking. Here Honch raised again his worries about his participation in the holiday. He dropped back a couple of spaces in the lineup.

Then the band had to make a run through the sagebrush to the old barn. Red made a darting and dodging run with his head held low. Each warrior followed him in turn. They were now completely out of sight. Honch had slipped back to the end of the group and said something about, "can't – School Board – President – look bad".

Free now to do anything they wanted, they slipped out of the north side of the barn and ran out to the middle of the old pasture. Honch had put a big gap between him and his friends now. When he joined them he shook his head, "I have to go back."

The others nodded. Honch left them and ran back to the old barn. Then the band made a run for the cottonwood trees along the river and disappeared from everyone's view. Well, everyone that is except Joe Charbonneau. He was standing on the top of Chalk Butte watching them through binoculars. "What the heck are they up to now?" thought Joe. He could see they didn't have fishing poles but knew they kept several hidden along the river. The Indian Boys could catch any number of fish they wanted, at any time. The Preacher's Kid would be illegal. Joe watched their progress from behind the cottonwood trees.

The boys had made good their escape from school but now found that they didn't have anything to do. No fishing poles, no guns, no cigarettes, no bubble gum. They waded across the Little Wind River to the eroded hills where Layman invented a game of jumping off cliffs. The idea was to see who could jump off the highest cliff. Layman started jumping off a low spot and they all followed him. Then he went higher, higher, and even higher. Red dropped out of competition. Layman won. They praised his jumping style, "How can you land from so high up?"

"You keep your legs bent," said Layman, squatting down to illustrate. "Then when you land you push up with your legs to absorb the shock." He straightened up.

No one said that it looked like a good way to get hurt. Besides, Layman was 18 years old and only with them in 8th grade because he had repeated so many years. Red remembered that Layman had engraved "OYW" on Ryan's necklace, instead of "WYO".

They idled around the river for a while, got completely bored, and decided to go up the river to Ft. Washakie. Joe followed them by staying hidden behind the cottonwood trees along the river.

The next stop for Chief Red Hand's band was the dump. They dug out beer bottles and threw them up in the air while the others threw rocks at them. They never ran out of beer bottles but they did run out of rocks. Joe lay on his belly on Signal Hill to observe the target practice. When the Raiders left the dump he slinked again through the trees until reaching Highway 287 and Ft. Washakie.

When the Chief Red Hand Band passed Hardin's house at the edge of the Fort, Beazel left them. Then they walked through the Parade Ground and they all scattered in their separate home directions. Red walked into the Rectory and Ryan told him, "Your sunburn looks just like a hand."

* * *

Joe realized he had wasted a lot of time. He gave up the game and trudged to the Jailhouse where he saw Tallboy's black and white Reservation Police Car.

"Tallboy," Joe asked, "can you give me a ride down to my truck at Chalk Butte?"

"Sorry, Joe, I just got called into Mill Creek for some commotion. How did you get up here?"

"Well, I, uh, thought it was a pretty nice day so I just walked right on up and left my truck." Joe realized he had made a mistake and started out on foot toward Chalk Butte and his Game Warden Truck. At home that night he picked 5 ticks off that he had got from skulking through the sagebrush.

* * *

The next day at school the entire Chief Red Hand Band was called into the Principal's Office. Mr. Brooks told them he was starting a special math class just for them. A big round table was placed just outside his door and the boys were assigned places around it. Their first assignment was to design a sprinkler system for the schoolgrounds. They were given little shapes of circles, half circles and quarter circles. Each one represented a sprinkler head. Then they were given a map of the yard and had to draw 25' squares all over it and then fit the little circles inside each one. They never had to go back to Miss Mitchell's Math class.

CHAPTER 20 How Pony Knight recruited the Preacher's Kid in dynamite cap fun

When Reverend B. made his house calls on his flock, he would drive the yellow Hudson and later, the pink Ford, up and down the gravel roads of Trout Creek, South Fork, and North Fork. He noticed the wide spacing between all the Shoshone houses. Perhaps the next house was built to be just out of earshot of the others. He did not know. The long driveways into each house gave the occupants plenty of time to hide when they saw Reverend B. coming.

The Trout Creek road, from Hunt's Corner, went west toward the Wind River Mountains. It passed the homes of Hines, Braman, Glick, Jarvis, Kniffin, Roberts, Chingman, Ward, Hurtado, Myers, Wadda, Wagon, Isis, Arrowsmith, Marshall, Tillman, Moon, Perry, Poire, Osborne, Day, LeBeau, McAdams. The School Bus picked up all the children from these homes. At Hunt's corner, it picked up Honch Hunt. It crossed US Highway 287 and drove on the Ethete Road to the big Russian Olive windbreak. It picked up Ronnie Beauclair. The driver was Dave Peters, a Montana Sioux. He was the Head Custodian at the school. His wife, Edith, worked at Hunt's Trading Post. The bus was the biggest one that the school had – a yellow 1937 White Motor Company bus that looked just like an oversized Yellowstone Park Bus.

No longer was the little white Wind River schoolhouse open. Now, all grades 1 through 8 went to the big government school on the Ethete Road. Between the road and the school was a huge playing field, including a dirt basketball court. Well, dirt and gravel. Red confirmed the gravel part when Dean Stockman tripped him for no reason and sent him sprawling. Little pieces of rock were stuck in the palms of his hands and in his kneecap. The next day

Dean said, "I probably shouldn't have thrown you down yesterday."

Red had no idea why anyone would throw him down.

During a lunchtime basketball game the next day, Red, Honch, and Beazel were playing against Dean, Pony, and Darrell Manning. Next to them, a bunch of girls were playing on the grassy slope between the basketball court and the school buildings. Dean patted his bulging Levi pants pocket, reached in and pulled out a handful of farmer matches. A great big sulphury farmer match was valuable because you could always light a cigarette in the Wyoming wind with its flare. This was called a sulphur light. It ruined the taste of your smoke and fouled your mouth.

"Want some matches?" Dean asked, holding a handful out under Red's nose.

Red looked admiringly at the handful of matches, but shook his head – no. Dean mashed them back with the hundreds of other matches puffing out his pockets.

Then Pony eyed the two White Boys, Red and Honch, and their Sioux friend, Beazel. Pony said, "All the Indians with their bows and arrows could defeat all the Whites with their Atomic Bombs."

No one knew what had prompted that remark. Pony only got nodding agreement from Dean and Darrell, but had distracted the Enemy. He dribbled down court and passed the basketball to Dean. The basket was open and Dean charged it. Unfortunately, he forgot about the rough, gravelly patch where he had recently thrown Red down. He tripped while running at full speed and went sliding along the ground. His pocket full of matches slid along, also. This ignited them inside his pocket with a big puff of smoke, followed by a howl of pain.

This scream attracted the attention of all the girls. While everyone watched, Dean jumped up off the ground and pulled his smoking pants down. He patted and blew on the fire in his Levis. The girls began to laugh and point. Dean had a great big purple and orange burn on his thigh and was jumping up and down alternately rubbing his burn and slapping at his burning pants. He looked up and saw all the girls laughing at him. They put their hands over their mouths. He tried to pull his pants back up but one leg caught on his boot and made him start to hop. With smoke and sulphur fuming from his pants he hopped around a while until he fell over.

Red knelt beside Dean and started throwing dirt on the smoldering Levis. Honch and Beazel joined him and helped screen Dean from view. Soon the fire was out. Dean stood and pulled his pants up. A great big hole exposed his purple and orange thigh. He pulled his shirt tail down to cover it up and walked around the rest of the day holding the shirt down with his right hand.

A few days later on the basketball court, Pony Knight asked Red if he would like some blasting caps.

"What are they?" asked Red.

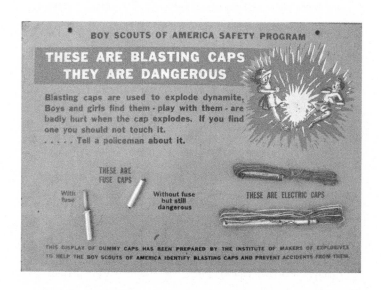

Red, Honch, and Beazel gathered around Pony, Dean, and Darrell. Pony pulled out a copper clad dynamite cap with two cotton covered wires attached.

"Where'd you get those?" asked Honch.

"I found them in an old abandoned cabin up in the mountains," said Pony.

Everyone made suspicious frowns but they all examined the caps with great interest.

"How many you got?" asked Beazel, with a light in his eye.

"Hundreds, we could split them up with you guys."

"How do you blow them up?" asked Honch.

"With a battery," said Darrell. He pulled a flashlight battery out of his pocket. "Just touch one wire to one end of the battery and the other wire to the other end. Make sure you're out of sight."

"How can you be out of sight?" asked Red, "those wires are only about five feet long?"

"Hang the cap over a cliff or put it in a hole. That's what we do. Pony blew one up on the ground and got a big piece of metal in his leg. Show them, Pony."

Pony rolled up the leg on his Levis. There was a great big black mark on his shin. "There's still metal in there," he said.

The wound looked pretty bad, but the three Buddies elected to take delivery on the ordinance anyways. The next day Pony and Darrell brought with them hundreds of dynamite caps, surprising their customers with their generosity. "Oh, boy," thought the White Boy and Beazel.

Pony was even kind enough to give them his D cell battery, so the boys could start blasting right away. They skipped the bus and started to walk home. Each of them had dynamite caps stuffed in all his pockets and under his shirt. They approached a culvert under the road with care and looked it over. They were apprehensive about their first dynamite job. Carefully they stuck the blasting cap in the culvert and laid the wires out the end. Lying on the ground, they prepared to cover their eyes. Red pulled out the battery and handed it toward Honch. Honch just looked at it but didn't take it. Red handed it toward Beazel. Beazel just looked at it.

"Okay," said Red. They covered their eyes. Red touched the wires to the ends of the battery. KKKKAAAABBOOOOM!

"AAAAhhhhh," not bad," they all thought. It was powerful, but not too scary. Then they all took turns using the battery while they popped caps in fence posts, prairie dog holes, cans, and sometimes just hanging over a cliff.

Joe Charbonneau was gassing up his great big green Game Warden truck at the Sacajawea Service Station when he heard the series of booms coming from down the Ethete Road. He finished filling and drove down the road. He saw Red, Honch, and Beazel turning on the dirt road at Ronnie Beauclair's house. He didn't see any guns. He continued to the Government School and turned around. On the way back he stopped at the Russian Olive Wind break. He searched around in the trees for a .22 or a shotgun. He didn't find anything.

The dynamite crew passed Winchell's and Highway 287. They entered the St. David's Churchyard and went into the parsonage and Red's bedroom. He convinced them to lock up all the dynamite caps in his lockbox, where they would be safe. They agreed. The blasting caps sat locked away safely on Red's clothes dresser.

When they wanted to go dynamiting, Red unlocked the box and they loaded up with some caps and the battery. Then, a series of bangs might be heard progressing around Ft. Washakie. Then, to the Little Wind River, where many caps were wasted attempting to dynamite fish.

So many booms were heard one Saturday that Joe heard a few of them when he stopped by the Reservation Jail. He waited. Soon the Subjects walked out of the woods. No rifles. After they passed he walked down to the Little Wind River and searched under the bridge. Nothing. Then he walked downstream to the Subjects' swimming hole and campsite. Nothing. Then he walked upstream to the big bend fishing hole. Nothing. No stashed rifles, no stashed fishing poles. "Darn it", thought Joe, "darn it all."

Red learned that he could twist several of the wires together to extend the safe working distance of the caps. Still, there was something missing – you couldn't see the explosion. They were too afraid of getting copper shrapnel from the explosion. And – Pony and Darrell had given them so many caps that they were even getting a little bored. Honch dropped out of the game. The explosions mysteriously slowed.

Joe discussed the situation with the Reservation cops. Tallboy agreed to help with surveillance. They refused to be beaten by the Preacher's Kid. They had cars, they had radios, they had time, they had badges. They listened to gossip.

One day, after school, Red got off the bus at St. Davids, and walked toward his house. He saw a police car drive off. He thought that it might have something to do with him. He entered the front door where he met his Mother.

"They took away your dynamite, Red."

"Oh."

He went into his bedroom and checked the lockbox on his dresser. Hmmm, it was still locked. He looked at the screws on the hinges. Uhhh, they must have unscrewed the hinges. Clever. He unlocked the box. All the dynamite caps were gone.

The next day at school, Red looked at Pony Knight, and Pony Knight looked at Red. They didn't say anything about the caps. No one said anything about the caps. The silence made Red feel guilty.

On Saturday, Red walked over to Beazel's house. As he passed the jail, Joe's Game Warden truck was parked beside Tallboy's Police Car and they were talking. Tallboy thrust his lips out in Red's direction. Joe looked at Red and studied him for a while.

"I think that kid is running off good Christians faster than his Dad can convert them."

CHAPTER 21 Red discovers a Hornets' Nest as big as a football and engineers its safe removal

When Russ Crossman built the new home for Reverend and Mrs. B. at Fort Washakie, he first built an outhouse. He simply dug a hole in the ground and over it built a telephone booth size wood shack with no wall or door on the west side. There was only the alfalfa field in view from there and, in the distance, the Sundance Grounds. In the far far distance the Wind River Mountains loomed over the Reservation.

When all the work was completed on the new Rectory, Russ decided to leave the outhouse where it was. He filled in the pit and replaced the open hole board with a solid plank. It didn't take Red long to acquire this property as a new one man clubhouse. He could slip out of the house, walk 50 feet out back over the irrigation ditches and disappear into his new retreat. He could smoke safely in there, having the three sided shack between him and the house.

This new clubhouse had come with remnants of a Montgomery Ward Catalogue and some Sears Roebuck pages. There were rifles and shotguns pictured in them, deer calls, decoys, and knives. Red would flip past the pages of women modeling underwear. At some point he began to realize the models' hourglass figures were like some of the older girls in school. This, apparently, was to hold their bras up and keep their skirts from falling down. Red soon restocked his club library with "Gun Digest", "Shooters Bible", "Car Craft", and "Hot Rod".

One afternoon little brother Douglas left his 3rd grade class and approached the lineup of buses behind the school. The bright yellow-orange buses with black stripes looked like bumblebees. Seeing a bus full of Indians watching his progress and licking their lips, he elected to walk the Windbreak Road home. Being Girls Catechism day at St. Davids, Vita, Mila, and Mona elected to jump off the bus and follow him. Dressed in bright blue, red, and green skirts, with white blouses, they alternately walked or ran to slowly close in on Douglas.

He had worried about just such an attack and watched them out of the corner of his eye as they raced towards him down the lane.

The Windbreak Road ran straight north from Beauclairs' for about a ¼ mile then turned due west for ½ mile past Winchell's farm. Douglas diligently streaked along the two sides of this triangle, continually looking over his shoulder at the cheering little waifs in pursuit. But, the three girls didn't square off on the road. They cut across the hypotenuse by slipping through the barbwire fence and streaking across the hayfield.

"Wait up!" they yelled at Douglas, "wait up!"

Douglas saw they could easily catch him due to their shortcut. He continued running down the road, monitoring the progress of Vita, Mila, and Mona. They leapt and surged and yelled. But – Douglas found himself unscathed and safe at Highway 287. The girls had somehow been unable to catch him, even on the hypotenuse. He crossed the highway and entered the safety of the new Rectory, Russ Crossman's handiwork. Having survived the run, he felt safe for the rest of the day in the safety of his bedroom.

The chase placed the girls at St. Davids too early for Catechism lessons from Reverend B. They looked around for some way to occupy their time. They saw a telephone booth/outhouse/clubhouse behind the Rectory and saw a puff of smoke rising from it. They decided to sneak up on it.

They tiptoed through the dry weeds, reaching the skinny shack unbeknownst to the innocent occupant within.

Red was puffing on a Bull Durham cigarette and reading about the 600 Nitro Express Elephant Gun.

236

Muzzle velocity, feet per second, foot pounds of energy, and knockdown power. Suddenly, a cute little brown face looked around the side of the clubhouse only inches away. Red jumped. Then another little brown face appeared beside that one – and – then – a third.

Red let out his puff of smoke, speechless.

"What are you doing?" asked Vita.

"What are you doing?" asked Mila.

"What are you doing?" asked Mona.

Red stood up and put his magazine down, "Nothin'". He gave a strict look at the girls, letting them know the seriousness of their crime – invasion of privacy. His 8th grade height towered over their 6th grade littleness.

They gave him innocent glances and then giggled back to the house.

Red, feeling that his clubhouse had been violated, sauntered over to St. Davids Church, sat down on the ground and leaned back against the logs. Soon, he became aware of some insect activity in the area. He looked up and saw a huge hornets' nest, bigger than a football, under the eave of the Church. Hornets would drop out of the hole in the bottom of the hive in pairs and fly out in search of food. Sometimes their flight paths came straight toward him but they didn't seem to mind and flew around him.

Red knew that hornets' nest would have to go. He picked up some rocks and tossed them up at the nest. His third throw hit the nest straight on and a blizzard of mad hornets burst out of the nest. They were looking for anything that moved or was warm. That was Red.

His ears were stung first and he began to run. "Ouch, ouch, ouch!" This was seen as an admission of guilt by the hornets so they increased their attack. Hornets stung his face, neck and arms. He swatted at them as he ran, then he rolled in the crunchy dry weeds to try to get them off.

Red jumped up and ran toward the front door of the house. Around the back, three little faces looked, giggled and watched in bewilderment as Red ran hopping and darting and swatting at invisible attackers.

Safely inside the house, Red looked in the bathroom mirror and saw the nasty red welts raising on his head. He went to the "Family Home Doctor" book and looked up "bee stings". It said to make a baking soda paste and daub that over the bites. He found the Arm and Hammer Baking Soda and stirred some into water in a cup. He spread this all around his face, arms, and hands. He felt better right away, so he pretty much put the white paste all over.

He sat down to let it dry while he pondered his next plan. Aha! He got the vacuum cleaner out and rounded up all the extension cords he could find. Then he plugged the cords all together from the house to the Church where the hornets' nest was. Then he set the ladder up under the nest, turned on the vacuum cleaner and climbed up. He held out the tube and aimed at the entry hole. Fwat! A hornet came out and was immediately sucked into the vacuum cleaner. Fwack – Fwack – two more. Red touched the tube to the nest and hornets streamed out. "Fwoot" – "Thunk" – "Thip" –"Shish" – "Flit" – they all got sucked into the vacuum cleaner.

Reverend B. was inside the Church trying to teach the catechism class. All the roaring outside concerned him. He excused himself and went outside to look around. The girls followed him. He traced the noise to the back of the Church, soon picking up the trail of extension cords. He saw Red, all splotchy white, standing on the ladder and holding the vacuum cleaner tube up to a hornets' nest. He turned around, held out his arms to protect the girls, and channeled them back inside.

Red tapped the nest and the vibration brought out the last of the hornets. He guessed a couple of hundred were now in the vacuum cleaner. What should he do with them? Well, he realized there wasn't anything that could be done, so he took the cords, the ladder, and the vacuum cleaner back to the garage.

Red retired to the peace of his outback clubhouse again and started reading the Warshawsky/J.C. Whitney Auto Parts catalogue about the four carburetor manifolds that fit the Ford flathead V8.

Meanwhile, Mrs. B. returned home and prepared to clean the living room. She retrieved the vacuum cleaner from the garage and plugged it in. It moaned strangely and didn't seem to have much suction. The bag was obviously filled up.

"Douglas!" yelled Mrs. B., "will you please take this bag out and dump it?"

Douglas dutifully took the bag out of the machine and went out back to the trashcan to empty it. Vita, Mila, and Mona had just finished their catechism and watched him from the Church steps.

Inside the house, Mrs. B. heard loud yelling coming from the back yard followed by a desperate clawing at the door.

Wind River Indian School, built 1892
Site of noon wrestling, fist-fights, the 100 yard
dash and recess intrigues

CHAPTER 22 How Red and Johnny Rodda drank wine in St. David's Church and fell down in the snow

Poor Mrs. B. had hoped all her three sons would be musical, but Red couldn't carry a note. Ryan, Red, and Douglas each dutifully took, per contract, one year of piano lessons. Ryan got through his year and somehow spun off into guitar, probably as an act of rebellion. Douglas continued forever with the piano and along the way picked up the organ, as well. He became so good that he could relieve Mrs. B., who often relieved Mrs. Barkley, the Number One Organist, wife of the Postmaster, and daughter of Reverend Roberts.

Red had walked the one mile in Durand, Michigan, to Mrs. Baxter's house for piano lessons after school. He squirmed and struggled with "Twinkle Twinkle Little Star" and "Mary Had a Little Lamb". He looked forward to the end of the year and asked to retire from the piano. Mrs. B. made no objection.

In the fourth grade they were asked to each bring $1.50 to school for the purchase of a Tonette. This turned out to be a plastic flute that would introduce the children of America to music. Mrs. Wakefield attempted to teach 30 tooting and squeaking 4th Graders how to read and play music. As a result of the program, Mrs. Hamm, the 5th Grade Teacher, declined to continue the training the next school year.

Then the B.'s moved to Walla Walla, where Ryan went to Pioneer Junior High and Red went to Birney Grade School. His 6th Grade Teacher, Mrs. Davis, was trying to build a school band, and needed a Bass Baritone player. All the good instruments were already taken. Red didn't mind taking lessons sitting beside Mrs. Davis, who was so nice and beautiful. He got so good that he could carry the huge Baritone home on his bicycle. He would clamp the handle of the case tightly to the right handlebar. Then, leaning far over to the left to counterbalance the weight of the big horn, he would pedal all the way home to Celestia Drive, bonking his right knee on the big black case with every pump. He never wrecked but he didn't make the band.

He did make the 6th grade baseball team. He got to wear a uniform. He hit the longest ball of the season, but it was straight up in the air and the Second Baseman caught it and put him out. Red bought a first baseman's glove and a pair of real steel baseball cleats. The players continued the next summer playing sandlot ball. Red was surprised to learn that Third Baseman, Eddie Matthews, sat by the radio, chewed bubble gum, and listened to "Earth Angel" in the dark. Red saw a shiny black 45 rpm record with a bright yellow Sun label for sale for $1.00 in a Walla Walla Drugstore. He bought it. The label read "Folsom Prison Blues" but Red didn't have a record player to play it on.

The music gene is strong, however, and seeks to perpetuate itself. Red somehow found himself looking through a big store window at a shiny new trumpet. Mrs. B. bought it for him. They brought it home and he tooted on it for a little while. They packed it up when they moved to Wyoming, and it sat in the closet until Johnny Rodda heard about it from Red and decided he wanted to buy it.

Rosette Rodda, Johnny's Mom, was one of the Robert's Mission Girls. She managed the Shoshone Craft Shop at Fort Washakie. She drove Johnny to the rectory and they looked at Red's trumpet. Johnny tooted it. Red sold it to him for $90.00 and in the future always remembered what an important part he had played in Johnny's education and musical development.

Red was just beginning to pay attention to the music on the radio – "Singing the Blues", "Hound Dog", "Sixteen Tons", "Don't Be Cruel". The other music in his life was the Church Hymns played on the Pump Organ by Mrs. Barkley.

Reverend B. had recruited Red as an Acolyte. During the Sermons, Red sat in the empty choir pew directly across from Mrs. Barkley at the organ. Red was dressed in his cassock and surplice. Mrs. Barkley told Reverend B. she thought Red looked angelic sitting there in his robes. Red was proud to survive the torture of the hard kneelers during the long prayers of the Episcopal Church. He would peek around to see who the less devout were that stayed seated and only slipped forward a little bit with one hand on the pew in front of them.

Red would dress in the small room behind the altar, strike a match to the brass candle wand, enter by the small door near the altar, and light the candles. At the end of the service, he would use the bell side of the wand to snuff out each of the candles. He also helped Reverend B. by passing him the water and the wine as it was being blessed. Then, he knelt and was given the first wafer of bread and sip of wine from the big silver chalice.

Ryan had never been an Acolyte. You had to get up early. Red didn't know why, but he eventually started losing interest in the Acolyte business. One Sunday he decided to skip. Instead of going into the Church and dressing, he snuck out to his clubhouse. He took out his Lucky Strikes. He lit one up. He started to think about what his Father would say. He thought about his obligation to the Lord. He started feeling guilty. He squirmed. He threw the Lucky away and went back to the Church and got dressed for the Service.

Johnny Rodda was his best friend for a while. They played Little League Baseball together in the summer. They roamed the hills hunting rabbits and pheasants. They walked the dirt road between Wind River and Fort Washakie with slingshots in hand

245

and shot pebbles at telephone poles. They played pingpong in the B.'s garage. Once they ran all the way from school to Fort Washakie on the dirt road from Norman Beauclair's house to Twitchell's. Red couldn't keep up with him. They boxed in Red's bedroom and got all sweaty. Johnny nearly knocked Red out. Dizzily, he said -

"Do you want to be my Blood Brother?"

"Yah."

Red took his pocket knife out and used his sweaty fingers to wipe the blade clean.

"You go first."

"That's okay, you go first."

Both boys punched their thumbs enough to draw blood. They mashed them together and held them for a minute.

"Now you've got White Blood in you," said Red.

"And you're a Shoshone," laughed Johnny.

* * *

Reverend B. found a cassock and surplice for Johnny. Just in time for the Christmas Holiday, the time husbands accompany their wives to church. Year long sinners and truants can also be seen in church on Christmas Eve, fidgeting in their tight suits and looking around to see if anyone sees them or smells the mothballs. Reverend B. was expecting the largest congregation ever and planned accordingly. He doubled the amount of wine and bread on the altar and then doubled it again. Three full chalices of wine stood ready on the altar. Best to not run out.

Christmas Eve that year was cold and snowy. The cars slipped and spun into the Churchyard and parked in the yard between St. David's and Father O'Connell's Catholic Church. Then they minced and tip toed in their dress shoes to the big log Church. They sat as far back in the pews as they could, but the Church kept filling up. Some people eventually had to sit up front. Red looked out on the big crowd. He saw Gwen Roberts, a teacher at the Indian School and Reverend Robert's daughter. The Shiptons, Bramans, Peches, Croskeys, Markleys, Rushes, Bybees, McGuires, Duffields, Parkers, including the rare Cecil. The Regulars. But Red was more interested in the large number of strangers. There were lots of Shoshones that he didn't know. Who were they? They filled the pews.

Mrs. Barkley started a rousing hymn and the procession of Reverend B., Johnny and Red slowly marched down the center aisle to the altar. Some sang along, but Red observed that the majority were lip-synching. During the sermon, Johnny and Red sat elevated above the congregation and observed the fidgeting, throat clearing, and tie straightening.

At the appropriate time, Reverend B. signaled the boys to join him at the altar for the blessing of the host.

Johnny and Red each stood beside Reverend B. while the bread and wine were blessed. There were three goblets of wine. Red had seen only a single one used before. The boys kneeled beside the altar, took the body and blood, and then waited. Reverend B. turned to the congregation in invitation. The Regulars slowly rose from their pews and soft footed up to the railing. They kneeled and took communion. Wave after wave of Communicants were expected to follow, filling the railing repeatedly. But – no one else came up.

Reverend B. stood waiting, holding the wine chalice. No one moved. This was a big problem. The sacrament had to be consumed right after use and could not be destroyed. That meant that Reverend B. would have to finish off more than just the remainder of one wine goblet. He turned to the altar. He raised the chalice and took a long drink. He looked at all the unused wine before him. He took another drink. He looked at Red. He looked at Johnny. He presented the cup to Red. Red dutifully tilted his head back. The Reverend didn't remove the cup. Red swallowed some more wine. The Reverend stepped over to Johnny. He presented the cup to him and force fed him also. Johnny and Red didn't quite grasp the problem, but, each time they were presented with the wine chalice, they drank. The Reverend drank, Red drank, Johnny drank. Pause. The Reverend drank, Red drank, Johnny drank. Pause.

In this manner, the three of them eventually guzzled down all the excess wine. Red let out a burp. The linens were placed over all the empty goblets and the service was wrapped up with the customary words and the closing hymn.

Reverend B., Red and Johnny slowly walked down the aisle to the rear of the Church. The boys were excused while the Reverend prepared to greet the exiting congregation. Red and Johnny hitched up the skirts of their cassocks and flew through the snow to the rectory. They had the great joy of being out of Church. In Red's bedroom they took off their robes and put on their coats. They wanted to play in the snow. They went out arm in arm singing "Sixteen Tons". They slipped, grabbed at each other, and fell down in the deep snow. They made snow angels. Churchgoers, through snowy windows, caught glimpses of two cherubs flapping their wings in the fluff - one white, one brown. They were filled with the Spirit.

CHAPTER 23 Red, Honch and Beazel get free boulders and Ryan does a high wire act

The first time Red visited his best friend Beazel's house, the strength and coolness of the home's thick stone walls impressed him. Highway 287 had severed it from the rest of the stone houses of Fort Washakie. Perhaps some Army Officer had lived there in 1900 when the Fort was still active. Beazel's Mom, Penelope, worked as an Accountant at the B.I.A. in Fort Washakie. Beazel's Dad, John, told Red that they could still see signs of Indian tree burials when the Hardins first moved into the house.

If Beazel walked out the back door of that stone government house he was only a couple of hundred feet from the Little Wind River and one of its best fishing holes. The River meandered around its little valley, cutting little horseshoes and loops. The water penetrated through the valley sand and watered a wide band of cottonwoods, willows, and stands of nearly impenetrable brush. The biggest cottonwood trees, though, were on the other side of the river. To wade across to them meant fighting a pretty good current and walking through unseen big boulders which busted your ankle bones if you were wearing traditional Converse high top tennis shoes. The best way to go was to walk along Highway 287 over the bridge, then duck through the right of way fence, and walk through the big cottonwoods.

On this route you might see a variety of animals: pheasants, rabbits, skunks, raccoons, badgers, squirrels, magpies, nighthawks, owls, snakes, sage hens, mice, and frogs. The deer were all shot out. You would pass over an oxbow pond and a small sandy beach where an old channel had been abandoned. Then, in the big trees you would come to a big turn in the river where it had hit some hard rock and been deflected southerly on its course. Here the River had carved out the Big Hole. Occasionally, the Little Wind would overflow its little valley and deposit big reefs of driftwood against the trees. This wood was completely dry in summer and had been debarked. It was perfect firewood and several big deposits of it were near the Big Hole. When Red and his friends swam there, they started a fire to dry off with before getting dressed. They also hid their fishing poles in the drift piles so they wouldn't have to carry them back and forth from home. Freckles had learned that trick from Dude Sawyer, a regular River Rat who often hung out with Harold Contado.

The friends spent a lot of time there, swimming, fishing and smoking. They raised a couple of big boulders out of the river, hefted them up the 20 feet of wellworn path to their campsite, and marked the corners of their fire pit. Red brought an empty five gallon paint bucket. They put creamed corn in it for chum and sunk it in the pond at the beach. When it was full of minnows, they slipped the lid on the can and pulled it up out of the water. After careful minnow analysis, observation, and inspection, the minnows were returned to the river to grow up into lunkers that the Boys knew they would catch some time in the future. Red used his swim mask for the job so he could see under water. He had taken it with him when they moved from their old adobe house to the new house near St. David's Church, so it survived the mysterious fire that burned down the old Rectory. He stored it in the bucket with their cigarettes, matches, gum, and candy. The bucket was hidden in the brush or deep inside the driftwood rubble.

Red would go up the river near the beach and float down wearing the mask. He could see everything – the boulders covering the bottom and the brown trout and rainbow trout that also favored the Big Hole. Imagine the surprise of a Reservation Trout when it saw a bone white human being with flowing red hair floating toward them wearing a white swim mask with a yellow lens.

Rainbow Trout

Beazel, Honch, and Red were swimming in the Big Hole one hot summer day, taking turns using Red's mask, and floating down the river. They saw two people walking down the riverbank. Soon, they recognized Hank and Harold Contado, moving with the searching pace of a pair of crows looking for something to do. Hesitant waves of greeting were exchanged.

Their two visitors were two to three years older than Red, so had to show little interest in childish things. Hank spotted Red's white swim mask with the yellow lens. "What's that for?"

Red held up his mask, "You can swim underwater and see everything. You can see further and your eyes are protected."

"Yah," piped up Honch, "look at the big boulders we got out of the River. Red got that giant one."

Now, Harold had been the Life Guard at The Plunge Hot Springs. He was muscular and specialized in underwater swimming. Hank was a natural athlete and was the Pitcher on Red's Little League Team. Harold looked at Hank and asked Beazel, "Is that the biggest one you could carry?"

"Red dragged up the biggest one," said Beazel, "he's strong!"

"Oh, yah? Watch this," said Hank.

The two brothers stripped down to their shorts. They left their tennis shoes on. They slipped into the water where the path met the Big Hole. They dove for boulders, picked them up, and waddled over the rocky bottom to the bank. When they had grunted one up on the shore, the three Builders rolled it or carried it to the fireplace.

Seeing the boulders having to be rolled away, not carried, gave more incentive to the Divers. They continued dragging up boulders. The fire pit soon became a complete circle of rocks. They also lined the path with boulders.

"We've got enough big ones," whispered Beazel to Honch and Red.

"Just a minute," whispered Honch. He picked up Red's mask and walked to the riverbank. He waved the mask in front of the Divers and said, "Red could see so well with this yellow lens that he could pick up rocks exactly the size of a basketball. Every time!"

"Oh, yah!" responded Hank to the challenge. They began pulling up the smaller size rocks and the boys used them for the next course on their fire pit and walkway.

When they had more than enough rocks lying all about the riverbank, Honch said, "You guys really can see without a mask!"

"You bet," said Hank with an I-told-you-so grin. "Got enough rocks?"

"Too many, too many," smiled Beazel, looking admiringly at the two Divers.

Hank and Harold climbed out of the water and grandly looked at all the rocks they had dredged up. They stood air drying proudly in the sun. They got dressed and started to go back up the river path. In parting, Hank waved his hand toward Red's white swim mask and said, "We don't need no stinking swim masks."

*   *   *

The next day, Hank appeared with his cousin, Freckles at the St. David's Rectory. They wanted to go to the Little Wind. Ryan and Alan were playing their guitars in Ryan's bedroom, and decided they wanted to go, too. Red telephoned Beazel and Honch. Beazel couldn't make it but Honch walked as fast as he could up from the Trading Post.

The party of six walked out the Catholic Church driveway and along Highway 287 through Fort Washakie. As they passed the jail near Beazel's house, Officer Tallboy saw the procession and immediately radioed Joe Charbonneau, "Possible Band of Poachers moving north on 287," said Tallboy, "over."

"10-4," came crackling back over the Police Radio, "any firearms or fishing poles visible? Over."

"Negative. Over."

"Any Shoshones in the Band? Over."

"Ah, let's see, you clearly got you-know-who glowing on the head, uh, looks like another White Boy, a Shoshone or two, no, Shoshone Lights, a skinny White Boy that has to be Ron Hunt, and Alan with the perfect flat top."

"Alan Beauclair?"

"10-4."

"Okay, he'll be the only one to catch any fish, I'm sure."

"Roger that."

So the expedition, without their knowledge, safely passed review and continued down to the Little Wind River Bridge. Feeling they had enough of the Big Hole yesterday, they crossed the barbwire fence on the West side of the Highway and walked through the big cottonwoods. They had their slingshots and pockets full of good stones. They looked for birds in the branches and took shots at day sleeping Night Hawks. Red's black inner tube rubber band broke when he pulled it back for a shot and it snapped him on the cheek. He covered up the accident by pretending nothing happened. He twirled the slingshot up and stuffed it in the back pocket of his Levis.

The woods were at their widest here and that was probably why Fort Washakie was built here on the south side of the Little Wind River. The North Fork and the South Fork met here. Across the river was sagebrush covered Signal Hill where any Attackers could be seen coming from north or south.

The river meandered through its valley, twisting and turning. Its turns created deep fishing holes that all the boys were familiar with. They could even remember each fish they caught at these holes. There were Browns, Rainbows, Whitefish, and Suckers in the river. They discussed whether or not you should eat Suckers and Whitefish.

Beazel said "Millman says Whitefish are okay, but there's lots of bones, like a Carp."

"Yuck - Carp!" they all shouted. They had heard that the Whiteman's dams had slowed and warmed the water and made Carp flourish.

But today they weren't fishing, just rambling, smoking, talking, and taking potshots with their slingshots. Eventually they came to the Cable Car where the Government gauged the flow of the river. It was at a fairly straight, deep, and boulder filled race on the North Fork of the Little Wind River. Water depth and rate of flow measurements were taken here. A big, rusty 100 feet long cable drooped across the river about 20 feet above the water. On each bank it was anchored to a wooden tower with a stairway up to a small platform. The cable was bolted to the top of each tower. On the north side of the river, a two man gondola was chained and padlocked to the tower. It hung on two pulleys from the cable so that it could be rolled out over the center of the river. At the stream's midpoint, the government agent lowered his instruments for depth and velocity of the water. This cable car fired the boys imaginations every time they passed it. They dreamed of rolling back and forth across the river and fishing from it. Every time they visited it they checked the lock and chain designed to keep this wonderful toy from being used by adventure seekers like themselves.

So, Ryan, Alan, Honch, and Red climbed up the tower, confirmed that the lock was locked, sat in the gondola and rocked it back and forth. Freckles and Hank started wading across the river.

"I wonder if you could cross over on this cable?" thought Ryan out loud.

The others looked at the great length of the big, rusty cable. Then they looked at the progress Hank and Freckles were making with wading. They were struggling to fight the current and their footing was getting difficult. They winced as their toes slid and got jammed down between the big boulders. Their ankle bones got whacked, making them "ouch" and sit down in the water to take the weight off their feet. There was no real danger as they could always abandon wading and just swim downstream into calmer water. But they kept trying to cross on foot.

The boys in the gondola took out their smokes and lit up. Ryan kept studying the cable. Suddenly, he grabbed the cable and swung himself out of the car. Everyone watched in surprise. Ryan started going hand over hand along and down the sagging cable, just like the monkey bars. He passed over the bank. He continued out over the water. He kept moving along, swinging back and forth, hand over hand, while his brother and his friends watched riveted. He got to the middle of the river and stopped. Far below him, Hank and Freckles struggled in thigh high water. Ryan took a big bounce and turned his right hand around so that his two palms and his body were facing up stream.

Some time passed. Red started thinking that Ryan was contemplating a jump into the river. If you looked at the boys standing in the river, however, you would conclude that you would probably break your leg or ankle when you hit the boulders in the river bottom. The water wasn't deep enough for a dive and the bed was too rough for a jump.

More time passed. Red thought maybe Ryan had got tired and was resting. He would soon continue his climb all the way over to the other side. No, Ryan just hung there.

They finished their smokes and watched as Ryan hung with his arms stretched tight at the low point on the cable.

Then, finally, he took another big bounce on the cable and flipped his left hand around so that he was facing back in the direction he came from. He started slowly going up the arc of the cable toward the tower where Red and the other two sat quietly. He got to the safety of the gondola and swung over the edge. He sat for a second and then turned his hands up and looked at them. Red looked, too. All he saw was raw meat, no skin. No one said a word.

The Boys scrambled down from the tower and joined the two waders on the bank. No one asked Ryan what had just happened. The group turned east and walked back down stream. Ryan didn't say anything all the way home and Red didn't hear him play his guitar for a long time.

CHAPTER 24 How to smoke in a hay stack

Beazel's Dad, John, had invented a cigarette holder for smoking on the front lines during a war. He knew some Indian Boys who had been in World War II. They told John they couldn't understand why the White Man sat still in his foxhole while they were being bombed. The Indians moved around a lot to increase their chance of survival. Everyone smoked the free cigarettes that the Army put in their

K-rations. John worried that the enemy might see the glowing ember of a cigarette along the opposite trenches, take a potshot, and kill the smoker. He made a perforated tin tube and attached it to the end of a cigarette holder. It held the cigarette and its ashes. It covered up the glow. Wars were temporarily over, so John changed the description of his holder to fire prevention device.

Red learned from observing John how to tap cigarette ashes into the palm of your hand when you were in polite company, dry woods, or in posh surroundings with no ashtray handy. He learned how to control fires by adding a blob of spit to your palm. The "ssst" Red heard when an ash hit the spit proved that there was still danger. Then, to extinguish your butt safely in a dried up cornfield or on someone's new sofa, you dipped the burning end into the spitball. Red and John's son, Beazel, didn't smoke in front of Mr. Hardin or Mrs. Hardin. A pack of Lucky Strikes could be smuggled around safely in your sock if your pants were long enough. Just don't get too sweaty.

One summer evening after they left the Hardin's house, they lit up their Luckies and walked along 287 through Fort Washakie. Beazel said, "There's an old army jeep parked in back of the garage." He pointed at the big old stone building where the

Government vehicles were repaired. Red's ears perked up at the mention of a Jeep. There were lots of them around for deer hunting and elk hunting in the high country of the Wind River Mountains. Cecil Barker even plowed with one for a while right after the war.

1898 Ft. Washakie Horse Stable = 1956 Auto Shop

Beazel led Red to a place in the high chain link fence where they could climb over and into the B.I.A.'s storage yard. Satisfied that they couldn't be seen, they climbed the fence and found an old gray Army Jeep sitting under a tin leanto next to a pile of hay bales. There was no top on the Jeep. They jumped in and looked around the wonderful round gauges and the shift levers with black rubber knobs. They took turns being the "Driver", spinning the steering wheel around, pushing in the clutch, and shifting through the gears. They read and memorized the metal plate on the dashboard that showed the shift patterns for the transmission and the four-wheel drive transfer case. They loved their Jeep. They snuck in many nights and drove their Jeep. When not driving it, they sat above it on the haystack, smoked, and looked down at their Jeep.

* * *

Scooter Ferris was Red's best friend for a while so Red told him about the Jeep. Scooter was with him the day Red stepped out of the Community Hall Gym and saw the billowing smoke rising up in the distance from Wind River. "Wonder what that is?" said Scooter.

They stopped by Scooter's house on the way to the B.'s. They stepped inside a one room house filled with bunk beds. Scooter's three younger brothers were home, but his four older brothers were gone. Red didn't mind not running into Sherman. Nor Nicky, either. They might want to play hard pitch baseball or do some force trading.

264

The Boys walked over to the St. David's Rectory and played ping pong in the garage. They shot baskets at the oversize backboard that Red had erected in the dirt beside the garage. Red asked Mrs. B. if Scooter could stay for supper. She set a place for him and they ate Tongue. Red told Scooter what it was after they finished and were outside walking in the dark. They ended up at the B.I.A. garage fence where Red was wondering if Scooter was too round to climb up the fence and slip between the top wires and the building's roof. But, he scrambled up effortlessly and they drove their Jeep and smoked in the haystack.

It was getting late and cooling down. Red suggested they camp out in the haystack all night. Scooter agreed. They arranged their smokes, matches, and Red's pocket watch where they could easily reach them. They rearranged the hay to make flat beds. They found that a big square bale of hay wouldn't lie on them like a blanket. They cut the binder twine on a couple of bales and pulled the loose hay over them. Their toes stuck out. They thrashed around throwing a thicker covering of loose hay all over their bodies. Now they found that little bits and needles of dried up hay had fallen down their necks and pants. They thrashed around trying to brush these out, but every movement they made allowed more dust and debris to get under their clothes. Their kicks sent stickers up their pant legs. The brittle straws stabbed at their hands and faces. They tossed and turned. Every once in a while someone said, "Are you asleep?" and someone else said, "No." They sat up and smoked. It was getting cold.

"Wanta be Blood Brothers?"

"Sure."

Red pulled out his pocketknife and wiped the lint off the blade. He punched a little hole in his left thumb and handed the knife to Scooter. Scooter looked back and forth from his left thumb to his right thumb and finally punched a little cut on his left thumb. They held their thumbs together for a minute.

"Brothers."

"Brothers."

Then the brothers tried again to go to sleep, but they were too cold and too itchy. Red looked at his pocket watch. It was 3:00 in the morning. "Let's get out of here!" said Red, "you can sleep on the floor at my house".

"Okay," said Scooter.

They slid down the side of the haystack, checked that the coast was clear, and climbed back over the fence. They headed along Route 287 toward the

266

Churchyard. As they passed the B.I.A. Hospital, Scooter said, "Hey, let's check out the boiler room."

He led the way to the back door of the hospital. They walked down the concrete steps and opened a heavy door. They heard a roar and saw a square line of flame flickering through a large furnace door. It was nice and warm in the room. They stood listening to the low rumble of the fire while their eyes got used to the dark. Red then saw that there was a small flat concrete area in front of the furnace and sloping concrete floors running in both directions away from the flat area. Scooter lay down on the floor near the furnace. "Try it."

Red lay down on the floor. He rolled a little closer to the furnace. Too hot – he rolled away a little. Scooter rolled himself into a good spot. Red wondered briefly if they might get gassed in their sleep, but he was too tired to think about it for very long. Although the concrete was hard, their coats cushioned them enough that they relaxed. A little time passed and the hissing fire soothed them to sleep. If the concrete started to pain a knee, hip, or shoulder, they would automatically roll over in their sleep.

Then, a noise brought Red into a semi-sleep. The door opened and someone walked into the room. Red, as in a dream, saw a Shoshone stagger over to him, look down, and say in a wine soaked voice, "Shosh-u-upan-gidda-yushe!"

The Drinker staggered over to Scooter and inspected him briefly. Then he lay down on the floor and went to sleep. Red drifted back to sleep, dreaming that the door opened several times and that others staggered around the room and then lay down.

Red got warm. Red got hot. He slipped out of sleep a little bit. He looked around. A whole bunch of Indians were sleeping all around him. They had rolled around to control the heat and everyone was stacked up against each other. While he watched, the one closest to the hot furnace got up, staggered up the concrete slope and lay down at the top of the heap. Red smelled beer and wine. Red dozed off again.

Shadows drifted across his face as each Sleeper turned near the fire until done, then woke and went muttering uphill to the coolest spot. The slope of the floor kept them all stacked and gravity fed.

Red was the first one to get up in the morning. He stood in the jumble of bodies and tapped Scooter with his toe. They opened the door and the sun blinded them. When they could see, they made sure the coast was clear. They slipped up the steps out of the Hospital basement and continued their walk back to St. David's. Mrs. B. asked them where they had been and Red said that they had camped out. Mrs. B. thought he meant " . . . in the back yard" and was not alarmed that her Son had been missing all night. Red and Scooter yawned all the rest of the day, shooting baskets and playing cards in Red's bedroom.

Douglas shared the bedroom with Red, but, besides his bed, there was no other sign that he lived there. The décor was all hunting and fishing. There were pictures of elk and deer on the wall. Fishing poles and rifle barrel ramrods stood in the corners. Field & Stream, Argosy, and True magazines were stacked on Red's dresser on top of his lockbox. The lockbox held .22 shells, shotgun shells, 30-30 cartridges, two packs of Lucky Strikes, a pack of Bull Durham, an orange sheaf of Riz La Croix cigarette papers, a slingshot, a corncob pipe, a cottonwood pipe, a can of Ronsonol lighter fluid, and 300 stick matches. On the wall was a wooden gun rack that Red had made. It held his .22, his single shot .410 shot gun, and his Winchester Model 94 30-30. A big old wooden desk with a dozen pigeonhole slots was against one wall. The table was marked with dents, saw cuts, paint stains, and burn marks. Out of the pigeonholes stuck a hammer, pliers, crescent wrench, soldering gun, solder, screwdrivers, sandpaper, steel wool, gun bluing, black paint, gun oil, wood stain, wire, one hunting knife, a jackknife and a sharpening stone worn down in the middle. A variety of fishing lures flies, and bait hooks were stuck in the wood. A big wad of forgotten pink bubblegum was stuck to the top corner of the desk. A 4 feet long harpoon leaned against the desk. Red had wired a four inch wide treble hook to the end of a stick. He then straightened out a two inch wide single hook and wired it in the middle of the treble hook. He could use this to either snag or stab fish as he walked or floated down a creek. Unfortunately, the fish were usually faster than Red and the only thing he had every caught was a dead sucker below the North Fork bridge. He jerked it out of the water and the disintegrating flesh shot all over him giving him such a stink that his dog, Duke, wouldn't walk close to him.

Red and Scooter had been playing Blackjack on one of Mrs. B.'s TV trays when Honch arrived. They were playing for matches. Red told Honch about their attempt to sleep in the haystack.

"Shit," said Honch, "there's a haystack on the other side of the Church. You could have slept in it."

Red and Scooter had to confirm this and wanted to explore the haystack. The bales of sunburned

270

yellow alfalfa had been stacked by Jim Hurst, a White Farmer who had leased Vernon's field that year. It was a couple of hundred feet south of St. David's Church and a couple hundred feet west of Highway 287 where the Young's driveway met the pavement. It was big. It looked inviting. The three waited until dark, slipped through the barbwire fence, and began construction on the haystack. First they woggled out footholes between bales so that they could have a ladder up the backside where cars on 287 couldn't see them. Then they hollowed out the top in its center by putting the extra bales on the outside, around the top. They ended up with a tall fortress where they had a commanding view and a safe place to smoke.

"You can see Jolee Young's bedroom window," said Honch. Red and Scooter looked. All they saw were cottonwood trees completely circling Norman Young's house. "Made you look!" laughed Honch. They arranged some bales for seating and then celebrated the completion of their work with a smoke. They climbed down. Only Red ever returned for a smoke in that Haystack — it was too safe and too close and right in view of all Fort Washakie.

But, in a few days, Jim Hurst's truck was parked in the borrow pit near Young's. Joe Charbonneau saw him sitting there and also pulled off the road.

He drove up alongside and said, "Howdy, Jim, whatcha doing?"

"Howdy, Joe," smiled Jim Hurst, pointing at his haystack. "Does that haystack look taller to you?"

Game Warden Joe looked across the Highway at the haystack out in the alfalfa field. He considered the facts and then said to Farmer Jim, "Well, I don't know if it's taller or not, but I do know that there's a bright green ring of fresh alfalfa on the top."

Farmer Jim nodded in agreement. The bales that had been dug out of the haystack had been protected from the sun and were still green. They stood out clearly against the dry yellow of the rest of the haystack.

"Wonder who did it?"

Game Warden Joe very slowly dipped his head and turned to look directly at St. David's Church. He rolled his eyes skyward and then pooched out his lips.

"The Lord?" asked Jim Hurst, smiling. Joe jerked his head twice to direct Jim just a little further north to Red's house and jutted his lips out twice. "Just so he doesn't burn it down."

Jim knew Red since the day they met at the Roberts Mission when Jim leased that property and had planted Alfalfa there. Red had borrowed a tractor one day and practiced plowing. When Jim

272

saw the evidence of the plowed field he was very happy that the kid hadn't flipped the little tractor and killed himself. He casually told Red, "I wouldn't have trusted it."

Hurst knew about Red's work at the Roberts Mission and had to admire him for it. He drove into the Churchyard at St. David's one day and knocked on the door of the Rectory. He proposed that Red work for him over the next year. Jim would put a water tank in the field behind the Rectory. Every morning, for $1.00, Red would fill up the tank with a hose run out from the Rectory. In the winter, Red would have to break the ice also, so that the cows could drink. Red agreed and got more income for .22 shells and Lucky Strikes while Jim got free water. Every winter morning before going to school, Red broke up the ice on the top of the water tank and threw the ice out on the ground. At the end of the winter the cows had eaten all the haystack.

CHAPTER 25 How Red, being One with Nature, grabs a friendly Yellowstone Park Wildlife

A Pink 1955 Ford two door hardtop replaced the yellow four door Hudson Commodore. The Ford Dealer in Lander sold it to Reverend B. when a Lander Training School Nurse traded it in on a new Mercury. It had a white roof and a white interior. Red had gotten so good backing up the Hudson at Wind River, that he was allowed to drive front ways in the Ford at the new house at Fort Washakie. Soon he was driving around the dirt roads of the Reservation without benefit of license.

When Red hung out with Beazel Hardin, he got a good education in mechanics from Beazel's Dad, John. There were cars and lawnmowers being fixed in their garage and lots of time was spent around the kitchen table discussing how camshafts and carburetors worked. John taught Red how to drive a manual transmission when they went elk hunting up at Togwotee Pass. In John's chained up 1950 Ford pickup, Red lurched and bucked and stalled on a snowy dirt road until he got the hang of it.

Red felt confident enough in his mechanical abilities that he climbed underneath the Pink '55

Ford and put glasspack mufflers on, called Hollywoods. Now the car purred with a mellow roar. As Reverend B. made his visits up and down the gravel roads of the Reservation, his flock could now see and hear him coming. This gave them plenty of time to lock the door, turn off the T.V. and pretend not to be home. The Reverend found that a lot of people out in the country were gone, even though their cars were still parked out front.

Reverend B. wanted to enjoy Grand Teton National Park and Yellowstone Park. They were only half a day's drive away. He found a small Terry Rambler camping trailer for sale, bought it, and had a trailer hitch installed on the Ford. The trailer was parked in front of the Rectory at St. David's. Red noticed that the stripes on the trailer didn't match the color of the car. He mentioned this to Honch and learned that Honch's big brother, Will, had a gallon of Ford's Tropical Rose paint. This was because he had planned to build a hot rod and paint it Tropical Rose. He had bought the paint and started looking for an old car. In the meantime, he invented wings that he could strap on his arms and fly. He took his first flight off the roof of their two story garage and broke his leg. His father, Paul Hunt, terminated all his projects. Red got a good deal on the paint.

Red painted the stripes on the camping trailer. Now it was color coordinated with the Ford in Tropical Rose. The trailer was loaded with their camping gear and food. Reverend and Mrs. B., Red, and Douglas drove off on vacation. Ryan stayed home because he had a summer job working in Lander at Clark's gas station on the Popo Agie River.

They crossed the Little Wind River Bridge. On the grade taking them up and out of the river valley, a California car passed them. Both cars had all their windows down, the natural air conditioning of the time. The Californians, in seeing the beautiful color matched Tropical Rose caravan let out a big wolf whistle. Red felt good and probably so too did Reverend B.

They passed through Dubois, recalling their first time there when the Hudson had broken down. Then they crossed Togwotee Pass and at Moran Junction they turned south and drove along the massive Teton Range looming above them on the west. They drove into Jenny Lake Campground, signed in with the Park Ranger, and located a camping spot on the lake. Reverend B., with great effort, backed the trailer through the trees to reach the picnic table and fireplace near the water's edge.

They unhitched the trailer and drove to the Forest Service Store for last minute supplies.

They were surprised to find Bill Milne, a Fort Washakie neighbor, working there. He was one of the few of the many applicants in the whole United States that had gotten a summer job in the Park. Many, many youth from far away had dreamed of a fun summer in the Grand Tetons, but here was Red's classmate with the job who lived only 80 miles away.

Mrs. B. bought some groceries and they browsed in the curio shoppe. There were salt and pepper shakers made out of pinewood. There were ashtrays made out of pinewood. There were pens, pencils, clocks, mailboxes, sandals, forks, spoons, knives, bowls, plates, cups, napkin rings, shoe stretchers, coat hangers, jewelry boxes, cookie jars, doorstops, footstools, chairs, picture frames, beads, jewelry, ear rings, wall plaques, mirrors, key fobs, clothespins, and clever signs made out of pinewood. There were even pine trees made out of pinewood. On the bottom of every piece it said, "Grand Teton National Park, made in Japan."

In the 1950s Bears still roamed freely in both the Grand Teton Park and Yellowstone Park. Bear jams stopped the traffic for hours while the Tourists took photographs of the bears looking for handouts from the people. Bears made regular loops through the campgrounds, checking the trashcans and sniffing around for any opportunity. Red would pass them when he walked around the campground. He kept his slingshot in his pocket. When he found one of the log Park Service toilets, he snuck in and smoked a cigarette in a stall while he read another chapter in a Lash Larue cowboy pocket book.

Mrs. B. was very concerned about the bear danger and made sure there were no scraps left about their campsite. But, as they prepared for their first night in the Park, she didn't think about the consequences of leaving one certain thing out within Bear reach – Red. Because the trailer was so small, the two B.'s and little Douglas were going to sleep inside the trailer, while they had brought a sleeping bag for Red. He was to be in the bag outside the trailer. No one seemed to think anything of this oversight, and they soon were snoozing soundly in the serenity of the Grand Tetons.

Some time in the wee hours of the night, Mrs. B. heard some clunking sounds. She got up and went to the window at the front of the trailer. When her eyes became accustomed to the dark, she made out the form of a black bear sniffing around the top of the picnic table and pushing around the green Coleman stove. As she watched, the bear sniffed around the base of the table and then discovered Red. It sniffed up the length of the sleeping bag and sniffed Red's face. Mrs. B. wondered what she should do. Right. The bear turned and took a step away but then came back. It sniffed Red's face again. Mrs. B. wondered again what she should do. Correct. The bear turned and walked away, drifting along to other campsites. Mrs. B. went back to bed and slept soundly. In the morning she told Red what she had seen. He had no remembrance of anything happening, so no one was alarmed. He continued sleeping outside and everyone relaxed. They got used to all the night time clanking and snorting.

The next day they hiked part way up Grand Teton. Red fished in Jenny Lake and caught a trout that already had four other hooks in its mouth. At night they went to the Fireside Presentations where Forest Rangers talked about the geology, animals, plants and history of the Park.

Red set up their horseshoe stakes and pitched horseshoes. He read a Zane Grey Paperback novel about a Gunslinger. Red practiced fast draws with his slingshot. He chewed bubblegum. Red hiked into a remote lake to go fishing. He carried his fly pole and had his flies and one emergency spinner in a tackle book in the pocket of his Levi jacket. Nothing was interested in his flies, so, in a last ditch attempt, he put his one spinner on and clumsily flung it out into the lake. Nothing. He decided to loop the lake. When he got to the base of Mount Moran, he found the stream that fed the lake. There was a thicket of willows and a fallen tree lay across the creek. Red started to cross the log but saw a motion in the willows and froze. A moose calf was standing there, looking completely unfazed by Red's presence. Hmmm, thought Red, this is cool. He watched the calf for a while. Then he started thinking that a great big Moose Mom was probably not very far away and that this was exactly the situation that he had been warned about so many times. He continued further along the log until he got to the middle of the stream. He thought he was probably safe there so he decided to sit down and have a smoke. It was a warm day and he had been carrying his jacket in his hand. Before he sat down, he flopped the jacket carelessly down over the log. It slipped right off and down into the water. The swift current swept it towards the lake. He lurched at it with the tip of his fishing pole. No good. He watched as his jacket, his fishing tackle, and his fishing license floated out into the lake and disappeared.

"Blank!" said Red. He continued around the lake. He started getting into an area of high banks and was surprised to look down in the water at one spot and see a dozen or so of the biggest trout he had ever seen. They were casually nibbling on some unseen fly larvae or other insects that were striking the water in that area. The perfect place for a fly. But, all Red's flies were at the bottom of the lake. He quietly pulled some line out of his fly reel and tried to flip the spinner out into the lake the best he could with a fly pole.

"PLLOOPP!" The fish were gone. "Blank!" He reeled in his spinner with disgust and abandoned fishing for the rest of the hike back.

The next day they decided to drive the car into Yellowstone Park for a car tour of the main sites. They stopped at Obsidian Cliff. The highway still passed right by the black obsidian outcrop and every Tourist hauled off the usual handful of this perfect arrowhead material. Millions of pounds and a good part of the mountain had disappeared and the highway would be relocated some distance away in future years. They visited the Petrified Forest, Lower Yellowstone Falls, and Upper Yellowstone Falls. They watched Old Faithful blow off and walked around the smaller geysers and Old Faithful Lodge. They made it all the way to Mammoth and drove into the picnic yard at the big grassy field at the edge of the mud pots. Prairie Dogs were everywhere. The B.'s prepared to eat.

While Mrs. B. set up the Coleman stove to warm up a meal, Red surveyed the 100s of Prairie Dogs all around that were obviously a Phenomenon of Nature and Tourist Destination in themselves. They were quite tame and were approaching people for food. Some were on the picnic tables. Some would eat out of your hand. Some were fat, some were skinny. Red armed himself with some pieces of bread and ventured onto the Prairie Dog Field.

He tossed around some chunks of bread. More and more of the tamish Prairie Dogs came up to him. He tossed more bread. They looked so cute. They looked at him. He tossed some more bread. They looked like little Teddy Bears. He wondered if he could grab one? He picked out the biggest, fattest, friendliest one and knelt in front of it. He tossed a little piece of bread down in front of him. The big, fat Prairie Dog took it. With lightning speed, Red grabbed the Prairie Dog by the back. He thought that his powerful grip would render the creature harmless. No. With lightning speed and with surprising strength, the Dog twisted around in his skin and bit Red clean through the meat on the web of his hand, between his thumb and forefinger.

"Blankin', blankin, blanker!" yelled Red, and he threw down the Prairie Dog as fast as he could. "Blank!"

This style and volume of yelling caught Mrs. B.'s attention, and she came over to Red and saw the blood streaming out of his hand. She dragged him back to the picnic table, cleaned up his hand and wrung the story out of him. Reverend B. and Douglas listened in.

"A Prairie Dog bit you?" asked Mrs. B., the Nurse, rising quickly to the emergency. "A Prairie Dog? Why, they have Rabies!"

"Do we need to take him to a hospital?" asked Reverend B. They all looked around. They couldn't see a hospital within 100 miles.

Red's Parents discussed Doctors, hospitals, Rabies, and 100 miles for a while. This started to make Red a little worried. He looked at the tooth marks on his hand.

"Then there's Lockjaw," said Mrs. B. "Red hasn't had his Tetanus shot."

Red's Parents discussed Doctors, hospitals, Lockjaw, and 100 miles for another little while. Red felt his jaw to see if it was locking up on him. "Then there's Bubonic Plague – Black Plague," said Mrs. B. "The fleas on the Prairie Dogs have it."

Mr. and Mrs. B. discussed the Black Plague, Doctors, hospitals, and 100 miles for a spell. Red looked around his shirt and pants for fleas. He bent over and brushed out his hair with his hand. He started to imagine fleas itching under his collar and in his pants.

But Red's puncture wounds had stopped bleeding and he seemed to be okay. It was a beautiful day in Yellowstone Park, they were 100 miles away from everywhere, so, the B.'s decided to rely on the Lord's good will. And - they did have other children.

Prairie Dog

CHAPTER 26 Finding out who had the biggest noyo

Reverend B. drove the yellow 1952 four door Hudson Commodore carefully as he made his Pastoral calls around the Reservation. It was pretty low to the ground for driving through deep muddy ruts in the winter. The pink 1955 Ford the Reverend traded for was an improvement and it was easier to see him coming. With his black shirt and white collar on, he carefully navigated from house to house through the dust, mud, or snow of each season. If only the main road was clear of snow, or if it was muddy, he might have to walk the long distance that each Shoshone had set his house back from traffic. This made him really easy to spot, but the smoke coming out of the chimneys encouraged the Reverend to trudge on. When he got there, they weren't home.

The Hudson had sometimes carried little Douglas to his second grade class at the government school on the Ethete Road. Ryan and Red both walked the short distance to the 7th and 8th grade Wind River schoolhouse. However, for lunch, they were driven to the government school in the big yellow White school bus. It was made by the White Truck

Company and looked exactly like a giant version of the Yellowstone buses used in the 1930s. This bus was such a powerful handful that Dave Peters wouldn't let anyone else drive it.

Loading up one day at Wind River, Red slipped into the seat behind Becky Wagner and Nora Singer. Becky said, "Red doesn't like us Indian Girls, do you?"

"Yes, I do!" Red instantly corrected her. He really didn't understand the remark.

The Bus Drivers had a big mirror on the sunshade above them. It was their only tool of discipline and control. Everyone knew that they were constantly being watched. Still, someone could easily slip a wet finger into the ear of the kid sitting in front of him or snap his ears with a flick of the forefinger. They might toss a tuft of horsehair insulation from the bus seats onto their groin. This was especially hilarious if the victim didn't know the fur was there and innocently continued the bus ride while around him were giggles of "Beechy die, enit?"

"Yih, beechy die, you could tell."

"Yih, you could tell real easy, enit Pard?"

After eating lunch in the Government School Cafeteria, the boys drifted out onto the sloping front lawn. There was a low, stone wall they could sit on. Layman Smart was one of the biggest and most

287

athletic 8th graders. He started a daily ritual with Ryan. He approached him and abruptly, but smoothly, started wrestling. Ryan took the invitation. They soon were on the ground, rolling around, trying different holds on each other, with only a little concern for their school clothes. No extremes were taken, no bloodshed.

The wrestling match between Layman and Ryan became a daily ritual. The other boys would gather around and watch. Every day they tumbled around. Everyone looked forward to it.

Red didn't understand it, but noticed eventually that Ryan and Layman seemed to be friends. Layman probably encouraged Ryan to play basketball and go out for Track the next Spring.

Coach Hand built a track and field area using the labor of the boys. They had a high jump, pole vault pit, and shotput circle. Their running tracks were 100 yards, 1000 yards, and one mile. The 8th graders easily trounced the 7th graders, so Red kind of felt out of it as he jogged around the big field in his gray sweatpants and sweatshirt. One day, during calisthenics, he spit on the ground. Coach Hand chewed him out and told him to do 50 laps. Red started to run off his sentence. The big schoolyard, however, was several acres in size and to circle it once took about five minutes. Red ran until the class was over and he was alone. He ran and ran. The school bus loaded and took every one home. He ran. He wondered if he should quit by his own decision. No, he kept running. He had run for about two hours and 25 laps, when Dave Peters came out, told him to quit, and offered to drive him home.

Dave was Sioux. His house was on the School grounds in view of the tracks and ball fields. One afternoon, the boys were trying out their new starting blocks, nailed down to the 100 yard dash track. Dave walked by on his way to the school. Someone challenged him to a race. To everyone's surprise, he accepted the challenge. "I can beat all of you," he said.

Hank Contado accepted the challenge to race. Red thought that was funny, because Hank was the fastest in the 100 yard dash. And — Dave was their 40 year old Head Custodian and Bus Driver.

While everyone watched, Hank crouched down in his starting blocks. Dave stepped into another pair of blocks, wearing his leather sole boots. Someone counted off, "One, two, three!"

The strangely matched pair burst out of their blocks. To everyone's amazement, Dave was slightly ahead of Hank. But, Dave hit some loose dirt and lost traction. He went down at full speed and rolled. Hank won the race and Dave got up, rubbing his roughed up hands and forearms. As he walked off he got looks of newfound respect from all the boys. Beazel told Red that Dave was only ½ Sioux, so it was probably that ½ that beat Hank, and the White ½ that fell down. The bell rang and they all ran in to shower and catch the bus back to Wind River.

When they had PE class at the old Community Hall gym there were no showers. They simply tossed their shoes off at the edge of the court, ran around in their socks, and went home sweaty. One day, when Red went to put his black engineer's boots on, he saw Hank Delgado stomping on something. As he passed by, he saw that Hank was trying to crush the big black square toes of Ryan's engineer boots. Beazel later explained to Red that Hank was only ½ Shoshone, so the White half had probably done the stomping.

Coach Hand had installed foot tubs in the shower room at the big school Everyone was supposed to shower after practicing on the Track Field. As they stepped out of the shower, each foot was supposed to pause in the tub and get soaked by foot medicine. Red noticed that everyone wanted to see everyone else naked. Ryan found all the 8th grade class watching him and Layman.

Red judiciously avoided a personal stomping that year. He and Freckles were lying on the schoolyard lawn in their tracksuits. Red was on his back with his hands clasped behind his back and his knees up. They were smiling from the glow of exercise. Hank Delgado ran up behind the two and leapt over Red by planting his right foot squarely in Red's groin. He was running laps far away on the schoolyard by the time Red recovered.

Hank was two years older than Red and a great athlete. Red didn't care. When Hank returned, Red confronted him with his fists up. The boys around them watched.

"Come on!" said Red.

But Hank didn't seem to have the degree of motivation that Red had. The "fight" was reduced to a war of words, while Red stood with clenched fists. Seeing the target of his wrath slipping away, Red proposed that they "...meet to fight at the Wind River School tomorrow (Saturday)."

Hank approved, "Six o'clock?"

"In the morning?"

"Yah."

"Okay." Red dropped his fists.

The next morning, (Saturday), Red was not at the Wind River School. He didn't know if Hank was there. At school the next week Hank didn't say anything to him. Red wondered if Hank had been there. Red wondered if Hank hadn't been there if he had wondered if Red had been there. Maybe Red should go up to him and yell, "Where the hell were you last Saturday?" Red wondered if Hank had snuck up through the Buffalo Berry bushes and watched to see if Red showed up. If he had, would he have come out if Red had showed up? Would Red have come out if it were he, instead of Hank, who had snuck up through the Buffalo Berry bushes and looked for Hank, and then Hank showed up? Maybe Red should go up to him and say, "I was a little late Saturday, where the hell were you?" No, that wouldn't work because then Hank could just say, "Oh, I got tired of waiting for you and left." Maybe that was what happened – but no – if that were true, Hank would claim to have brought a witness. Then he could say, "I got tired of waiting for you and left – just ask so-and-so here." But, no, Hank would worry that so-and-so might not be a convincing liar. Or, someone might accidentally mention that they saw Hank at 6 o'clock on Saturday at Hunter's Trading Post listening to "Honky Tonk Man" on the jukebox. Freckles told Red that Hank had never been up at 6:00 AM on any Saturday his whole life.

Red's 8th grade year brought more fighting opportunities. Red had luckily brought all his toys from the old adobe house in Wind River before the unknown source fire that leveled it. Among these toys were two pairs of boxing gloves. These were in Red's bedroom at the new house near St. David's log Church at Fort Washakie. In the garage was their pingpong table. Red would invite his Shoshone buddies over to play pingpong and then he would pop a bunch of popcorn for everyone. One night they decided to have boxing eliminations. Red's first and last fight of the evening was going to be with Johnny Rodda. As soon as they started, Johnny delivered a rain of blows on Red's head that drove him up against the wall. As his skull dribbled back and forth between the wall and Johnny's fists, he started to feel a little light-headed. Johnny noticed this and stopped punching. Red stayed out of the ring for some time.

*   *   *

Red's 8th grade class was now on the top of the heap at the Government School. Red was surprised one morning to get off the bus and find a large circle of Indian kids gathered in front of the old original stone grade school 1/2 gym. He walked over and saw that, in the center of the circle, two of his classmates, Ronnie Beauclair and Bud Graybow were faced off against each other with their fists up. The two fighters stepped around in their own little circle and sized each other up. Several minutes passed in a staring contest. They traded punches. They circled. They bobbed, they circled, they ducked, they dipped, they danced. Finally, Ronnie got a good right cross on Bud's nose and it shot blood all over his white cowboy shirt. They stepped back a little from each other. Everyone saw the blood. Bud worked to stop his nose bleed and the fight was over.

Red heard whispers about the fight: "full blood versus half blood, Shoshone versus Arapaho, half Shoshone versus half and half Shoshone/Arapaho."

No teacher interrupted that fight, but perhaps as a result of it, the boys found themselves having boxing for the first time in their P.E. class. The boiler room in the new school addition was selected as the boxing ring. The long steps into this subterranean room would allow first class viewing for the audience. The round robin began. Red was paired with Robbie Beauclair. Red accounted for himself better in that contest. He was getting big for his age and had a long reach. Robbie was also a very good sport.

The boiler room had thus been brought to their attention. Red popped out of the hall once as he passed its entrance and explored the big cavern. It had a giant boiler roaring away with pipes running all over. It was clearly Dave Peter's territory and he had his coats, hats, and a sweatshirt hanging in the room. Red saw that all the heating pipes ran into a low concrete passageway under the floors. He mentioned these interesting things one day to Tommy Singree. They decided to play hooky right under the noses of their teachers. The two boys jumped through the boiler room door, found no one there, and slipped into the utility corridor. Wow, this was neat! They were in the dark, duck walking in the low passageway. It was toasty warm. They lit a match. From the ceiling of the concrete utility tunnel hung some heating pipes. A sewer pipe ran about two feet above the floor. They explored the tunnel, getting familiar with the layout so that they could duck walk around without a light. Eventually, they had looped the entire school and came out on the other side of the boiler room. They looked around and tiptoed up the stairs and into the hall. They returned to their classroom and found that they had not been missed during their adventure. How handy. They could dart into the utility tunnel, have a smoke right under their teachers' feet, and never be missed. This little mini-hooky was fun.

Being deep below the school, they could talk or yell in the tunnel and not be heard. They tried rhymes about their teachers,

"Mrs. Franny came in through the door,

Smacked little Tommy with a two by four."

"Mr. Wolcott said, "Hey, listen, Red.

If ya' don't straighten up, I'll smack yo' head."

During one of these hooky escapes after a really big lunch, the boys had a good smoke and started duck walking back out of the tunnel. With the meal, the smoke, and the exercise, Tommy suddenly and urgently had to move his bowels. Right now! They tried to hurry — but — too late. Tommy threw his pants down and sat over the sewer pipe. "AAAhhhhhh."

Red heard powerful noises in the dark and soon smelled powerful odors in the dark. "RAAAhhhhhh!"

"Oh, no," said Tommy, "I think I shit on my shirt."

"No shit?"

"No, shit."

"On shirt?"

"On shirt!"

"Shit!"

"No shit."

"No shit?"

"Yes shit."

"On shirt?"

"Wod-I-say!" yelled the desperate Tommy.

"Got any toilet paper"?

"Of course not."

"Shitass."

Red struck a big farmer match to give some light to his friend. Tommy confirmed the mess he was in. He put his chin on his hand and sat slung over the sewer pipe, stinking and thinking. "Hey, Red, remember that sweatshirt hanging in the boiler room."

"Yah, Dave's sweatshirt?"

"Yah, can you go and get it for me?"

"Okay." Red duck walked out of the tunnel, checked that the coast was clear, and ran for the sweatshirt hanging on the wall. He grabbed it and returned undetected to the tunnel. He delivered the shirt to Tommy.

"What are you going to do with your shirt?" asked Red.

"Bury it," said Tommy. He kicked a hole in the dirt on the floor and covered up the shittyshirt.

They crawled out of the tunnel, paused at the entry, eyeballed the boiler room, and then leapt into the hall. Back in the classroom Red noticed that big letters on the back of Tommy's new sweatshirt read, "DAVE PETERS 14". Red wrote out a note and had it passed hand to hand up to Tommy. After reading it, Tommy looked back at Red with a worried eye. Red made the time out sign and then held his finger down in the pee pee position. Tommy brightened up, raised his hand and asked for permission to go to the bathroom. He walked backwards and sideways out of the room. When he came back the sweatshirt was on inside out.

They felt bad about Dave's sweatshirt and realized that it was only a matter of time before they were seen hopping out of the hall into the boiler room.

Later that winter, when Red went Elk hunting with John and Beazel Hardin and Dave Peters, Dave gave him some of the best advice he ever got. They were puffing through the snow, packing their rifles in the cold clear air high up in the Gros Ventre Range. "Always stop once in a while and look behind you. Get familiar with that view. If you don't, everything will look strange on your way back and you could get lost. And – you might just see a deer or elk watching you."

Red put great value in that advice.

On another cold day after that, Dave mumbled something to Red about, "Never could find that sweatshirt I always kept in the boiler room."

CHAPTER 27   Red paints the log Church and Rev B. learns how to tell when Shoshones are home

Luckily, Russ Crosman had completed the new Rectory at St. Davids before the old one at Wind River burnt down. It was a Pre-Cut home and arrived by way of a couple of semi-trucks. Every stick of wood that would go into the house had been laid out on the ground beside the Church. This deeply offended Russ, who was a Carpenter who expected to measure and cut every board himself. Now he just wandered around looking for a number on the end of each piece. The house was the new ranch style and had an attached garage. Reverend B. thought that the big log St. Davids Church should also get spruced up, so he bought a dozen five gallon cans of brown oil stain and hired Red for 25 cents an hour.

The Church was built in 1941 of Pine logs and had been drying in the Wyoming wind and sun. They were drier and thirstier than a cowboy on Saturday night. Red was provided a 30 feet long ladder, a 5 inch wide paintbrush, and a gallon of turpentine to clean the oil stain from the brush each night. He started one day by opening a five gallon can and using a big stick to stir up the stain. The brown glog in the bottom slowly mixed with the lighter oil. Next, Red would pour some stain into a one gallon can and run up the ladder one handed with the paintbrush clenched in his teeth. The Church had a steep roof and deep overhanging eves. This meant that Red had to do a lot of reaching up under the eves with his paintbrush. The light oil stain flicked off the bristles and sprayed him, giving him a face full of brown freckles. Soon the brush got saturated and the stain ran out of the brush and down his hands and arms. The stain got on his Bull Durham and he smoked it. The stain got on his food and he ate it. He got blisters from holding the brush. They popped and bled and he got stain in his blood.

Standing on narrow ladder rungs all day in tennis shoes killed his feet. The sun scorched him. He started wearing a long sleeve shirt and a straw cowboy hat bent low. He learned to paint in the shade, hopping back and forth from one side of the Church to the other as the sun crossed the sky. In the evening he had to clean the brush with turpentine. The first night he cleaned himself with turpentine too, but very quickly wished he hadn't. The turpentine burned. The fumes attacked his brain. He decided to just leave the brown stain on his skin while he did the job. The spatter and spray turned him brown.

St. David's Episcopal Church, built 1941

Red did a little painting on the south side. He did a little painting on the north side. He did a little painting around the front door. He left the west side to last because nobody looked there. He would position his ladder in one place and paint. Then, while at the top of the ladder, he would bounce it along the logs to the left and paint that. Then he

301

would bounce back to the right and paint that. He stood back and admired his handiwork. He realized that the old natural dry looking logs looked better than the stained logs that now looked like Lincoln Logs. Oh, well.

When he needed a smoke, he rode his bike over to the gravel pit near Youngs and Winchells. He rolled a Bull Durham and smoked it while he sat in a pile of rocks. He got brown stain all over his bike. He didn't seem to be making much progress. He needed a plan. He decided to paint the front first, where everyone could see his progress. He jockeyed the ladder around the concrete steps to get up in the gable. It wouldn't reach. He spattered the stairs with brown freckles. He was getting tired of this job and he had a big scab growing under his nose that looked like a big booger. He wished it was a booger because he could have wiped that off, but this thing wouldn't go away, so everyone thought he had a big booger. Then the next week when he still had a big booger they would think he was crazy. When people talked to him he watched to see if they looked at the scab. Then he wondered what they were thinking. Occasionally, he would touch the scab to show the person that he knew it was there and that it wasn't moving or going anywhere, therefore, it couldn't be a booger. He examined it in the mirror. It was getting bigger.

Mrs. B. finally observed Red's scab and hauled him into Lander to see Dr. Ward. The Doctor examined him and then lit up a Camel. "You've got impetigo. I'll prescribe some salve for you. It's a good thing we caught it when we did. If it had gone up into your brain it would have been really bad."

"Phew," thought Red. He salved up his scab thoroughly and hoped that everyone who had seen his scab would see his salve and know that underneath it wasn't a booger. He was still bogging down on his painting.

Mr. Hunt rang him up when he stopped in the trading post to buy some hamburger for Mrs B. "Aren't you supposed to be painting a Church?" Mr. Hunt peered into the brown face before him. It had blue eyes. "What's that under your nose?"

"Salve."

"Oh, I thought it was a booger."

Red started playing hooky from Church painting. He rode his bike down to the Little Wind River and went fishing. He tied his fishing pole across the handlebars. He crushed his hat down low to keep it from blowing off. He was peddling along the shoulder of Highway 287 when Joe Charbonneau pulled up along side of him. Joe looked at the fishing pole and then he looked at the brown person riding the bike. Then he looked at the thing under his nose. Joe smiled and rattled off something in Shoshone. "Shosh-u-upan-gidda-yushe booger!"

Red, without missing a beat, answered, "Yah, you could tell real easy, enit, Pard?" That was the only Shoshone he knew that wasn't dirty.

Joe waved and drove off laughing. Red went down to the Swimming Hole and caught a two pound Brown Trout.

That evening they ate it for dinner. Mrs. B. had always cooked every thing that Red had brought home – rabbit, pheasant, sage chicken, fish, deer, antelope, and elk. Reverend B. seemed to be in an especially good mood. He was even whistling when he came home. Red thought it might be a good time to tell him that he was having trouble getting the painting done.

"Don't worry, Son," said Reverend B. "I've been talking to Wayne Larrabee and Jessie Danson. They want to finish the job."

"Oh, good," thought Red.

Mrs. B. inspected Red's nose. "It looks like it's healing."

Ryan looked at it and said, "It looks like a booger."

"It's not a booger!" Red snapped back.

304

Mrs. B. looked at her husband and asked, "whats got you in such a good mood, Dear?"

Reverend B. laughed an embarrassed little laugh and even turned a little red. He looked down and confessed, "I found a surefire way to tell if an Indian is at home."

They all knew his frustration with trying to make his house calls around the Reservation.

"What happened."

"Well, I was up at Champlins and knocking at their door."

"Yes?"

"And no one was answering."

"So?"

"I kept on knocking. No one answered. Then, I heard little voices giggling right behind the door. They were only a foot away from me. Someone whispered, 'What did he do?' and the other voice whispered, 'he farted!'" The Reverend laughed and turned redder. Everyone laughed with him.

CHAPTER 28 How Ryan put an engine in his 1948 Dodge Convertible in only one year

When Ryan got a driver's license he got to take the Pink Ford into Lander on Saturday nights. A stream of cars circled up and down Main Street, making a turn-around at the High School on the north and at Clark's 66 Service Station on the south. Occasionally, two cars would leave the circle, drive a block or two away, pull alongside each other, and talk. On Station KOVE the Everly brothers harmonized with "Bye Bye Love," "Wake Up Little Susie", and "All I Have To Do Is Dream."

Ryan was making a lot of requests for the Ford. He wanted to go to movies and ballgames and drive in to school, thereby escaping the bus ride from Fort Washakie into Lander. Red wasn't interested in such things, but once or twice Reverend B. insisted that Ryan take Red into town with him. The relationship between the two brothers suffered. Red was two years younger than Ryan. He didn't yet understand the magic of cars nor the possibilities that they might bring.

Ryan got a job at Clark's 66 Gas. Then one at the Lander Creamery and a weekend one at American

Laundry. He would miss the Yellowstone Vacation and needed his own car. J.P. Folsom, who had an auto shop and junkyard near Hunt's Corner, drove over to St. David's one day in a shiny black 1948 Dodge Convertible. Reverend B. bought the car for $250. Ryan started driving with his guitar across Highway 287 to practice with Alan.

Ryan first became fully aware of Alan's Sister, Nora, when all Ryan's friends and all Red's friends, the B Band, were walking one night on the Old Wind River Highway. Their path was toward the empty adobe Rectory the B's had previously lived in. Red had a key to the door. Nora walked beside Ryan. She jumped up and kissed him. "Ohh, I'm not ready for that yet," blurted Ryan. He always remembered that night because it was the night of the mysterious fire that burned down the old adobe at Wind River.

Ryan was playing guitar a lot with Alan. Nora listened to them. The threesome would ride around in the convertible. They went in to the Drive-in theater in Lander. KOMO in Oklahoma played "Sweet Little Sixteen." Reverend B. worried about Ryan.

Ryan started his senior year at Fremont County Vocational High School in Lander. He drove his Dodge to school every day. He worked before school and he worked after school. He wanted to rent an apartment in Lander. Reverend B. didn't like that. Ryan took it out on his Dodge. He drove it everywhere with his foot to the floor. Naturally, the ancient flat six engine gave out and started producing a distinct knocking sound deep inside the engine block. John Hardin told Ryan the bad news and volunteered to help install a new engine. Ryan accepted this great offer and the Dodge went into John's garage. The work commenced.

A new engine would be expensive. They looked around for a rebuilt engine or a good used one. Jett and Robert Ring lived at Fort Washakie and had several Plymouths and Dodges in their family. Jett ran all around in a 1952 Plymouth and, hearing about Ryan's plight, told him that he had a used engine that they had just taken out of one of their cars. They would sell it for only $50. Ryan jumped at this chance. Red and Ryan stopped by Jett's garage and looked at the engine sitting on the floor. It looked okay, so they went in to Jett's house to get a bill of sale written out. Jett put on his favorite record, "Mule Skinner Blues". He turned it up to full volume and played it over and over.

The engine was hauled over to Hardin's garage. For a while, Ryan showed up dutifully every day and was learning a lot from John. But winter came. Ryan lost interest. John had to take Beazel and Red deer hunting and elk hunting. The Dodge got pushed out of the garage and sat through the winter with a tarp covering up the hoodless engine compartment. It looked like it might stay that way forever, just another used up car on the Reservation.

But warm weather returned in the Spring and the car was again worked on. They got the "new" engine bolted in and all the wiring hooked up. Every one gathered around for the big event – starting it up.

Ryan turned the key on, pulled the choke button, pumped the gas pedal, and pushed the starter button on the dash. "Ur-uh-ur-uh-ur-uh-vrooom!" It started. Ryan revved it up and adjusted the choke.

As the engine warmed up and began to idle smoothly, Red leaned toward Ryan and said, "Is that a knock I hear?"

"No, that's not a knock!" said Ryan.

Red walked around to the right front fender where John was looking under the hood.

"Is that a knock I hear?" asked Red.

"No, that's not a knock!" said John.

"It's not a knock!" re-emphasized Beazel.

The proud Mechanics got in the car and they drove all around the streets of Fort Washakie. Ryan had learned a lot and Red noticed that he treated the car a little better after that. Reverend B. still worried.

Ryan kept his bedroom door closed, reading all night and playing his guitar. Ryan asked Mary Arroya for a date. She was Chief Washakie's great granddaughter. Her parents said that she couldn't date a White Boy. One day Red saw a hole in Ryan's bedroom door in the shape of a foot.

The next Saturday night, Ryan joined Red and Honch in their Walk Around. They crossed the cattle guard in front of St. David's and ambled south along Highway 287. Before they passed Young's house, Ryan said, "Watch this."

He lay down across the northbound lane of Highway 287. "What the heck are you doing?" asked Red.

"Are you crazy?" asked Honch.

"Just stand back," said Ryan.

The two younger boys were dumbfounded. They walked down into the borrow pit. They saw a car's headlights approaching fast from the south.

"A car's coming!" they yelled at Ryan.

He lay still. The two observers held their breaths. They looked at the approaching headlights and realized that the driver could be drunk and run right over Ryan. Ryan lay still.

The car slowed. It stopped. Ryan lay still. The car didn't move. Red and Honch watched. Then, the car slowly started moving over into the other lane and went around Ryan. As it passed, an incoherent voice yelled down at him, "Shosh-u-upan-gidda-yushe!"

Ryan stood up, still alive. That was the last time he walked with them.

Ryan rented an apartment in Lander on the second floor above Hub's Menswear. He worked at both the Lander Creamery and the American Laundry that school year and the next summer. He graduated as Salutorian in his class and applied for the University of Alberta. He would also be in the Army R.O.T.C. and spend his summers at an Army base in the East.

When Ryan left, he locked his Dodge Convertible up tight and took the keys. He gave strict instructions that the car was not to be driven by anyone while he was gone. The car sat in front of the St. David's Rectory.

This was a terrible waste. Red clearly saw this waste. Ryan was 500 miles away and couldn't see this clear waste. Nobody liked waste. Red looked over the driver's door and found that it was relatively easy to squeeze around the canvas convertible top and flick up the door handle. He did that and slipped in behind the steering wheel. Then he looked at the ignition switch and the starter button on the nice shiny black dashboard. He lay down on the floor and looked up at the back of the ignition switch. There were three posts on it, with three wires coming out of it. Red got a little piece of copper wire and wrapped it around those three wires. Then he hit the starter button. "Ur-uh-ur-uh-ur-uh-vrooom!" It started. It knocked.

Red went for a little drive around Fort Washakie and Wind River. Oh, boy! What fun having your own car. However, the car started to overheat, so Red drove back home and parked it in exactly the same spot that it had been in before. He filled the trunk with water in milk bottles and his Army Surplus Canteen. After that, whenever he wanted to go somewhere, he would fill the radiator full of water and then jump the ignition switch. Eventually, the battery started to fade away. He parked only on hills when he was away from home so that he could start it rolling and pop the clutch to start the motor.

He took Larry Brickman, Honch, Freckles, or Beazel with him. They went hunting. They went fishing. They wallowed around muddy roads. They knocked around the Reservation. They developed an effective way to start the car when they had to push it. Red would roll down the driver's window and push alongside the car. Someone would push on the back of the car. When they got up to starting speed, the guy in back took a running step up on the rear bumper and dove through the open back window, which they left unzipped. Red then jumped in the driver's seat, threw in the clutch, shifted into second gear, and popped the clutch. "Ur-uh-ur-uh-ur-uh-vrooom!" It started. It knocked. Then they could drive around some more until the engine overheated again and they had to stop and let it cool down.

Red was so confident in the Dodge's dependability that he invited his Mom, Mrs. B., to the Diane Drive In Theater in Lander. Would she like to accompany him and Honch to the picture show?

"Yes."

Red stashed a five gallon can of water in the trunk and they drove in to Lander without event but blew off a lot of radiator water on the way. They went to the Drive In and saw a double feature. They enjoyed some popcorn in Ryan's car while he studied Math in the frozen North.

When the show ended and it was time to go, the car wouldn't start. Red and Honch did their startup routine a couple of times in the gravelly hummocks of the Drive-in movie lot. Mrs. B. sat in the Dodge and howled with laughter at this sideshow and at their efficiency. They left the movie, drove out Main Street and left town. However, the car was boiling hot right at the Reservation Line. Red stopped on the shoulder and they sat for 15 minutes, enjoying pleasant conversation. Then they did the starting routine again. Mrs. B. howled again with laughter. "This is just outrageous, Red," she said.

They performed again at Ray Lake and again at Hunt's House after they dropped Honch off. Mrs. B. was in tears. Red drove back to St. David's and parked in exactly the same spot. He reached under the dashboard to unwrap his copper wire ignition key.

"Is that a knock I hear?" asked Mrs. B.

Now Red burst out laughing and that fueled even more laughter from his Mother. He helped her out of the car and into the house. Reverend B. was surprised by all the giggling and wondered if they had been drinking.

The Dodge continued to secretly serve Red until he accidentally delivered the coup de grace. He was at Young's driveway and drove down into the borrow pit. There was a really steep dirt trail climbing up out of the borrow pit onto Highway 287, close to where Ryan had lain down on the road. Red wondered if he could stop at the bottom of this hill and then start up it in second gear? He gave it a try. It didn't have enough power to do it. He revved the engine higher. Knock, knock, knock. He slipped the clutch out. No go. He revved it way up.

KNOCK – KNOCK – CLUNK! He heard the sound of rod hitting crankcase and the engine locked up solid. "Holy shit," said Red. He knew he was in deep trouble. What could he do now?

He walked across the highway, past the log Church, and into his house. He telephoned Honch and asked him if he could come quick with his pickup and a chain and give him a tow from Young's?

"Be right there," said Honch.

Red soon saw Hunt's Ford Pickup coming down the road. He guided Honch as he backed up close to the Dodge and then he hooked up the chain. Red threw the clutch in and waved Honch forward. The pickup spun out a little bit on the asphalt and then got traction and pulled the Dodge out of the ditch. Then they entered the Churchyard and pulled the dead Dodge over to the Rectory. Red explained to Honch that it had simply, "thrown a rod". They maneuvered it back and forth until it occupied exactly the spot that Ryan had left it in. Red locked it up carefully and threw away his copper hot wire.

"Do you think he will remember what the odometer reading used to be?" Red asked Honch.

"Do you remember what it was?"

"No"

"There ya go."

315

1948 Dodge Convertible

CHAPTER 29 Payday

The uniform all the boys wore in summer was Levis, white T-shirt, and a pair of white hightop Converse running shoes. Red found out that prickly pear cactus could stab you through canvas running shoes. Wading across boulder filled rivers crushed your toes and ankle bones. By the end of summer, the running shoes were grass stained, ripped, and fermenting with foot rot. Red saved his money and bought a pair of Red Wing Irish Setter boots. Red wasn't afraid to get his boots wet and would wade anything to get to a better fishing hole.

On a June Saturday morning, Red sewed the laces through the 200 eyelets of his Red Wing boots. Virl Crow stood in his Velcro Snap black shoes and patiently watched. "How many years of your life have you spent lacing those boots?" Red realized that his Indian Buddies all wore easy-on and easy-off boots and shoes.

"You're right," said Red, "there's better things to do." Then Virl, in his snap button cowboy shirt, watched while Red buttoned up his shirt, his collar and his sleeves.

Red and Virl wandered over to Fort Washakie looking for something to do. Chuck Barris drove by with a stock truck full of sheep. He lifted two fingers above the steering wheel. They came to the little old country Post Office that Charlie Barkley ran, and saw the whole gravel parking lot filled with cars and pickups. It looked like every Shoshone on the Reservation was there. Green Chevy and GMC pickups were filled with the kids. Grandmas sat in the back, with their colorful shawls pulled around them. "What's going on?" Red asked.

"Payday," said Virl, "we're going to get $600 each today, so everyone is here."

"$600 each?"

"Right, our per capita payment."

"Who pays it?" Red looked around and saw lots of people he had never seen before. He calculated that a grandma, mother, and four kids would get $3600 that day.

"The B.I.A. pays us for oil leases and stuff," said Virl. "Everyone who is 1/4 or more Shoshone gets a check for Tribal Oil Leases."

Red looked in some of the cars. "I think I see some white people. Are they all Shoshone?"

"Oh, yah, everyone's at least 1/4."

"Red hair and freckles?"

"No problem."

"Wait a minute. If he's ¼ Shoshone, isn't he a White Man with ¼ Indian in him?"

"No, he's an Indian."

"Why isn't he a White Man?"

"White Men don't get per capita."

"Oh. What if a ¼ Shoshone marries a ¼ Sioux?"

"No deal. The kids are only 1/8 Shoshone."

"What if they lie?"

"Never happens."

"1/4 Shoshone and ¼ Arapaho?"

"Shut up, Red."

"What about this Land Bridge business where you are all Chinese and you walked over from Asia?"

"Shut up, Red!"

318

The two boys crossed the cattle guard into the Fort Washakie parade grounds. The big central park was surrounded by The Shoshone Agency, the hospital and the government housing section. They walked past Beauclair's house, Markley's, Vanoss', Davis', Bennett's, Milne's, Twitchell's, Duffield's, Bell's, Rush's, Roger's, Jolly's and Buckman's.

"You get $600 today?" asked Red.

"I'll probably get $601. My grandma is picking it up for me."

Red was confused. "What's the $1 for?"

"My Great Grandpa's old place has an oil lease on it to Pan American Oil."

The boys reached the Old Flour Mill sitting on the bank above the South Fork of the Little Wind River. They cupped their hands and tried to look through the cracks in the shuttered windows. They glimpsed some long leather belts running between big wheels on the ceiling. A great big government padlock was on the front door.

"Why only one dollar? What's the deal?"

"My Great Grandpa got a 160 acre allotment on South Fork." Virl pointed down the slope at the trickle of water below them. "It's a mile up the river. He was supposed to become a Farmer, but no one could live on 160 acres. After 25 years he sold everything except where the house sits. Some White

319

guy farmed it until he went broke in the Depression. Now it's part of Meriweather's farm. The oil lease is for the land where the house sits."

"It's only worth $1?" asked Red.

"It's worth more than that, but there's lots of uncles and aunts and grandkids, so I only own about 1/1000 of it. Uncle Chuck calls it Virl's six inches." He laughed. "Indians can't own Reservation Land anymore, so the B.I.A. takes care of all the land and money."

"Can the Whites farm it?" the confused Red asked. He ambled with Virl down Black Coal Drive, named for Arapahoe Chief Black Coal.

"Sure, the Government fixed everything. They straightened out Crooked Creek. In the '30s they built Washakie Reservoir on South Fork. They built ditches from North Fork and South Fork, crossed over Trout Creek, went past Ray Lake and down to Boulder Flats. That's where some White Farmers who bought Indian Allotments got their irrigation water. That's why there's no water to run the Old Mill anymore."

"Great White Father take good care of Red Brother," smiled Red.

"That's nothing," laughed Virl, "They moved the Northern Arapaho onto our Reservation. There were twice as many of them as us. Then we ceded a

320

big chunk of the reservation north of the Wind River for the Riverton Reclamation Project."

"You seeded it for corn, or wheat?"

"Not 'seeded', I said 'ceded' - gave it up."

"That was nice of you. Did you get paid?"

"Yah, for all that land and the water of the Big Wind River they paid us with TB and measles."

"Great Spirit forsake Red Brother?"

They giggled as they walked along the old warehouses on the edge of Fort Washakie. Virl peeked in the half open door of an old warehouse. "Hey, look at all the telephones!"

Red joined him at the door and looked in the old shed. He saw a jumble of telephones and wires. They entered the room and explored. There were dozens of old wall phones, candlestick phones, and lots of wires. They found a big switchboard console which clearly must have been the old Fort Washakie telephone center. They experimented pushing and pulling wire jacks in and out of the switchboard. Red found the Operator's headphone and put it on. Then he pulled a wire jack out of one hole and stuck it in another. In a shrieking falsetto, he said, "Calling Mr. Virl Crow, Mr. Virl Crow."

Virl laughed. He picked up one of the candlestick phones and held the receiver up to his ear. In a deep bass voice he said, "This is Mr. Crow, Mr. Virl Crow, who's calling please?"

"This is the B.I.A.," shrieked Red, "and this is your lucky day!"

"I can hardly wait," sighed Virl.

"The Government has just found that you own a large piece of land and has written up a deed for you to sign."

"Thank you very much," sighed Virl.

"Mister Man would like to have a meeting with you right away. Say at Ellshire's Bar for drinks?"

"Now you're talking," giggled Virl, and hung up.

Red screeched, "Wait, I didn't tell you what time to meet."

"Oh," laughed Virl. He picked up the phone again and said into it, "What time?"

"One hour," screamed Red with a burst of laughter. "Oh, by the way, you're talking into the wrong end of the phone."

Virl looked at the telephone and then swapped it around. "How did you know I was doing that?"

"Your voice sounded so far away."

"Well I am far away," said Virl, "I'm way out here in Wyoming and you're way back there in Washington."

"You're right. I'm sitting here in the Great White Father's House. I'll tell him you said hello."

They hung up with big smiles, slipped out of the shed, and walked back up the North Fork Road. Now Ellshire's parking lot was all filled up. Further up the road they saw that Joe Moore's lot was full also. They peeked around the west side of the Bar under a leanto and saw a bunch of drinkers sitting in a line passing wine bottles around. They went into the restaurant and bought two RC Colas. They drank them down. They burped.

"Wush yor deal, Mr. Man?" ashed Virl.

"Ids jus wunnerful, jus wunnerful, Sir," shed Red.

"How mush?"

"25 shents."

"No shid?"

"No shid!"

"Waredo I sine?"

"Ride here."

"Gimme that pen."

"Here diz."

"Shanks."

"Shank you! Keep the pen."

"No shid?"

"No shid."

"Shanks."

"Shank you."

Virl signed the imaginary deed with a flourish. Then he sunk his head down on both hands and said, "Oh, my aching hed!"

Red pulled a stick match out of his pocket and offered it to Virl, "Wanna ass-burn?"

"Shanks."

"The Guvmint will straighten yew out."

They laughed, slid out of the booth, and stepped out the door. Virl struck out in the direction of his home and Red aimed for 287. Before Virl went out of sight, he turned and yelled at Red, "Hey, you furgot the 25 shents and my pen!"

"The check is in the mail!"

On his way home, Red came to the now empty Post Office. He went in and stepped to the wall full of little brass mailboxes with combination locks. He looked through the little glass window and saw a couple of letters lying inside. He spun the combination on the brass dial and flipped open the door. Oh, boy! He saw a letter from Argosy Magazine. He tore it open. Inside were a letter and an award. It was the coveted Winking Bull prize. The letter said that his story had won that month's competition and would be printed in the upcoming edition. He became the first of his contemporaries to appear in print, with the following tale -

He had gone pheasant hunting one day and, unnoticed by him, dropped a shotgun shell into a puddle. The shell sat in the water for several days until he happened across it on his next hunting trip. He picked it up and returned it to his ammunition belt. Some days later, he hunted again and a pheasant broke from cover in front of him. He fired and brought the bird down with one shot. But when he dressed the bird out he could find no birdshot wounds anywhere. Upon further examination, he determined that the bird had drowned. The water from the puddle had been in the shotgun shell. As proof, he still has the empty shotgun shell.

THE "HONEST ABE CLUB" TROPHY
ARGOSY MAGAZINE

The 1957 win of this prestigious award by a 13 year old Wyoming boy made Red think of a literary career. In the 8th grade, Red was given a sheet to fill out. It was a list of High School courses that he could sign up for in Lander at Fremont County Vocational High School. The choices were Auto Mechanics, Agriculture, and College Preparatory.

Red also wanted to work on cars, but he felt a large, invisible pressure to sign up for College Prep. He thought he would do both. Checking off everything on the list that he liked, he found that he would have to go to school 16 hours a day. He raised his hand and Miss Franny, the pretty young teacher from New York, came to his side and reviewed the instructions with Red as a gaggle of boys and girls clumped around them.

Niles Ramshire sat beside Red but seemed to be interested in something else, his foot thrust out and dancing around. While everyone else was staring down at Red's desktop, Niles was staring down at his shoe.

When the problem was solved and the huddle broke up, Red focused on what Niles was up to. On his shoe was a little piece of broken mirror. Niles looked at Red and then very quickly picked up the mirror. "Oh, oh," thought Red, "7 years bad luck."

Then, on the bus ride home that afternoon, Red found himself sitting in front of Chester Lavoie. He didn't wince when his ears were snapped. Then he heard a strange sales pitch made to Dean Stockman.

"I bought a pair of X-ray glasses."

"Oh, yah? Do they work?"

"Hell yes, they were selling them in the back of 'For Men Only' magazine."

"What can you see with them?"

"Everything! If you were to look at Ayleen up there, she wouldn't have any clothes on."

327

"No shit!" How much do they cost?"

"Well, I got in on the last bunch so I only paid $2.00."

"Let me try them out."

"Oh, I never carry them around - too dangerous."

"Ahhh, would you sell them?"

"Well, for you, maybe I could figure something out. Course there was postage and everything."

"Sure, sure, how much would you take?"

"How 'bout $3.00?"

"I don't have $3.00."

"How much do you have?"

"Err, well, actually I only have $1.00."

"Well, maybe for you, we could do a deal."

"Wait a minute, what if I get caught with 'em? I think I'll pass."

"Whoa, Pardner, just don't let anybody else try 'em on. Tell you what, I'll let you have them for just one dollar."

"Oh, I don't know, I'm kinda worried."

"Ok, Ok, I'll tell you what. I'll sell you the glasses for a dollar and, if you're not completely satisfied, I'll buy them back from you."

"How much you give me?"

"50 cents."

"That's only 1/2."

"100s of other people would pay big bucks to get their hands on a pair of these glasses. You could make a lot of money."

"Okay, it's a deal."

*   *   *

A few days later, Red sat behind Chester on the bus and heard him whisper to Willy Sorrel, "I bought a pair of X-ray glasses."

CHAPTER 30 Red makes another big grab

Every time Red walked along Black Coal Drive he looked at the warehouse that held the Fort's old telephone system and wondered what he might do with all the gadgets stored there. The first phone he remembered when he was growing up was an oak wall phone that hung on the wall, had two bells on top, a little notepad, and an earpiece hanging on a cradle. A hand crank signaled short or long rings in the sequence representing the number you were calling. Short – long – short. The phones were on a party line so that anyone could pick up their phone and listen to your conversation. There were lots of wall phones here going to waste. There were also candlestick phones like Humphrey Bogart used to talk with Lauren Bacall. They had a tall slender black stalk and an earpiece hanging from a cradle. These were sitting unused. Red knew that anyone he told about the phones would agree that they shouldn't go to waste. Red told his best friend, Beazel. They went to the old shed and looked around through all the ancient equipment. Red cranked the handle on a wall phone and realized that there had to be an electric motor inside. If they had an electric motor they could make electricity. If they could make electricity they could shock fish. The Little Wind River was only 200 feet away. Red and Beazel took apart one of the telephone cases with a pocketknife. Inside was a little generator that the crank handle spun around. They removed this little dynamo from the box. They coiled up several feet of wire and headed directly to the first fishing hole north of the 287 Bridge.

At the Little Wind River, they hooked two lengths of wire to the plus and minus terminals of the generator. Then they stuck the wires down in the deep water of the River. Red spun the crank. They hoped to see big trout popping up to the surface and throwing themselves in surrender on the bank. But, they didn't.

They moved their operation upriver to the next good fishing hole. Beazel cranked and cranked with no results. Red pulled the wires out of the water, "Maybe the currents too low."

"It's over your head," said Beazel, looking at the river.

Red looked at him. "I mean the electrical current. I'll hold the wires in my hands and you crank."

"Okay," smiled Beazel. He spun the dynamo.

"Hah," laughed Red, "it barely tingles. You couldn't shock a minnow with this."

"Let me try it," said Beazel. He took the wires and held each end.

"Walk over to that shallow spot and stand in the water. Splash some on your hands."

"Okay," said Beazel. When he was in the water, holding the wires, Red gave the generator a fast spin.

"EEEEE-YUDAR-OOOOO!" yelled Beazel. His hair stuck straight up in the air and his eyes bugged out. His leg muscles snapped tight and flipped him out of the water onto the bank. He flipped and flopped for a while until Red remembered to stop cranking. Beazel went limp. Red looked concerned. He reached out with his toe and gave him a little push to see if he was still alive.

"Are you okay?"

Beazel made a great big fish eye at Red. His lips were pumping like a goldfish "Ohhhh, you Yogo Horse!"

His voice sounded okay, so Red felt it was safe to start laughing, "Hah, hah, hah, Beazel, you're so funny!"

Beazel examined himself a little, determined that he was okay, but was done with electricity. "Let's go swimming."

They coiled up the wires and stashed the generator in a pile of driftwood. They walked and waded downstream to their rocklined hideout at the Big Hole. Red dug around in the bushes and brought out their five gallon paint can. He opened it up and took out his swim goggles. There was also a sack of Bull Durham, some matches, and a Three Musketeers candy bar. They ate the candy bar. They stripped down to their underwear, walked down the boulder lined path to the swimming hole, and slipped slowly into the cold water. They swam upriver and down until they no longer felt cold.

Red put on his facemask and floated underwater looking for fish. He saw a couple of big Browns and some Rainbows. He surfaced where their path met the riverbank.

"Hey!" yelled Beazel, "a Coon's up in that tree!"

"Where?"

Beazel pointed at a big cottonwood tree growing out over the river. "He went in a hole right above that limb. Let's check it out!"

Red pushed his facemask up on his head and the two wet swimmers daintily tiptoed barefoot through the thick brush around the cottonwood tree. Bezel pointed up at the big limb over the water, "I know he disappeared right there."

Even though Red was barefoot and his underwear was dripping wet, he thought that he could easily climb up a leaning tree to look for a Raccoon den. He hugged the tree trunk and shinnied up it. He swiveled around and sat on the limb. "Yah, there's a big hole up here!" He looked down at the river.

"What do ya see?" yelled Beazel.

Red leaned down over the hole to see what was in there. His big freckled face and wild red hair with a white swim mask on top scared the wits out of the Raccoon down in the hole. It came shooting out of its den right at Red. Red thought he was being attacked and automatically jerked back. This made him lose his balance and he flipped upside down on the limb. The Raccoon cleared Red in a single bound, took one step on the limb, and then jumped into the river. It swam safely away as Beazel tried to watch everything that was happening both with Red and with the Raccoon.

Red tried to hold onto the limb with his legs but only swung a couple of dangles and then fell upside down into the river. The frigid water stripped his shorts down to his ankles. He instinctively reached up to pull his face mask on. With all the excitement and the rush of the current, Red only got the mask on over his nose and mouth, not his eyes. It was full of water as it snapped tightly on his face. He thrashed and paddled wildly with his feet tied together by his shorts. When Beazel saw him surface he thought it would be safe to laugh. "Hah, hah, hah!"

Red floundered in desperation toward the bank, unable to breathe. As he got near, Beazel saw that Red's eyes weren't under the swim mask. The mask was full of water and it was sloshing around over Red's nose and mouth. This made Beazel laugh harder. "Hah, hah, hah!"

Red scrambled up on the bank and immediately tore off the facemask and gasped for air. Beazel saw he wasn't drowned so released even bigger peals of laughter. Then he saw that Red's underwear was knotted down around his ankles. Beazel pointed at Red's naked crotch and stopped laughing enough to choke out, "You're shriveled up! Hah, hah, hah!"

Red could only make some soft squeaky "glurps" as he swallowed down some of the river water. He moved toward Beazel to punch him but his underwear tripped him and he fell in some fresh spring nettles. "EEE – YUD – AROO!"

Beazel screeched even louder. He took his gum out of his mouth to keep from choking. He wiped tears from his eyes. "Oh, Red, you're so funny, hah, hah, hah!" Red stood up, untangled his shorts and pulled them up. He rubbed the water off his arms and legs with his hands. "Harumph." He stood with crossed arms while he waited for Beazel's hysteria to wind down.

"I think there's babies in there."

"Oh, yah? Why?"

"Why else would a Raccoon be in a hole in a tree? I'm going back up."

Red climbed the tree again and swung on to the limb. He reached down in the hole and felt something furry. He pulled it out. It was a baby raccoon and it was the cutest thing that Red had ever seen. "Grab this little guy," he yelled at Beazel. Beazel positioned himself as close to Red as he could get. Red swung his arm down and dropped the baby into Beazel's arms. Then he went back, "There's more." Beazel set the kit down. It was too small to walk. Red handed him another one. "Let's take them home."

"They're so cute," said Beazel, "we've gotta show everybody."

They took the kits back to the fireplace and got dressed. They walked back to Beazel's house with the babies. Before they got there, they were having second thoughts about whether or not they should have taken the little Raccoons.

"What do they eat?"

"Do they need their Mother's milk?"

"What if she won't take them back?"

"She'll smell humans and she'll abandon them."

"They always do."

Where are we going to keep them?"

They decided to hide the babies for a while. Turning into Hardin's driveway, they saw Ryan's Dodge Convertible sitting out beside the garage. "Ha," pointed Red, "that's been there forever. No one will look in there." They opened the car door and slipped the two babies into the back seat. Then Red and Beazel separated and each boy went home to a nice dinner and a peaceful sleep.

But, the peaceful sleep of those around Fort Washakie didn't last very long. Over at the jail, Dean Millman's bloodhound, Scout, started baying. His long, deep howls pierced the night. A few porch lights were turned on. Scout broadcast with all his strength and in all directions. A Prisoner woke up out of his winedream and yelled "I surrender." Some phones rang. Dean got dressed and went outside. He saw John Hardin walking out his front door with a flashlight. Dean slipped through the fence and went over to him, "Hey, John."

"Hi, Dean, what's your dog up to?" They walked together toward the sound and found Scout on point at Ryan's car. John flashed his light into Ryan's Dodge and glanced around. Four little eyes glowed back at him in the dark. "Coons!" said John, "Baby Coons!"

Dean looked at the two Raccoon babies. "I'll call Joe."

Joe picked up his phone and got the news from Dean. "At Hardin's?"

He looked at his watch. "It's 2:00 in the morning!" Joe hung up. Should he go right now? What damage could two raccoon babies do in a car? He got dressed.

Joe drove down to Fort Washakie and into Hardin's yard. John was waiting for him at the Dodge. Joe took a wire cage from his truck and the two went to the car and opened the door. Joe put on a big puffy pair of leather gloves. The babies were easily picked up and caged.

337

Joe tried to get information from John, "How do you think they got in there?"

"I don't have the slightest idea. All I know is that Beazel and Red were swimming down at the River today."

Joe nodded and swung the cage up into his Game Warden pickup. "Tell any interested parties that Coons can have rabies, and tell them it's best to leave critters in their own homes."

Trooop F, 10th Cavalry, Ft. Washakie, 1904

Tribal Council 1940
l to r: Marshall Washakie, Johnnie Boyd, Sam
Nipwater, Charles Washakie, Pete Aragon, Lanjo
McAdams, Cyrus Shogutsie, Gilbert Day

CHAPTER 31 Red catches a Little Wind River trout with his bare hands

If Red wanted to go to Beazel's house after school, he stayed on the bus and got off at Fort Washakie.

The children of the white government workers disappeared into the stone and frame government houses that ringed the B.I.A. offices, but Red and Beazel walked north on Highway 287 to where Hardin's house perched above the Little Wind River. One early fall day as they walked along they heard a yell behind them. "Hey, want some fish?"

They turned and saw Harold, Hank, and Freckles Contado running toward them. They had run all the way down from Wind River. "They channelized the Little Wind," said Harold, "there's tons of fish caught in the shallows! They're puddled!"

Red and Beazel joined them in their race to the River. "How do you know?"

"Our Dad was on one of the Cat's that dozed it out."

"Where abouts?"

"Below the bridge."

The five boys rushed to see all the fish cut off from the river by the Dozers. They crashed straight down the south bank of the river. There they saw that the bends in the river had been straightened out and the rocks from the bottom had been spread out on the gravel bars and banks, creating the puddles that trapped the fish. At the first puddle they saw a bunch of big trout struggling in the shallow water.

"Those are monsters!" said Red.

"Come on," yelled Hank, "make a chain!"

The boys stepped into the water, close to each other, and walked slowly towards the fish. As they got close, they put their hands down beside their feet with their fingers wide apart. They closed in on the fish. When they touched them they darted and thrashed, trying to get away in the shallow water. They bumped into the boys' hands and feet. Hands grabbed for the fish. Everyone got very excited. The Fishermen broke ranks and tried to chase the biggest fish. The fish were slippery. The fish didn't like being grabbed. The fish were fast. The fish got away and huddled at the other side of the puddle.

In his head Red heard Sam Cooke singing "Chain Gang."

"Stay together!" yelled Harold. The boys again made their moving net of feet and fingers and stepped in unison toward the fish. Giggling with joy, the boys hooted every time a fish bumped into them and they tried to grab them. This time they were successful and caught some of the big Browns and Rainbows. They looked over the big beauties that had been condemned in the shallow little ponds. "They would just die in these puddles, anyways," said Harold.

"Where have these lunkers been hiding all these years?" asked Beazel. They looked up from the fish and at each other. "What we gonna do with them?"

The Fishermen paused. At first, they had only thought of the thrill of catching the fish. If this had been a normal fishing trip they would think how many they were going to take home to eat. But this was different. The way they had been caught seemed somehow unfair. What would they tell others they did? After only a brief hesitation, the boys carried their catches over to the river, set them down carefully in the water, and let them go. Then they returned to the puddle, caught the remaining fish and put them back in the river.

They went to the next puddle. There they saw that it was close enough to the river that they could make a ditch from the trapped fish back to the river. They dragged their feet, scuffed, and kicked to dig through the gravel. Then they made their human fence and herded the fish toward the ditch and down to the river. Now they felt really good. They continued downstream, rescuing stranded fish. The size and number of fish surprised them.

Red started to look at the other changes the Bulldozers had made. The deep holes were gone, the banks straightened, and trees near the water were gone. He looked toward the Big Hole. He couldn't tell where it was. "Where's our swimming hole?" yelled Red.

Beazel wanted to go and look for it. "Our stuff's still over there."

"We're going to keep going," said Hank. "This is fun!"

Red and Beazel left the others and waded the now smooth bottomed river to the north bank. They estimated where the old rock firepit and the swimming hole used to be. They looked for the five gallon paint can that was always stashed in the driftwood. There was no driftwood. All the overbank flotsam and brush were gone! Their fireplace and pathway boulders were gone. Their swimming hole was gone. They weren't even sure that they were within 100 feet of where it had once been. Before them was now a ditch, not a river.

Oh, well, the government knows what they're doing. Red and Beazel walked back up the river to Highway 287 and then crossed the bridge back to Hardin's house. They told Beazel's Dad, John about the big trout and the bulldozers.

"They channelized it," said John.

"Why?" asked Red.

"The government had the money and the machines, so they ran the bulldozers down it."

The swimming hole was gone. The fishing holes were gone. Their rock hideout was gone. They changed their routes to skip this portion of the river. They were getting older. A driver's license could make a big change. One day John Hardin asked Red to accompany him and Beazel into Lander for a surprise. Red jumped into their pickup and rode along. They went to the Ford Dealer. John walked Beazel and Red over to a green 1948 Jeep CJ2A that he had bought for Beazel. The boys were overwhelmed.

In their excitement they didn't realize that they had passed a milestone - from Walkers Around to Riders Around. Beazel drove the Jeep back to Fort Washakie with Red in the passenger seat. The canvas cab fluttered and the gears whined as they reached the Jeep's maximum speed of 50 miles per hour. John followed them in his Ford Pickup. Somewhere around Ray Lake he decided that the boys weren't going fast enough in the Jeep. He sped up and gently kissed the back of the Jeep with his front bumper. Then he went even faster and pushed the little Jeep far beyond its own speed range. At first Red and Beazel thought that was kind of fun, but eventually the Jeep was screaming and complaining. The wind thrashed through the canvas and the steering got very loose. Red looked back through the scratched and discolored plastic back window. John had a great big smile on his face, just like a kid. He was sitting in a tight modern truck while the boys were bouncing around in a 1/2 worn out Jeep. He finally backed off and let them slow to a safe speed.

John was like a second Dad to Red but he was also like a big kid. John once had Red and Beazel on the front of his car with their rifles and Ryan was on the trunk. They were driving down the dirt road toward Chalk Butte, looking for rabbits. Red looked at Ryan on the trunk and signaled to John to speed up for Ryan's benefit. John started bouncing down the sagebrush lined trail really fast. Red watched as Ryan laid flat across the trunk, hooked his toes and his fingers on the side of the car and rode out the bumps. Red was the one that got tossed off. He was spit off into the sagebrush holding his 30-30. He tried to run, but couldn't run fast enough. He tripped on the sagebrush and cartwheeled through the brush and prickly pear. He got clubbed by his own rifle. Fortunately, he had been catapulted away from the car instead of under its wheels.

John helped Red set the record riding a bicycle 60 miles an hour past Signal Hill. Red had grabbed the passenger door handle of John's brand new Mercury Convertible. The bicycle was wobbling so much that it almost threw Red under the wheels. When he did let go, the equal and opposite force Law of Physics shot him sideways off the road and into the usual sagebrush and prickly pear cactus.

When Beazel and Red were employed to drive Elk toward John above Togwottee Pass one year, he took pot shots at them with his 30-06 as they returned, aiming "way far to your right so you were safe."

Red learned a lot on their weeklong elk hunts and deer hunts. He remembered the taste of raw liver from his first deer kill. He also remembered the pain of carrying the front half of that buck 10 miles on his back.

Red started bluing old rifle barrels and restaining stocks under John's tutelage. He ate lots of meals with Beazel and listened to John's stories of deer hunts. John gave Red a hunting knife. When Beazel and Red were old enough to get hunting licenses they got their deer every year with John. The Reservation game had all been shot because there were no hunting limits for the Shoshone. To get elk they went to Jackson, the Gros Ventre, and Pinedale. For deer they went to Lander, Pinedale, and Meeteetse. For antelope they went to South Pass.

Red's earliest practice with a single shot rifle had helped make him a good shot. One of his great shots was with the Stevens single shot .22 that he had given himself for Christmas. Beazel had been driving his Jeep along the base of the big sagebrush hills north of Chalk Butte. They saw a rabbit run away from them and up the hill. Beazel slammed on the brakes and Red jumped out. The rabbit was running at full speed up the hill, darting around the sagebrush. Red knew it was an impossible shot, but he took it. He hit it! Red let out a whoop and started to run up the hill. Beazel followed along by driving at the base of the hill. The hill got steeper and steeper. Pretty soon Red was panting and stopped to rest. He heard the Jeep below and looked down. Beazel was trying to drive further up the hill to get nearer to Red. That seemed unnecessary because Red was almost on a cliff and there was no way the Jeep could get very close. But, as Red watched, Beazel continued to drive, bouncing through the sagebrush and up the hill. All his tires soon lost traction. He was in four-wheel drive low range and first gear and he just couldn't go any further. To Red's surprise, Beazel jumped out and started to run excitedly up the hill towards Red.

If there is one thing you must know about old CJ Jeeps, it is that they can get on a slope much steeper

347

than a little emergency brake on two rear wheels can hold. If you get out of one on a steep hill, say, to open a gate, you have your passenger mash his foot down on the brake pedal as hard as he can while you're out. Maybe Beazel was fooled because the last big sagebrush clump he stopped on helped hold him. For a while.

When Red saw the empty Jeep start to roll backwards down the hill he yelled at Beazel, "Look out!" and pointed down the hill. Beazel turned around and saw the Jeep slowly gathering speed through the sagebrush. He turned and started running after it. "Oh, no," thought Red. He watched as Beazel ran downhill and got close to the Jeep bouncing through the brush. The Jeep wobbled side to side as it hit sagebrush clumps. The canvas door that Beazel had left open flipped in and out. He had to leap over sagebrush, get around the flapping door, and jump in the driver's seat, all while the Jeep was hopping and leaping and going faster and faster downhill and over the brush. Red was worried.

Red pictured Beazel getting run over by his own Jeep. He pictured the Jeep flipping over in the ravine at the bottom of the hill. No possible ending looked very good to Red, standing helpless high up on the hill. He couldn't imagine any possible way that the leaping Beazel was ever going to save his leaping

Jeep. But, 16 year old boys live charmed lives and Beazel actually flipped aside the door, jumped in the seat, mashed on the brakes, and saved his CJ from destruction at the bottom of the hill.

Red collected his rabbit and walked back down to the Jeep. Beazel was still puffing. They relaxed with a cigarette. Then Red jumped up on the hood of the Jeep with his .22 and they drove around in the sagebrush to the west side of the dump. Beazel thought he would have a little of the same kind of fun with Red, so he started driving fast through the tall sagebrush. The hard-sprung and rough riding Jeep started bouncing Red around. He looked for something to grab onto. The only things he saw were the windshield wipers. Beazel went faster. Red now actually pictured himself going off the front of the Jeep and being run over. He yelled at Beazel, "Knock it off!"

As Red made his slide back towards the windshield to grab the wipers, Beazel realized he was serious. He hit the brakes. Too hard. Red went sliding off the hood. His butt raked over the hood ornament. He tried to run as fast as he could in front of the Jeep. He tripped on a sagebrush and fell on prickly pear again. His .22 barrel jammed in the dirt and got plugged up. Beazel at least did not run over his friend when he disappeared from view in front of the Jeep's hood.

Red and Beazel slowly learned to drive a little better. They learned to stay inside moving vehicles. They loved that Jeep. The exhaust rolled forward from the tailgate and percolated through the old canvas cab. They smelled exhaust fumes all the time, except when they smoked. Once in a while a telephone would ring, maybe number 030R4.

"Want to go get stuck?"

"Yah."

Red got a little revenge in the winter when he drove Beazel's Jeep into Washakie Reservoir. When they finally realized they were impossibly stuck, Red did the honorable thing. He let Beazel slip into the driver's seat and he jumped out into the mud and freezing water. He pushed and pushed and tried to dig with his feet. He tried to jack up the Jeep from the muck of the lake bottom. Red's legs and feet were soaked and freezing. He told Beazel that he would have to walk out to get help, so he picked him up and waded him to shore. Beazel walked all the way down to McDaniel's place in the cold winter air. It seemed like it took hours. Red eventually saw him coming back riding on a tractor. He must have confessed that they really had driven right into the lake. McDaniel chose to bring his serious pulling machine. It wasn't the first time that McDaniel had pulled a vehicle with Red in it out of a mess. Being the first house down off the mountain could be a big pain. At the next Tribal Council Meeting, Dutch McDaniel collared Game Warden Joe Charbonneau.

"Hey, Joe, what's the chance of getting paid a little something for rescuing White People in the mountains. Maybe a little gas money at least?"

"Who did you save?"

"Red and Beazel."

"Well, Beazel's an Indian."

"Yah, but he's a Sioux."

"And Red thinks he's a Shoshone."

"I know."

"I think you see the problem."

"Yah. Maybe next time I'll just let 'em die."

CHAPTER 32 How Red interacted with a skunk and was barred from school for one full week

The Wind River Agency, Fort Washakie, and Hunt's Corner made a perfect little triangle. The Soldiers of the 9th and 10th Cavalry marched between the Little Wind River and Trout Creek from the 1880s to 1910. Highway 287 was built by the State of Wyoming and the original dirt road was named The Old Wind River Highway. State Route 287 went from Lander, through Hunt's Corner, Fort Washakie, over the Little Wind River and north to Dubois, Grand Teton Park and Yellowstone Park. Trout Creek Road went from Hunt's Corner to the Wind River Agency, continued up Trout Creek past the Roberts Mission and then climbed the Wind River Mountains. South Fork Road and North Fork Road started at Fort Washakie and then followed the creeks west to the mountains. Red and his friends had walked these roads many times and now were driving on them.

They learned to drive young in the country. By the time they turned 16 years old and took the Drivers License test in Lander, they had several years of experience already. Red first steered when he helped load three Ford Tractors onto a flatbed trailer at the borrow pit pond near the Wind River Agency. Beazel's Dad, John, let him drive whenever the three of them were out hunting. They also hitched rides with older boys, like Harley Brickman, who showed them how to keep a vehicle sliding sideways as long as possible on a gravel road, on snow, or in mud.

This rewarding style of driving left a huge plume of dust in the air along all the gravel roads on the Reservation. The rocks hammered a steady beat inside the fenders and on the car's frame. If another car approached them they dropped to an extremely slow speed so they would not break the other driver's windshield. This was one of the Codes of the Road. As they passed, everyone flicked fingers above the steering wheel as a wave.

Red's driving ability made him very helpful to his Father. He could drive the Indian Girls home after Sunday School and after their catechism lessons at St. Davids Church. Vita, Mila, and Mona, in bright white shirts and colorful skirts, rode quietly with him.`

Red could also drive up Trout Creek Road to help take care of the now closed Roberts Mission. The Reverend John Roberts had built the big two-story brick Mission next to his original Episcopal Chapel on 160 Trout Creek acres given by Chief Washakie in 1883. The Mission educated Shoshone girls who missed out on what their brothers were taught.

In 1892 the Government built a large school half way between the Shoshones and Arapaho. Students attending "Gravy High" lived in a 3-story dormitory.

The dormitory was torn down and a new classroom building replaced it in 1956.

By 1956 all eight grades, boys and girls, Shoshones and Whites, were consolidated at the Government School. The Arapaho attended St. Michaels and St. Stephens.

The Roberts Mission School was closed in 1945 and the house was sitting unused and aging. Someone had installed chickens and pigs in the outbuildings. Laurence Higby, from Ethete, put his horse there. It may have been the last attempt to fulfill the United States Government's desire to have the Indians settle down and take up farming.

Someone was needed to feed the chickens and pigs. In the winter someone would have to fill the coal stoker in the Mission. The Reverend drafted Red for the contract at $1.00 a day. Red was happy and settled down to take up farming. He got money for guns and cigarettes and got to drive up to the Mission and back every day.

Roberts Mission

Red's glass pack mufflers on the Reverend's pink '55 Ford two door hardtop guaranteed everyone could hear him coming, as well as see him. Just like his Father.

Red would hop off the school bus after school, drink a quart of milk and then drive up to the Roberts Mission to do his chores. If it was muddy out, he would splash and skid sideways across the Sundance Grounds to maximize his contact with nature. If dry, he raised a glorious cloud of dust over Trout Creek Road.

Red first filled the coal stoker for the furnace. He shoveled a bucket full of coal from the bin and waddled stooped over down the tunnel into the basement of the Mission. He dumped the coal into the stoker. Then he checked the water level in the boiler. It was always low. He would turn the water on to top it off and then do some other chores while it was filling. One evening he forgot to turn the water off. When he came the next day he found the water had run out of the radiators' pop off valves and flooded the second floor. He ran down to the basement and turned off the water valve. Then he got some old blankets and laid them out on the floor. He soaked up the water and squeezed it out into the bathtub. It gave the floors a good mopping, Red thought.

The next chore Farmer Red did was feed the chickens and gather the eggs. Armed with bucket and feed, he entered the wire cage and then the log shed where the chickens roosted. He had some training from the Barkers at their farm up on the hill above Ray Lake, so he knew how to treat a chicken. If you had to reach under them to take their eggs, you showed no fear. After the first few pecks on the back of your hand, you realized they weren't so tough. You had to be firm with these girls and grab those eggs. After filling the egg bucket, Red fed them and watered them.

Then Red would feed and water the pigs and give some oats to Higby's horse. There was always something that could be repaired in the old house and plenty of work around the barns and fences.

Red had spent his life until then studying the lives and ways of wild animals and fish. This new farming business supplemented the critical knowledge he had already acquired and increased his harmony with Nature. For example, he accidentally dropped an egg one day in the henhouse. The chickens immediately charged and devoured the broken egg lying on the floor. Red tried another one with the same results. Regarding the behavior of roosters, Red had never seen a single example of their great reputation. Using his keen powers of stalking and observing motionlessly, he went a good way off and then froze perfectly still. Sure enough, the roosters lived up to their reputations, and fast.

The chicken coop was a log building with hay bales stacked all about the outside walls to insulate it. One day Red opened the door to the coop and found a skunk inside who apparently dined regularly on chicken eggs. Alarmed at being caught red handed, the skunk retreated to his exit hole in the wall. Red made mental note of the location of this hole and then went outside and around to that same site on the building's exterior. He knelt beside the hay bales and began pushing them around in an attempt to find the skunk.

Skunks are pretty cool customers who have no need to rely on speed for escape, and they do have pretty good sets of teeth and claws, if they ever wanted to defend themselves physically. Red had great knowledge of the lore of this creature, however, and he knew he had nothing to worry about. Chuck Barris had told him that a skunk can't spray you if you hold its tail down. Therefore, when the skunk was revealed hiding behind the hay bales right where he had exited the coop, Red felt no fear in reaching in and grabbing the skunk by the tail.

Now Red had a nice, healthy, wellfed, fullgrown skunk hanging by his tail in front of him. He looked him over, up and down, and especially read the look emanating from the creature's eyes. Red saw that there was no animosity on display and that courteous relations could be maintained by two of Nature's creatures one unto the other.

Red had some understanding of how the skunk's defenses worked, being the veteran of several previous meetings in the woods. He now found it true that a skunk could not squirt you when he was hanging upside down. If he couldn't lift his tail – he couldn't aim – he couldn't shoot.

Red put his left hand under the belly of the skunk, lifted him up, wrapped the tail underneath, and laid him flat along his right forearm, close to his belly.

All this was accomplished without any protest of any kind from the skunk, further telling Red of the harmony the two had between them. Red carried him around the barns. He even petted him like a kitty-cat.

Soon though, Red realized he would have to leave. What should he do with his new friend? He didn't want him eating eggs, but he didn't want to hurt him. He decided to imprison him in the pump house where the concrete floor and walls would hold him. So, Red unlocked the pump house and set the skunk down. The skunk didn't do anything, further cementing the bond between them. Red locked the door and went home.

The next day when Red did his chores, he realized that he must feed his prisoner. The only thing that he could think of that the skunk might like was – egg. So, he took an egg to the pump house and unlocked the door. The skunk wasn't there to greet him so Red had to crawl around a bit to try to find him. He was in the extreme corner of the building underneath the hot water heater. When Red stuck his face under the water heater, the skunk clicked his front claws on the concrete floor – tap, tap, tap. But he didn't do anything else and Red rolled the egg towards him and left him alone to dine.

Red kept up this egg a day diet for about a week. Everyone who heard the story told him to shoot the skunk, like any proper farmer would do. But Red and the skunk were good friends now, so Red thought he might just let his friend go free. He couldn't keep him locked up forever.

Then, one day, Reverend B. got a call from Jess Crossman. Jess had been working at the Roberts Mission when he found a blown circuit in the fuse box. He replaced the fuse. Then, to insure the water pump was working properly, he went to the pump house and unlocked the door. "A skunk sprayed the hell out of me when I opened the door!"

"Where's the skunk now?"

"It's still in the pump house."

"Can't it get out?"

"No, apparently not."

Reverend B. thought about that for a little while. "Let's see – if it can't get out, then how did it get in?"

"I don't know, maybe you should ask Red."

So Reverend B. collared Red that afternoon when he got home from school. When he had all the facts, he told Red about Jess Crossman's meeting with his skunk and told him that would not do. Red nodded with a small grin and agreed to get rid of the skunk.

He grabbed his .22 and drove off in the pink Ford towards the Roberts Mission.

Red was not planning on using his .22. With parole or pardon for his fellow creature in mind, Red opened the pump house door and found the skunk still in the corner under the water heater. Probably he wanted to stay and live with friend Red. But – Red knew that he couldn't stay there. Red got a rope. He reached under the water heater and got a noose around the skunk's neck. For the first time there was disagreement between them. Red tugged. The skunk did not come. Red tugged harder. The skunk began to click his claws on the concrete floor. Red dragged him into the open with full force. He again grabbed his reluctant pet by the tail and held him upside down while he untied the rope. Then he again wrapped the tail underneath the skunk and laid him flat on his fore arm. He carried him out into the light of day.

Red now had to plan for the release. Should he take him out to the trees along Trout Creek? Should he put him in the alfalfa field? Ahh, they were good friends – he would just toss him down on the ground right here.

At this point, Red found his belief in his oneness with Nature challenged. His trust in fellow creatures was shattered. His confidence in his ability to communicate with all living things was destroyed. The skunk didn't just mist him, it hosed him down! Pure skunk juice poured onto Red's body from close range. This wasn't the long range scent of common experience – this was the Nuclear Bomb of Skunk.

Red could see the pure liquid on his arms. He ran to the Mission, threw his clothes on the floor and drew a tub full of water. He lathered up and scrubbed all over. He soaked. He scrubbed again. Soap and water didn't seem to have any effect. He dried off and smelled himself. Peewwww! He filled the tub again and did it all over again. Peewwww! – he took a third bath. Red thought he was making progress, but, actually, his nose was just adjusting to his new essence.

Red wrapped himself in a towel, threw all his clothes out in the yard, and slipped into the car. He spun out in front of the house and spun sideways out onto Trout Creek Road. He had accelerated up to 50 when he heard a siren screaming behind him. He looked into his mirror and saw Joe Charbonneau's big green pickup about five feet behind him with its big red light flashing. He slowed down and pulled over.

Red kept his window rolled up while all the dust cleared around him. He watched Joe's progress from his truck to Red's car. When Joe got up to

Red's window, he saw that Red only had a towel on. Joe started to smile and motioned for Red to roll his window down. Red sat still, stewing in his stench. Joe reached out and tapped on the window, "Roll your window down."

"Are you sure"?

"Hurry up."

Red rolled his window down. Joe, thinking that he had caught Red in some illegal act, took off his cowboy hat and stuck his head inside to look around.

"Hey Zeus Cristo! Where the hell you been?" Joe jumped back waving his hat back and forth in front of his nose. "Get the hell out of here!"

Red idled off as slowly as he possibly could. Joe slapped the rear fender with his hat as it went by. "Gittyup!"

Now a little smile began to wrinkle Red's lips. He was sure the smell was disappearing. He drove slowly to Ft. Washakie, put the car in the garage and treated his Mother and Father to his new look and smell.

"Peewwww!" They stepped back and waved their hands under their noses. Several different chemicals were added to his next three baths – vinegar, lemon juice, and tomato juice. None of them seemed to work and poor Red was forced to miss a whole week of school and try to fill his time fishing the big holes in the Little Wind River.

Reverend Roberts with the Shoshone Girls
and his own children, 1906

CHAPTER 33 The White Man makes Red run the gauntlet

As he became a Shoshone, Red may have started seeing things differently. He had walked so many miles on the Reservation with his Blood Brothers that he had become One with Nature. He hunted, he fished, he swam, he climbed mountains, he camped, he smoked, and he lived off the land. He didn't apply for the per capita payment – he didn't want the White Man's money. Freedom from materialism also freed him from worry and guilt. He forgot about the strange fire that burned down the adobe house the night he and his friends went there to wrestle and smoke.

He thought of the White Man's tricks and forgave them. Once they had rounded up the Indian Kids and bussed them into Lander for a Spelling Bee. Mrs. Marshall accompanied Red and Beazel into the old High School Study Hall. Beazel was eliminated first. Red kept going, word after word. He started to think he liked competition and that he might win. But, the lady reading out the spelling bee words gave him, "liqueur", a French Word. Red couldn't spell it. He was eliminated and the Shoshones' chance to beat the White Man in English was lost. The word given to the next contestant after Red was "canoe". Red could have spelled that.

After graduating from the eighth grade at Fort Washakie, a couple of kids went away to Indian High Schools at Flandreau and Haskell. Most went into Lander to Fremont County Vocational High

School. Red thought he could take both the Auto Mechanics Program and the College Preparatory Program, but he had to settle for just one. F.C.V.H.S. also taught Agriculture. A bus picked up the students at Fort Washakie, stopped for Red and Ryan in front of St. David's Church, and then stopped at Hunt's corner. On the 15 miles to Lander, the bus was filled up in about a dozen stops where farm and ranch roads met Highway 287.

The society inside the bus was loaded with emotion. The serious and the quiet would sit up front near the Driver, where peace and safety could be found. The clowns and the troublemakers went to the back end. In between the two extremes were clusters of friends who sat together. The oldest boys went in back to stay away from the silly freshmen and freshmen stayed up front for safety. A few quiet senior girls scattered around created little zones of dignity and safety for the defenseless. A couple of these girls had mothers who had attended the Roberts Mission and their kids excelled in school.

When a little 13 year old Red first climbed up into the Lander Bus, swiveled at the top of the steps, and faced down the aisle, everyone wondered where he would sit. Red walked right to the back and sat down with the Seniors. As he walked down the aisle he picked up a variety of smells; shampoo, no shampoo, Spearmint, Juicy Fruit, Doublemint, bubble gum, cigarettes, toothpaste, no toothpaste, Vitalis, Brylcream, Butchwax, new shoes, old shoes, daily bath, monthly bath, no bath, deodorant and no deodorant. Freshmen started High School in their Reservation uniforms of oxfords, Levis and H Bar C or Panhandle Slim cowboy shirts with snap buttons from Hub Cramer's, Baldwin's or Hendershot's. The boys all wore army surplus flat tops from World War II and Korea. Without much hair, they all looked alike. The girls had to wear dresses and they froze in the winter. Conformity was important.

Nobody knew what to do with Red. No one tripped him as he walked down the aisle of the bus. That would be too easy. Faces watched to see where he was going. No boy could sit with a girl on the bus. Some small kids wanted anybody to sit beside them to make sure that a troublemaker couldn't slip in beside them. Freshmen couldn't sit with Seniors. The White kids whose parents worked for the BIA sat near the front. Where you sat was a powerful statement. Red knew none of this. He walked right to the back of the bus and sat down. The only physical test he was given was when Bud Morton squeezed his little finger over as hard as he could. Red never made a sound and Bud finally let him go.

The Mortons were White Farmers who lived on what was once an Indian Allotment.

There were educational and entertainment benefits that came with sitting in the back of the bus. Chuck Barris came one day with a wooden clothespin that was adapted so that you could shoot a farmer match. As the sulphury matchhead shot out of the wood pin, it ignited. Red spent some time that evening at home trying to build a replica. There was also an era of the hairpin snapper. A simple spring steel hairpin was borrowed from one of the girls. With two bends in just the right place, it became a spring-loaded snapper that was jammed against a thigh. The pressure on the thigh triggered the pin and it gave a crisp, but bearable, sting. Red bent many hairpins that evening trying to get the geometry just right.

Spring always had a squirt gun season. They were routinely confiscated in school and they sometimes leaked and made an embarrassing wet spot in your front pocket. In the summer the bus roasted. All the windows would be thrown wide open to let the 90 degree air blow through the bus.

In the winter, everyone froze. The windows iced up with their breath and they rode blind into Lander, occasionally rubbing little peepholes on the window glass. Their toes nearly froze on the metal floor. For a joke an older boy might open a window and leave it until someone jumped up and quickly slid it shut. Snow could be carried into the bus or scraped off the sides of the bus through an open window. This would be slipped down the neck of those in front of you. The only protection was to be all the way back.

The older boys also had more interesting gossip and news. Harold read a sensuous poem about The Love that he pressed to his lips. On and on it went and at the end revealed that the great love was a cigarette butt.

One snowy morning when Red was waiting for the bus, he saw the big Highway Department snowplow coming towards him at 50 miles an hour. A huge white stream of snow was pouring up off the blade and shooting into the ditch. Red thought it would be fun to get dusted by all that snow. He positioned himself on the shoulder of the road where the snowplow would pass safely but would blast him with fluffy snow. The driver saw Red and accommodated him. What Red didn't realize was that snow plows not only throw up snow but also ice, sand, gravel, and empty beer bottles. And, a plow at 50 miles an hour throws snow at 50 miles an hour. THWAACK! Red blew over backwards feeling like he had been sandblasted. He was flat on his back with a foot of snow, ice, and dirt on top of him. He couldn't see. He rubbed his eyes clear and spit the grit out of his mouth. He picked up his scattered books and notepapers. He still had a rind of wet sand all over him when he climbed into the schoolbus.

The Indian boys would stand in the snow in oxfords wearing only Levis, shirt, and a light jacket. Hats were apparently illegal, no matter how cold it was. The school lunch was the only meal of the day for some. They were tough.

The goal for Juniors and Seniors was to get a car and be able to drive into school. Ryan was able to do that in his Senior year by working at jobs in Lander. Red rode the bus every morning into Lander. Every night he rode the bus back to Fort Washakie. It was nearly impossible to play sports, music, or be in extra curricular activities because the bus left promptly after the last afternoon period. There were very few who could afford to drive 30 miles a day so a student could stay late for sports or band.

Red's Freshman and Sophomore years passed by riding in a yellow school bus. After school he watched Chubby Checker do "The Twist" on American Bandstand.

Back and forth, back and forth, Jack Norwoski drove the bus morning and evening and worked the rest of the day at Fremont Motors Ford. His presence up front made a safe zone on the bus. His occasional glances in the big mirror above him let the free spirits in the back of the bus know that he was watching.

When Red started his Junior year at age 15, the High School started a "Late Bus" that left the school one hour later than the regular bus. Honch and Red decided that they would go out for football. They got a partial practice in until the bell rang for the late bus. They would have to shower and catch that bus or else be stranded in Lander. Because Red and Honch hadn't played the first two years of High School, they weren't Coach Rupe's boys. He assigned them to practice with the Freshmen. Red's outdoor years had strengthened him and he was starting to get his big-for-your-age look. Honch was a fast runner and a good player. The two of them were moved up to practice with the varsity. After a few days of practice with Juniors and Seniors who were on the starting team, Coach Rupe called all the players to huddle and told them that Red was going to run the gauntlet. The Coach had all the players line up with Red confronting them. "I'll throw the ball to you and you run at these guys as hard as you can!"

Red caught the ball and charged the first player. He got tackled. "Run straight at 'em!" yelled Coach. Red got up and threw the ball to Coach Rupe. He jogged back to his starting point, caught the ball and tried to mow down the next player. Down went Red. Each player who tackled him went to the back of the line. They rested while Red ran and ran and ran. The Coach yelled him on. "Straight at 'em, straight at 'em!"

Red assumed this was a standard drill, but, it seemed to go on forever. Some of the players would dive at his feet to trip him and his shins and knees got beat up on their helmets. Red faced the 40 players time after time. Not until the late bus bell rang did Coach Rupe let Red go. He and Honch showered and caught the bus home.

Honch asked Red to get off at his place to help him with his Math. They got a snack in the Hunt's kitchen behind the store. Then they studied geometry for a while. When Red got up to leave, he felt a little sore. He left the store and started walking down 287 toward his house. Just after he passed the Mormon Church, he heard someone slow down. He looked around and saw that it was Joe Charbonneau in his big green game warden pickup. It stopped beside Red and he got in, "Thanks."

"You looked like you needed a ride. What you limpin' for?"

"Oh, we just got back from football practice. I had to run the gauntlet."

"What do you mean?"

Red explained the routine he had been through.

"That's not what running the gauntlet means in football," said Joe. "The other players only try to strip the ball out of your hands and push you around. That makes you get used to being roughed up and learn to hold onto the ball. No one could survive being tackled that much. I heard Rupe tells his Tackles to hurt their opponents and he got them to beat up J.R. McConnell for not showing up for a game."

The truck slowed at the driveway to St. David's. "I guess that's why I'm limping," smiled Red.

"You're lucky to have such great White Leaders and role models."

Red opened the door and stepped out on the shoulder of the highway. "Thanks a lot." Joe drove away and Red limped into the Church driveway and over to the Rectory.

In a few days he had to go see Dr. Ward in Lander. An x-ray was taken of Red's knee and leg. The Doctor lit up a Camel and invited Red to sit down with him at his big desk. He looked at Red's x-ray and smiled, "You have big prayer bones."

Red imagined that the prayer bone must be right below the kneecap. He wondered if he had damaged them by kneeling on the hard Episcopalian kneelers that didn't have pads on them. Lots of Christians just touched the kneeler with one knee, held on to the pew in front of them, and put most of their weight on one cheek or the other. If things got painful, they turned the other cheek.

Then Doctor Ward added, "Your Fibia and Tibula have separated. Or is it Tibia and Fibula?"

The doctor prescribed an Ace bandage for Red. He would have to wind it around his leg, below the knee, to keep his two leg bones together. They went to Noble Drug Store and bought one. He put it on as they drove north out of Lander. They crossed the North Fork of the Little Popo Agie River and were safely back on his Reservation. Red thought about football. The White Man called it a game but in all the practices and all the games he had never once seen a smile or heard a laugh.

CHAPTER 34 Red falls in love

When the summer of 1960 arrived, Red was 16 years old. The State of Wyoming had given him a Driver's License so that he could drive legally. Officer Mitchell of the Wyoming Highway Patrol gave him his driving test. When Red passed, Officer Mitchell smiled, "It looks like you've had lots of practice." Brother Ryan helped Red get a summer job at the Lander Creamery.

The two boys got up at 4:00 in the morning and drove from Fort Washakie into Lander. Ryan loaded a delivery truck with milk, butter, cheese, and eggs, and delivered them around town. Red dumped the 10 gallon milk cans the dairy farmers brought in. He weighed them, sampled them, and then poured them into a pasteurizer. When the milk and cream were separated, pasteurized, and piped over to the bottling room, he spent hours cleaning the piping and vats. At 30 cents per hour, he was feeling pretty rich. The Boss, Roger, often didn't keep him a full eight hours, so he would walk around Lander until Ryan was ready to go home.

One day, as he walked past the used car lot at Guschewsky's Fremont Motors Ford, he saw the most beautiful thing he had ever seen. It was a red 1950 Jeep CJ3A. He walked over to it and looked it over. It had a weathered gray canvas cab. He flipped the door handle, leaned in and inspected the interior. The seats were fairly worn and the paint was scratched on the floors from 10 years of use. His heart beat a little faster. He went into the Dealership and asked a Salesman about it. The price was $600. Red figured that was only 2,000 hours of work for him. He walked out of the store.

Every day after work Red somehow managed to walk by the Ford Dealership. He would look at the Red Jeep. He would open the hood. He would slip in the driver's seat and grip the steering wheel. He shifted the transmission and the transfer case. He tapped the canvas roof. He unchained the tailgate. He thought all day long about the Red Jeep.

Red had to have it. He was getting lovesick. He told Reverend and Mrs. B. about the Jeep. They were surprised. They couldn't see how they could possibly afford it. Red was crushed. His budgeting hadn't considered taxes, plates, insurance, gas, oil, and interest on a car loan. He quit visiting the Jeep every day but found a way to pass by to make sure it was still there and that no one else had bought it.

At some point Mrs. B. must have decided that Red had mooned around long enough and that his health might suffer. She told Red that she would go to the Bank and sign a loan. He could buy the Jeep, with the understanding that he would have to make all the payments, as well as pay all the expenses of driving it. Red was excited. He contributed $100 in cash and his Mother handed him a Bank Check for $500. On a Saturday he walked into Fremont Motors and bought his Jeep. The Salesman suggested that he have some extra oil with him when he drove. Red was so happy! He bought four quarts of oil and started driving the Red Jeep home to Fort Washakie. He noticed that the oil pressure gage read 0, so he stopped, checked the oil, and put in one quart. That filled it up, but the oil pressure remained 0. Red thought that the gage must be broken, but he was worried. He stopped about halfway home, near Aragon's Corner. He had to add another quart. He stopped a third time and added another quart. The Jeep was burning oil at just about the same rate that it was burning gasoline.

1950 Jeep CJ3A

As he passed Hunt's Corner, he saw Honch pass him in his Chevy. Honch recognized Red and immediately turned around. Red floored the Jeep, drove through Fort Washakie and went up to the dump. Honch was right on his tail. Red left the road and got on the 4X4 road along the fence, which climbed the steep hill east of the dump. As was the custom, he turned around and backed up the hill. Honch's Chevy was stopped on the dump road and couldn't follow. Red wondered what Honch was thinking. He topped the hill and then drove back down. He came up to Honch sitting in his Chevy and let him have a good look. Honch had a huge smile as Red told him that he had bought the Jeep. They bounced around in the sagebrush for a while, and Red happened to mention that he had used three quarts of oil to drive from Lander to Fort Washakie.

"Let's go talk to Harley Brickman at the Conoco Station," said Honch, "He's a good Mechanic."

Red thought that was a good idea, so he delivered Honch back to his Chevy and they both drove to the Sacajawea Service Station. Red told Harley his problem. Harley had taken Auto Mechanics at Fremont County Vocational High School in Lander. Mr. Ward had trained him well and he also had a lot of experience at the Conoco Station. He suggested that Red first try pouring valve and ring oil down the carburetor. That would burn out any carbon deposits. Red bought a $1 can from Harley, started the engine, opened the hood, and started pouring the oil down the carburetor. This started to kill the motor, so Honch reached over and pulled the throttle wider. Smoke started to blow out the tailpipe. That gave them the feeling that they were accomplishing something so they poured more and revved the engine more. The smoke cloud became huge. The Jeep was in front of the Conoco Station just 50 feet from the intersection of Highway 287, the Ethete Road, and Trout Creek Road. The smoke

379

cloud forced passing cars and trucks to slow down. Red stuck his head up from his pouring, looked east at the giant cloud stretching toward Ethete, and was scared. "It looks like a forest fire!"

"Ahh, it's okay," said Honch, "it's supposed to do that."

Red kept pouring and Honch kept the engine screaming. The billowing gray cloud could be seen by everyone on the Reservation who happened to be outside that day. The telephone started to ring at several places at Fort Washakie and Wind River. Several members of the Volunteer Fire Department got calls, including Game Warden Joe Charbonneau who got called on his radio from the Police Dispatcher at the Jail. He looked up into the sky and saw the billowing smoke filling the sky by the junction. He pushed his foot to the floor and raced towards Hunt's Corner. When he arrived, he saw traffic stopped on 287 and a circle of people standing around in front of the Sacajawea Service Station and beside Hunt's Store. His eyes jumped to what they were all watching. The clouds of smoke were emanating from the tiny little tail pipe of a little red CJ Jeep sitting near the Highway. He drove up close and jumped out. He saw two boys leaning into the engine compartment and working. He put his stomach on the radiator and leaned over between them. Red and Honch saw Joe at their elbows at the same time. Honch let off the throttle and said, "Gleep." Red lost his aim at the carburetor, started pouring the oil all over the motor, and said, "Ooops." Some oil hit the fan and was misted all over their faces.

The smoke stopped coming out of the engine, but the oily fog bank hung over them. Joe took off his sunglasses and tried to wipe off the oil. He wondered if there was any kind of law that had been broken. He couldn't think of any kind of ticket that could be written. He just said to the two guilty looking mechanics, "What ya doing?"

Red recovered enough to show Joe the can of Ring and Valve Oil. He looked at it and thought for a minute. Then he just sighed and walked away saying, "you may need new rings."

Red hoped that the $1 treatment had worked. As the cloud slowly dispersed, he and Honch drove around. They checked the oil. It was still disappearing at the rate of about five miles per quart. They returned to the gas station and Harley Brickman.

Harley told Red what a ring job involved. Red could borrow his cylinder hone and wrenches. He could borrow a torque wrench from the government garage. It would be easy.

Red bought the piston rings. He read Harley's Motors Manual on ring jobs. He borrowed Harley's tools. He and Honch went to the government garage and asked Ben Winchell for a torque wrench. He loaned it to them. The Red Jeep went into the narrow single car garage at the St. David's Rectory. The boys dropped the oil pan off and pulled off the head. They unbolted the rod bearing caps and pushed out the pistons. They honed the cylinders. They couldn't get the rings on. They took the pistons and rings down to Harley. He put them on without a ring expander but didn't break a single one. They went back to Red's house and put everything back together. The Jeep started. They returned all the tools. Red drove around. The Jeep used no oil! The oil pressure gage still read 0, but Red didn't care.

Red drove over to Hardin's and showed off his new Jeep. He took Mrs. B. for a four-wheel drive ride up a steep hill until she screamed for mercy. He took off the canvas cab and drove around topless. He bought Select-O-Matic free wheeling hubs and installed them. He painted the whole Jeep with a paintbrush and a can of red house paint.

Red could now drive himself into Lander to start work at 5:00 A.M. His top went back on. It was cold early in the morning and the little heater in the Jeep only kept his right foot warm. If it rained, the vacuum wiper on his side could be manually assisted with a little chrome knob. The passenger's windshield wiper was completely manual. A rider would have to continually sweep the lever inside the windshield to keep the glass on the outside clear.

* * *

The B.'s went on vacation. Ryan was living in Lander. Red drove his Jeep home to Fort Washakie one afternoon and lay down on top of the bed. Starting work at 5:00 in the morning is hard. He thought that he would just take a little nap. But, he woke up and saw that it was 6:30! He looked outside and saw that it was light! Oh, no – he had slept in! He jumped into his Red Jeep and headed for Lander. He roared the little four cylinder along as fast as he could. He passed Dead Horse Slough and Ray Lake. Then he noticed that it wasn't brightening up very much. It must be the change in light that comes with fall weather. He roared on. He went around Aragon's corner and past Kniffen's. Something didn't seem right. It was actually getting darker out, not lighter. He started to think that it might be 7:00 at night, not 7:00 in the morning. He turned his headlights on. He crossed Boulder Flats. He let his foot off the gas a little. It was night, not morning. He crossed the Popo Agie North Fork, turned around and went home. The next day after work he saw Honch.

Ray Lake

"I saw you driving into Lander last night," said Honch. "Know how I could tell?"

"How?"

"The space between your headlights. And - your right headlight shoots up high and to the right. Where were you going?"

"Oh, uh, I was just riding around."

Honch admired the Red Jeep very much. He borrowed it one day to drive Ken McCaw up to Dickinson Park. He drove it down Main Street from the High School during lunch one day with Red and a bunch of friends in it. As he passed the Lander Sporting Goods Store he saw three girls walking on the sidewalk. Honch eyed them too long. The station wagon in front of them stopped and Honch smashed the Jeep right into the tailgate of the wagon, leaving a long crease in the shape of the Jeep's front bumper. The Driver jumped out and rushed back to evaluate the damage. He saw the dent in his car and then looked back at the Jeep full of High School students that had hit him. He shook his head, got back into his car, and drove away.

Cecil Barker also borrowed his Jeep to drive up the Wind River Mountains to check his cattle. Sven Anderson borrowed it once and brought it back with the muffler dragging. Red drove around for a while without a muffler and Harley Brickman called it the Hotrod Jeep.

The little ten gallon Jeep gas tank was right under the driver's seat. One day Red drove down into a steep gulley out past Chalk Butte. He was so low on gas that the Jeep died on the steep hill. Red figured out that the gas was all downhill of the tank outlet. He took off his sock, tied it to a string, and dropped it into the gas tank. Then, when it was soaked with gas, he ran around to the engine and squeezed the gas into the carburetor. Then he started the engine, popped the clutch and the little bit of sockgas got him down to a flatter spot where once again the gas could flow out of the tank. He saved himself a very long walk home.

* * *

Red worked at the A.G. grocery store when his senior year at High School started. He took four classes in the morning and then worked in the afternoon and on Saturdays. The B.'s moved to Douglas, Wyoming, and Red convinced them that he should stay and finish his last year of High School in Lander. He moved in with the Barkers. Cecil suggested he brace his Jeep's radiator with a strut. He offered one from an ancient truck in his debris field. Red cut it down, drilled holes, and mounted tabs. The strut ran from both sides of the firewall to the grill. It stopped the vibration that broke the radiator spigots and cracked the fenders. Then he cut the tread off a bicycle tire and replaced the old liner between hood and grill.

Red went deer hunting with Hardins one warm October day. Red had his Red Jeep and they had their Green Jeep. They drove through the red, orange, and yellow sandstone cliffs of Red Canyon.

As usual, John sent Red and Beazel out on a long walking circle which would surely drive deer to John

Red Canyon

as they doubled back. Beazel and Red walked for some time and then heard shots from where they thought John was. Red suggested he go get his Jeep and drive over in case John needed to load up a deer and drive it out. Beazel would walk over and continue hunting. Red set out for his Jeep. Just as he arrived he saw a beautiful buck standing in front of him. He shot it with his 30-30 Model 94 Winchester,

387

then drove his Jeep the few feet over to it. He cleaned it out. John and Beazel arrived. They hadn't seen any deer. They agreed that Red should leave right away due to the warm weather. If he stayed to help them his deer would be spoiled with the heat. Red tied the buck to his tailgate and drove back to Barker's farm. Cecil helped him hang it and cover it and suggested they let it hang for three days.

* * *

Red, Honch, and Butch Wallen went to a Lander versus Thermopolis football game in the Jeep. Wallens were Farmers who had been on the Reservation at Mill Creek for three generations. Butch's Grandfather had known Shoshone Chief Washakie and Council Chairman George Terry. Red and Honch picked Butch up at his farm north of Aragon's Corner. They were cold in the canvas cab as they roared across the Reservation to Riverton. Butch pointed out the farms, ranches, mines and canals along the way.

When they came in sight of the Big Wind River, Butch pointed to the Owl Creek Mountains, "The Government took back all the Reservation from the river to the mountains. It was sold to White Farmers. Then they diverted the Big Wind River with Diversion Dam to irrigate the land. Project farmers got Indian water but had bad soil, alkali, and a short growing season. Water flowing out of the Wind River Mountains is high in sodium. A lot of the farms were turned back to the government."

The three friends watched the cold, winter football game and then went to swim in the big hot springs in Thermopolis.

"Reminds me of my Washakie Hot Springs," said Red, bobbing in the mist, "but mine is warmer."

Butch told them that the Thermopolis Hot Springs had to be sold by the Shoshone and Arapaho. "Did you know that Lander used to be in the Reservation?"

"Nope," said Red.

"What do you know about the Reservation?"

"Not much, apparently, confessed Red.

"Gold Miners forced out a big chunk of land from Lander to South Pass." Butch got splashed and jostled by a crowd of Lander High School fans who were sliding down the Giant Water Slide and roughhousing. They decided to dry off and start the long trip home.

On the way home, they stopped in the Wind River Canyon to read the sign at The Wedding of the Waters where the Wind River's name changed to Bighorn River. They cut off to go through the Midvale Irrigation District. "This is the land the Government took, but, a strange thing happened."

389

"What," asked Honch.

"The Government gave most of it back."

Then they roared back home with Butch sitting between them on the wood toolbox that filled the space between the two seats.

*   *   *

As the really cold weather came, Red had to plug in his headbolt heater in the morning so that the little 6 volt battery could start the Jeep. He had to dress warmly and wear gloves to drive. He could see his breath so he didn't have to smoke. Every once in a while, he would reach up with a windshield scraper and scrape the ice off the inside of the windshield. Ray Lake froze over and by December Red thought that it was probably thick enough to drive on. It was covered with a couple of inches of fresh snow for lubrication. He drove down to the edge of the lake across from Becky Wagner's house. He knew there was a CJ Jeep in Wagner's garage because he had seen Becky and Judy Contado come sliding down the muddy Old Wind River Road one day, giggling and throwing mud clumps 20 feet in the air from each tire. Now Red shifted into four-wheel drive and slowly drove out on the ice. Someone in Wagner's house saw him and said, "Some genius is driving out on the ice to go fishing."

Becky glanced through the window, "That's no genius, that's the Preacher's Kid."

The fishing season was closed and it was risky business driving out on ice that might still be thin. The snow made it impossible to judge the ice's thickness. As they watched, the Jeep slowly went out on the ice and drove around. It explored the edge of the lake all around and then drove into the middle of the lake over the really deep parts. It seemed to be working up its confidence. Then it started driving around really fast and spinning in circles. In two wheel drive the Jeep could spin around and round forever on the ice. And it did. The spectators lost interest. Red spun his brains out on the ice. Eventually he had enough spinning and left the lake on the north side where the wind had blown the snow away.

About an hour later, Joe Charbonneau's big green Game Warden Pickup pulled into Ray Lake. He was using one of his favorite tracking tricks – looking for tire tracks. He saw the narrow tire tracks that only a little CJ could make. "Ah, hah, someone is ice fishing." Maybe they left some evidence at their ice hole that would identify them. Joe was too smart to drive on the ice with his heavy truck, so he started walking along the tracks on the ice. He walked and walked. "This guy either knows where he's going or he's an idiot", he thought. The tracks went on and on. Joe dragged on through the snow, slipping on the ice underneath. He started getting tired.

Len, watching from across Highway 287, noticed this and started feeling sorry for Joe. Then Joe saw small snow piles right in the middle of the lake and he walked over to them. Maybe they marked the spot where the Jeep broke through the ice and sunk to the bottom. He found that endless doughnuts spun by the Jeep had swept the ice clean and blown the snow into little windrows that stood above the ice. They were having some fun, he thought. Now where is the hole they cut? He walked some more. He came to more clear ice. Maybe they fell through and the ice has already frozen over. Joe lay down on the ice, cupped his hands around his eyes to block out the sky, and peered into the ice. Len noticed this. When Joe didn't get up right away, he began to worry. He got in his car and drove across the highway and down to Ray Lake. He wouldn't drive on the ice either, so he stood at the lake's edge beside Joe's truck and waved Joe to come back. Joe recognized Len's car and walked over to him. He arrived, cold and puffing. "Hi, Len."

"What you doin', Joe?"

"I'm looking for where this Jeep stopped to fish or else where it fell in."

"Ain't no Jeep been fishing out there."

"I mean the driver. Did you see him?"

"Didn't need to. It was a red Jeep and all it did was spin around in circles for half an hour while we waited for it to fall through the ice."

"Red Jeep, huh?"

"Yep, the Preacher's Kid."

"Did he fall through?"

"Nope, no such luck. Preacher's Kid have heap big medicine."

"I know," said Joe. He got in his Game Warden Pickup and drove away.

The Red Jeep survived Ray Lake but it didn't survive long. Red picked up three of his Buddies one day and they rode around town with the top off the Jeep. He decided to drive up on the High School Football Field and race around the track. On the third corner, he felt the inside tires lift. The Jeep slowly rolled over. Red and Kirk were under the Jeep with the windshield lying on top of Red's right arm. Carl Adams and Phil Barrow were thrown clear. Kirk crawled out of the Jeep and the three of them lifted the Jeep off Red's arm. Then the four of them flipped the Jeep back up on its wheels. They bent the windshield and the steering column up enough to make the Jeep driveable. Red started the engine and the other three jumped in. They started to drive off the field with the windshield crunched down on the hood and the steering wheel bent down. They looked around at all the houses, wondering if anyone had seen the incident. Just when they thought they were safe, they saw a city police car driving toward them. He stopped them, asked a few questions and then wrote Red a ticket for careless driving. Reverend B. told him to settle down. He sold his Jeep. First love hurts.

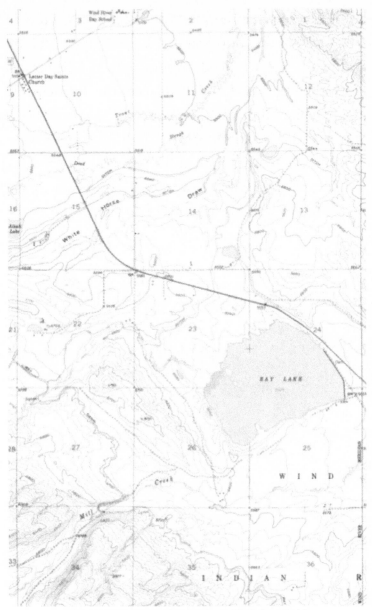

Ray Lake Quadrangle, USGS, 1952

CHAPTER 35 The Preacher's Kid climbs from the sewer to become the World's Greatest Shot

The Hunt's septic tank and grease trap were plugged up. Honch and Red were given the task of digging it up and cleaning it out. Two 55 gallon barrels without lids were put in the back of the Hunt's 1950 Ford pickup. With shovels, the two boys dug down to the lid of the grease trap where all the slurge from the butcher shop, the store, and the Hunt's house was filtered before entering the underground drain field.

They unbolted the lid to the trap and studied the creamy light brown stinking slurge with the smell and texture of vomit. Honch backed the pickup near the trap and handed Red a five gallon bucket. "You've got longer arms, so you can stand on the edge of the trap and hand the bucket up to me."

"Oh, okay." Red stepped down onto the slippery tank edge and scooped up a bucket of slurge. He lifted it up high for Honch to reach from the bed of the pickup truck. Unfortunately, as Honch jerked a hold of the bucket, a wave of the nasty goop sloshed out of the bucket and onto Red's head.

"Shit!" yelled Red.

396

"I know," said Honch.

Red tried putting less slurge in the bucket to stop the sloshing, but it still happened and pretty soon he had the slippery goop all over himself, his shoes, and the lid of the grease trap. Even Honch, in the bed of the truck, found that pouring the bucket into the 55 gallon barrels created a backsplash of odorous blurp. His feet and the bed of the truck got slippery. Honch held onto the barrels to stay upright but Red's feet started to slip off the lid and down into the trap. It wasn't long before both of them gave up all hope and abandoned themselves to a total soaking in slurge. Honch had to take off his glasses and lay them on the roof of the truck.

Once committed to their fate, they sloshed and slurged happily until both barrels were full. Well, maybe too full.

"You hold onto the barrels and I'll drive," said Honch.

"Okay," said Red, climbing out of the sewer trap and up into the bed of the pickup. He grasped the tops of the two barrels and steadied himself against the back of the cab.

Honch put the truck into gear and slipped out the clutch. The truck jerked and the barrels slid backwards and hit the tailgate. They dragged Red with him and then gave him a nice slosh of slurge when they hit. He pushed the barrels back up front.

"Shit!" yelled Red.

"No shit," said Honch.

"No – shit!" yelled back Red.

"I know." Honch kept driving, oblivious to the fact that every bump in the road was giving Red a good slopping. The barrels slid up – the barrels slid back. Red tried to steady them as they made their way through Ft. Washakie and up to the dump. The bumpy dirt road generated a misty spray over the back of the truck. Honch picked a good dumping spot and backed into it. When he hit the brakes, the two barrels and Red whacked the back of the tailgate in just the right spot for unloading. Only half the slurge was left in the barrels and the rest had painted a stripe on the highway all the way from Hunt's Corner to the Ft. Washakie Dump. Luckily, the evidence and smell would disappear in only one month.

Honch jumped out of the pickup and unchained the tailgate. He jumped up in the bed and helped Red slide the barrels out onto the dump. Splash! They flipped the big drums up and loaded them back on the truck. They were soaked. They reeked, but their noses had mercifully suspended normal operations due to overload.

398

Now it was time for some fun. They had brought their .22's with them and two boxes of shells. They wiped their hands dry on their pants and pulled out the rifles.

Red had been reading in Argosy Magazine about the old Sharpshooters of the past. Apparently, they shot small wood blocks out of the air by feel alone – they didn't aim with the sights. The trick was to start out shooting with a bee-bee gun and look for the bee-bee. If you tried to see the bee-bee you could and you would develop the "feel" for the rifle, rather than using the sights. When you had mastered this with a bee-bee gun, you graduated to a .22 rifle using short shells. Very soon you would be able to see the bullet flying through the air, something you ordinarily wouldn't think about. Sure enough! With just a little practice looking for a bullet rather than staring through your sights you saw the bullet. Now you could learn to swing and shoot your rifle without use of the fixed sights – just the feel of where you knew the bullet was going.

Red had advised Honch in detail about this interesting and important phenomenon. Honch had been doubtful, so Red proposed that Honch provide a couple boxes of shells and some ½ inch washers and the proof would be shown to him.

Before them now lay the prime shooting grounds of the dump.

"When you get good at this," said Red, "you can shoot a .22 right through the center of a washer. "It's easy."

"Let's see," said Honch.

Red handed him a fistful of washers. "Instead of throwing up beer bottles to shoot at – throw these. I'm going to shoot right through the center of the washer."

"Okay," said Honch. He positioned himself at a safe distance from Red, who was poised for action with his .22 rifle.

"Go!" yelled Red.

Honch flipped the washer up into the air. Red quickly threw his rifle towards it and fired, "CRACK!" The washer fell to the ground.

They ran to the washer. Red picked it up, inspected it, and handed it to Honch. "See, right through the hole – not blown away or marked by the bullet."

"Oh, yah!" exclaimed Honch, "you did it. I believe you now."

Red shot a couple more washers successfully and then they drove back to Hunt's house. Honch's Dad thanked them for cleaning out the grease trap but waved his hand under his nose and suggested that they both needed a shower. "Phewww!"

CHAPTER 36 Honch dares The Preacher's Kid to grab a rattlesnake

The Ford pickup that Honch drove on errands for the store was one day employed by Mrs. Hunt, Honch's Mother. She wanted to put some flagstone steps in her back yard garden. She learned from neighbors, the Crosscuts and the Shipoffs, that good sandstone rocks were found on the ground in the area of the Winkleman Dome Oil Field. The area was just a few miles north of Ft. Washakie.

The bed of the pickup had dried off from its recent soaking, so Honch and Red were employed by Mrs. Hunt to search for appropriately sized flagstones in the sandstone outcrops.

Winkleman Dome Oil Field was discovered in 1944. It produced oil from the Tensleep Formation, Phosphoria Formation, and the Nugget Formation. Joe Charbonneau used to joke that the big semi-trucks would leave Winkleman Dome with a load of oil and then return to the Reservation with a load of Coors Beer.

Honch and Red were assigned to drive around the sagebrush hills of Winkleman Dome and look for suitable rocks. They drove off early one morning with Honch shifting the crashbox transmission through the gears – raaack – raacck – crash! Even double clutching couldn't completely tame the unsynchronized four speed transmission. Honch's brother Will's tassel from high school graduation hung from the rear view mirror. His brother Larry's girlfriends' earrings were pinned to the sun visors. They hoped they could get stuck and have some fun.

They drove around the oil field roads and up on the ridge tops. There they found some nice flagstones and put them in the bed of the pickup. Then they got the idea that they should search for the ultimate and biggest flagstone. They screeched through the sagebrush and came upon a great big slab of rock right on top of a ridge. Honch backed up to it. They jumped out and took its measure – that is – they tried to lift it. Impossible! It was a really big rock. Honch took out a shovel and began to dig around the edge of the rock. They determined that it was a good thickness for a flagstone but it was about 10 times bigger than any normal flagstone.

All the better they thought. They would take this world record flagstone home and make everybody happy. They got out the Handyman Jack and tried to jack up one end of the giant flagstone. No luck. It was too awkward to get a hold of. They paused. They looked around.

Red saw an oil pump working not far away. "Hey, maybe we can use that pump jack to lift up this rock!"

"Yah," said Honch, "we've got a chain!"

"Let's drag her over," said Red.

The boys wrapped the tow chain around the big rock and hooked it up to the trailer ball on the back bumper. All the clumping around in the rocks and sagebrush scared out a rattlesnake and it started buzzing its warning signal to them.

Now, Red and Honch had scared up many a rattlesnake before. They had prodded them with sticks in an attempt to get them to strike and they knew that it took a warm body to get a snake to strike. Also, snakeskin made nice belts, wallets and hatbands. Snakes squirmed around after they were killed for a couple of hours, so you usually had time to take one home and scare your Mother with it.

As the snake gave its rattle-rattle—rattle warning with the buttons on its tail, Honch thought of the movie, "Trappers" where the hero grabbed a snake by the tail and killed it by snapping it like a whip.

"Hey, Red, I dare you to grab that snake!"

"Oh, Yah?" Red answered defiantly. He thought of the same movie and how easy it made it look to snap the head off a snake and kill it. But Red also knew that a snake could move faster than he could so he simply took the big old Handyman Jack and pinned it down.

Oil Well Pump Jack

He took out his pocket knife and cut off the head. He threw the writhing and squirming body of the snake into the back of the truck and it wriggled its way out of sight under the flagstone rocks.

Then the boys drove the truck over to the pump jack, dragging the giant flagstone behind them. Near the pump was a metal sign saying, "Pan American Oil Company, Winkleman Dome Number 1, 1944". The big donkey was gently going up and down, pumping out the Indian Oil.

The donkey had a bridle of cable. The cable was attached to sucker rod that went deep into the earth and was attached to a pump swab. Just like a giant waterpump, it suctioned up oil and sent it down a pipe to a storage tank nearby. Up and down, up and down, the gentle giant lifted the sucker rod in the well casing to pull up the oil.

Honch and Red positioned their rock under the well, got out of the truck and looked over the pump donkey and its controls. They saw that there was a convenient switch that apparently turned the donkey pump on and off. They tried it – it worked. Now all they had to do was harness the power of the pump to lift their rock and they could drive under it for loading!

As they looked between oil pump, pickup, and flagstone, they caught glimpses of the still writhing headless snake coiling around under the flagstones.

Red walked over to the control panel and turned off the electricity exactly at the moment that the pump donkey was at its low point. In the Oil Field

Office, the Pan American Manager saw a red light come on.

Honch wrapped the chain around the flagstone and then over the head of the pump donkey. Red turned on the electricity. The pump of Winkleman Dome #1 started up. The world's largest flagstone rose up off the ground. The donkey raised to its highest point. Red turned off the electricity. The pump again signaled that it was off to the Winkleman Dome Oil Field Office.

Honch backed up the truck so that it was nearly centered under the flagstone rock suspended in the air by the pump jack. Red turned the electricity on and the pump descended, lowering the rock into the bed of the pickup truck. The pump signaled that it was on to the Winkleman Dome Oil Field Office. Then off again. Joe Charbonneau drove up.

"I've got 'em, I've got 'em, I've got 'em now!" sung Joe under his breath. He jumped out of his big green Game Warden Pickup and ran over to where Honch and Red were doing their who knows what.

"What the hell are you two doing?" yelled Joe. He looked at the giant rock chained to the pump jack. He peeked at the flagstones strewn around the bed of the pickup.

Red and Honch were completely confused why any Game Warden would appear out here in a sagebrush and cactus country oil field and confront them for gathering garden flagstones.

"Joe, Joe, we're just picking up rocks!"

"Yah, yah, I bet!" said Joe, grinning over the contents of the pickup truck. He reached into the bed and began to move the rocks around. He knew there were probably fish or birds hidden under those rocks so he kept stirring them around until the writhing coils of the rattlesnake flipped into sight. The flash of the snake near his hand sent Joe jerking violently away with a loud, "Hey-ah!" He fell backwards into a patch of prickly pear cactus, "EE-YUD-AR-ROO!" The Pan American Oil Company Man drove up.

"What the hell are you doing?" he yelled. The Winkleman Dome Number 1 Well had been signaling its off-on-off-on condition and he was there to find out what the problem was. He looked at the dead pump. He looked at the rock chained to the pump and laying in the back of the pickup truck. He looked at Joe getting up and pulling his Levis gently away from his backside.

The Pan Am Man and Joe had a consultation in whispers? Was there any crime committed? Who had jurisdiction? They cast occasional cloudy looks at Red and Honch.

At the conclusion of this PowWow, the Pan Am Man said, "I think all of you should get the hell out of here and I'll try to fix up anything that's left." This order was firmly seconded by Joe who got slowly and sideways into his green Game Warden Truck and drove away.

The Pan American Oil Company Man climbed up the pump donkey to straighten out the bridle and undo the boys' chain. He dropped it into the bed of the pickup. Red and Honch wasted no time in jumping into the truck and driving away. But, the rocks were so heavy that Honch could hardly steer. The front wheels were hardly touching the ground and the truck wheelied whenever it hit a bump.

"Go sit on the hood," said Honch.

"Okay" said Red, and he got out and sat on the hood. His weight helped to keep the front end down so that Honch could steer. As they drove away, Red looked back and saw the white Pan Am Man astride the pump jack ready to pump up and down into the earth.

The Boys drove with the nose of the truck high in the air and the big flagstone dropping the tailgate in back almost to the ground. Red sat in the wind like a big smiling hood ornament. They drove over the grass in Hunt's back yard to deliver the flagstones. They were able to slide the giant rock off the tailgate and then jack it up so that they could let it fall on the grass. When they did so, the big rock cracked in half.

All that work! Gone! They were too depressed to even say, "Shit" out loud. They stared at the rocks and then the still writhing headless rattlesnake flipped into sight.

"Ah, hah!" said Red.

"Ah, hah!" said Honch. He grabbed the snake and took it over to the Hunt's back door and called his Mother to come and take a look. She did and seemed to enjoy the snake very much from a distance. Then the boys drove to St. Davids Rectory where Red's Mother could enjoy it also. She rewarded them with some whoops and shrieks from behind the locked screendoor.

Then they skinned the snake. Red looked at his knifeblade. "Hey, Honch, want to be Blood Brothers?"

Honch looked at Red's knifeblade. "You just skinned a rattlesnake and your hands are probably covered with old sewage from riding in the truck. Who ever heard of White People becoming blood brothers?"

Red thought about that for a while. "I guess you're right. You wouldn't have anything to gain.

Anyway, you're blood brothers with Johnny and Alan, aren't you?"

"Yep."

"So am I, so – that makes us automatically blood brothers."

"Yah, sorta like blood brothers in law."

"Nah, you could only be a blood brother in law if one person in the circle is a girl."

"That sounds right – kinda a blood sister. I'd like to be blood brothers with Ayleen!"

"Yah, who wouldn't!" laughed Red. They forgot about their snake.

Maverick Springs Oil Field, 1917
located on ceded land

CHAPTER 37 Red catches a Whitefish and Game Warden Joe catches a White Boy

When summer came to an end a boy would look to be worn out if he had made maximum use of his summer vacation from the White Man's School. His flat top would be grown out and fallen over from gravity. His tee shirt would have holes in it from being snagged going through barbwire fences. The shirt's neck would be stretched two sizes bigger from wrestling and playing football. His Levis would have holes in the knees and permanent grass stains. They called them High Water Pants because the boy kept on growing while the pants kept on shrinking. His once white Keds would have turned brown, have holes in the toes and the sole on one shoe would be flapping. He lifted that foot a little higher as he walked to keep from tripping. Every once in a while, he stopped and hopped to clear a rock or sand out of it. Fermentation and putrefaction were fed by regular wading in creeks and irregular changing of sweaty socks. The shoelaces had broken. Knots were located carefully between two eyelets. The worn ends of the laces puffed up so thick that they wouldn't go through an eye again, no matter how much you spit on it and tried twirling it into a point.

One sunny September day Red couldn't find anyone to go fishing. He decided to go alone. He asked Reverend B. for the use of the new 1960 Ford that had replaced the pink 1955 Victoria. He took his Wright and McGill fly rod and headed toward Chalk Butte. When he got to the fence north of Chalk Butte, he parked snugly up near the barbwire. With his fishing pole in hand, he walked through the sagebrush to the top of the cliff overlooking the river. He stood near the top and looked down at the big, deep pool hitting the Butte and being deflected hard right. Every time he stood here he visualized Hoagie Barton riding his bicycle off the cliff and into the Little Wind River. He would have to go fast enough to clear the big red and white boulders at the base of the cliff. The water was deep and fast moving – too fast to make a good swimming hole, although it looked like it would be perfect. The fish must have agreed because Red rarely caught anything right at Chalk Butte.

So, he climbed down on the north side and started fishing up river in the shade of the cottonwood trees and willows. He had a white floating line with a tapered six feet long 10 pound test nylon leader. On the end was a number 14 McGinty Bee. After a few casts upstream, he caught a nice little 12 inch trout. He cut a willow fork, slid the trout on it and dipped it in the water to stay cool while he continued fishing. He worked his way upstream and while he was still in sight of Chalk Butte he caught two more trout and added them to his willow fork. Then he let the Bee tumble on the bottom and he caught a Whitefish. Millman said the Whitefish and Suckers were increasing because of the lowering and slowing of the river through the irrigation projects. Millman said you could eat Whitefish, but Red unhooked this one and threw it back into the river.

Red left his string of trout in the shallows and walked farther upstream. He cast his fly upriver again. He kept the slack out of the line on the way down and then paid it out to let it float downstream. As he watched it float toward the Butte he saw someone walking up the river. It was Joe Charbonneau in a pair of rubber waders coming up the shallow south side of the Little Wind. "OOPS!" thought Red. He was caught fair and square. He wondered if Joe had seen his three trout cooling in the river below.

Joe waded across the river and came up beside Red, who stood looking sheepish with his line cranked in and the hook stuck in the cork handle.

"Practicing casting?" asked Joe, looking at Red's Wright & McGill rod.

Red wondered if he was going to confiscate it and was glad his fish were out of sight downriver.

"Looks like I caught a Sucker," smiled Joe, "Eeny meany miny moe."

"Let him go!" answered Red.

"What would you do if you caught a Sucker?"

"Let him go," said Red.

"You're going to have to get out of here," Joe smiled, pointing down the river.

"Okay."

"When you get back to your car you'll find that I parked a little close. You can get out but it might take you a little while."

"Okay, Joe, thanks." Red walked away on the riverbank in a path that would take him to his fish, cooling in the shadows. He occasionally looked over his shoulder and saw that Joe had continued walking upstream. He wondered why he was doing that, because Red rarely saw anyone else on the river trying to catch Red's fish. When he got to his trout, Joe was out of sight. He picked them up and continued back to Chalk Butte. Then he topped the hill and walked through the sagebrush. He could see the tar seep where someone had tried to drill an oil well and where Beazel had been mauled by the Cottontail Rabbit. In the distance Red could see Joe's big green Game Warden pickup parked behind Red's Ford.

When he got to the car he saw that Joe's truck was only about two inches away from his back bumper. He jumped in the Ford and started the motor. He cranked the steering wheel hard left and went slightly forward, kissing the barbwire. Then he cranked full right and backed up until he tapped Joe's truck. Then he spun the wheel full left and touched the barbwire again, then back to Joe – on and on, back and forth, making progress toward freedom at a fraction of an inch at a time. Spin – forward – spin – reverse. He eventually had crabwalked sideways enough to drive clear of the pickup. He drove out to the fork in the road and turned downriver instead of homeward. Then he stopped, broke off a chunk of sagebrush and used it, walking backwards, to obliterate all the tire tracks and his footprints. He then drove off the road and through the sagebrush to turn around and go home.

Joe was extremely tired the next day. Based upon tire track evidence, he had looked downriver all the way to Ethete for possible Poachers and got home very late. When he met up with Tallboy at the Jailhouse he said, "Guess who I caught RED handed yesterday?"

"Uh, uh, let me guess," laughed Tallboy, "uh, uh, the Preacher's Kid?"

"Yep, but I was using Catch and Release!"

CHAPTER 38 Red goes elk hunting and saves an Eagle

When Red's little brother, Douglas, was in the second grade at the Government School, his Teacher was Mrs. Thom. She had a son the same age as Red, named Thomas. Naturally, everyone called him Tom Tom. Tom Tom's father was a very old man who only had one eye, the left one. Like Russ Crosman, he had made a living logging in the Wind River Mountains and building houses in Lander. He hunted every year and had taken over 60 elk in his lifetime. He shot his right-handed bolt action Winchester 70 left-handed. He hunted successfully and drove around safely, so far. When elk season came around Tom Tom invited Red to go with them to the Big Sandy area north of South Pass. Red had learned to hunt big game with Sioux and Shoshone Indians. He thought maybe he could learn something from the Whites also. He agreed to go along. The three would go and would spend up to a week if necessary for everyone to get an elk.

Red woke at 5:00 A.M. at Ft. Washakie and put his sleeping bag, knife, hunting clothes, and Remington Model 700 30-06 into his Jeep. Being the first day of Elk hunting season, Joe Charbonneau was also up early. He knew the Preacher's Kid was going hunting when they passed each other on Highway 287. In Lander, Red parked his Jeep and put his equipment in the Thom's Chevy pickup.

The Thoms had a big wall tent and a half barrel stove to keep it warm. They loaded it and a week's supplies into the back of their Chevy pickup. Mr. Thom drove them out of Lander, through Red Canyon, and up South Pass. Red was feeling a little worried about Mr. Thom's one eye. He wondered if he could judge distances well enough to drive. After a few miles, Red relaxed a little when he saw that Mr. Thom seemed to have depth perception. They topped South Pass, turned onto the Big Sandy Road and headed north to get to the big timber country. The high country. Moose country. Elk country.

417

The road was sandy with hill after hill like a roller coaster. Sven Anderson once drove them so fast on this road that he flew over one hill and smashed all their heads against the roof. Red's rifle was standing on the floor beside him with the barrel pointed up. It flew up with Red and punched a hole in the headliner. But Sven had then been only 16 years old and Mr. Thom was now 70. He couldn't see if another car was coming up the other side of a hill toward them. The rule in the West is that you can drive anywhere you want on a dirt road unless there is another car coming or you are going up a hill. Then you drive on the right side. Period! Red became alarmed to see that Mr. Thom was going up every hill on the left side of the road. He looked out of the corner of his eye at Tom Tom sitting in the middle. He didn't seem to be worried. He looked at Mr. Thom to see if he might be going to sleep at the wheel, but he could only see his bad eye, so he couldn't tell. Maybe he's having fun, thought Red. It seemed that left side driving was all that Mr. Thom did the minute he turned off asphalt.

On a long flat stretch of road, Tom Tom said, "What's that?" He pointed straight ahead. It looked like someone was standing right in the middle of the road. Red saw it and hoped that Mr. Thom did too. The truck slowed. As they got closer they saw that it wasn't a man. It was — an eagle! Mr. Thom stopped. "It's a Golden Eagle!"

"Why didn't he fly away?"

"Must be hurt," said Mr. Thom.

Carefully, they slid out of the pickup and approached the Eagle. It didn't seem to mind. Its eyes just looked straight ahead as if nothing was happening. It was almost four feet tall with golden brown feathers riffling in the cold wind. Its beak and long talons looked deadly. Its majestic appearance made them stand back a safe distance.

"It might have been shocked on a power line and it's still confused."

"Maybe it ate some coyote poison and is sick."

"Maybe it's been shot."

"Hit by a car?"

"Snake bit?"

"What should we do?"

"Leave him alone."

"He'll get run over standing in the middle of the road!"

"Someone might come along and shoot him!"

"You're right. But he might be a goner anyways."

"Let's take him with us," said Red.

Golden Eagle

They thought about that for a while. "He'll have to be in the tent with us for a week," said Mr. Thom.

They thought about that for a while. They looked at the Eagle. He didn't seem to mind people talking about him. They stepped a little closer to him. The giant bird still didn't acknowledge their presence. Such a majestic creature had to be helped.

"Okay," said Mr. Thom, "let's make a place for him in the pickup." They rearranged some of the gear in the bed of the truck. Then Red and Tom Tom very carefully stepped near the Eagle and studied how they might lift him up off the ground. They didn't know the correct way to grab an Eagle and they didn't know if it would tear them to shreds with that fierce beak and claws. Red had the most experience grabbing wildlife and knew they were natural brothers. He leaned over and put his arms around the Eagle. Nothing happened. Red lifted him up and carried him to the back of the pickup and set him down in the bed. The big Golden Eagle stood motionless while they softly closed the tailgate.

The three got in the pickup and continued their drive on the wrong side of the road. They got into snow and slid around for a little while until they got stuck. They got out and put chains on the rear wheels. All the time the Eagle sat unmoving in the truck bed. They drove the rest of the way to their campsite and unloaded the truck. They shoveled the snow off the ground and set up the wall tent. They pounded the tent spikes into frozen ground. They put the half barrel stove in the middle of the tent and stuck the chimney pipe out through the canvas roof. They started a fire. They unrolled a big canvas tarp on the ground and then laid out their sleeping bags. Then they brought the Eagle into the tent.

"Who wants to have him next to you?" smiled Mr. Thom.

"It's okay with me," said Red. They set the Eagle down at the end of the tent next to Red's sleeping bag. It remained motionless with its eyes looking straight ahead. As they cooked and ate they wondered if they had any food that it might like. Red set a chunk of beef stew on the ground. The Golden wouldn't even look at it. "We could shoot a rabbit tomorrow and see if he would eat that."

Then they planned the next day's hunt. Red and Tom Tom would head for the higher ridges and Mr. Thom would stay lower. They would take lunches with them and meet back at the tent in the afternoon. They didn't want to be far out from camp when it got dark.

When they slipped into their cold, cold sleeping bags, they shivered and lay still, waiting for their bags to slowly warm up. The air in the tent was fairly warm, thanks to the stove. Red looked at the big Golden Eagle standing a few feet away from him. His mind played out a few fantasies. What if the Eagle came around to his senses in the night and went berserk? His huge hooked beak and giant talons could rip your face off. What if it just stepped on your nose like a tree branch and sunk his claws into it to hang on? But, Red didn't let those thoughts worry him. He soon fell asleep.

The next morning there was no change with Mr. Eagle. He was like a statue standing in their tent. They dressed, ate, grabbed their rifles, and tromped off in the snow for their first day of elk hunting. The tent flap closed loosely on the Eagle. It could leave if it wanted to.

As soon as they were a little distance away from the tent, Red asked Tom Tom, "Why does your Dad drive on the left side of the road?"

"He says that it's smoother on that side."

Red knew that was true sometimes, but not all the time. Experience proves it's true half the time. He didn't say anything more about it.

The first day they made small loops through the timber. They all agreed that they didn't want to get an elk down too far away. It becomes too big a job to pack the meat out a long way through deep snow. No one saw any animals the first day, but they did see lots of elk tracks. In camp at evening, they again placed some tidbits of beef on the ground in front of the Eagle. He showed no interest. At bedtime, Red thought again about the consequences of the Eagle going berserk in the middle of the night. But he just stood silently through the night.

The next day, Red and Tom Tom worked a little higher up. Then they agreed to split up. Tom Tom went north, Red went south. They heard distant shots, a good sign that there are animals in the area. Other hunters often drive animals to you. Red stopped, turned, and looked behind him regularly to familiarize himself with the way things would look when he wanted to find his way back.

By noon, Red was seeing lots of tracks. He smelled the warm must of a big bull that must have crossed his trail only seconds earlier and then disappeared in the timber. Red stopped walking and stood motionless beside a tree. This worked well. A big cow elk came into sight and within shooting range of Red. He waited to be sure that it didn't have a calf with it. He shot and it fell. He approached it and made sure it was down. Then he cleaned it out but realized that Tom Tom had the hatchet so he was unable to cut the sternum. He did the best he could but cut his hands a lot working up in the chest. Red's blood mixed with the elk's. He cut the hindquarters off and started back to camp with one. He heard shots ahead of him.

In a few minutes he saw Tom Tom coming through the trees. He had an elk down also. "Come over while I get a quarter. We can pack out together."

They went to Tom Tom's elk. Red noticed that Tom Tom was bleeding too. "Want to be Blood Brothers?"

Tom Tom looked at his hands and stretched out toward Red. They clamped together for a minute, mixing their blood and the elks' blood.

"Blood Brother."

"Blood Brother."

Tom Tom and Red each lifted a hindquarter. Then they struggled with their heavy loads through the snow back to the camp. When they returned to their elk, Red found that some kind hunter had happened by and sawed the sternum for him. They made four trips to camp, taking out one quarter at a time. Only together could they lift a front quarter and get it secured on a Hunter's back. They didn't want to set it down even to rest so they just leaned against a tree when they were tired. They didn't think they were going to have enough time in the day and maybe not enough strength, but the adrenaline of the hunt kept them going. Mr. Thom congratulated them on their kills. That night Red looked at the Eagle and wondered if it would make a good pet. He sliced off some fresh elk meat and put it on the ground. The Golden didn't eat and again stood motionless through the night.

425

The fourth day of the hunt they hoped for Mr. Thom to get his elk. He had no luck and decided to call it quits. They broke camp and loaded the pickup. The last thing they loaded was the Eagle, still standing quietly. They faced him forward, behind eight elk legs sticking straight up in the air.

Mr. Thom drove back on that same hilly road. He drove all the way on the left side. That was the old bad side that he didn't want to drive on during the drive in. Now it was good when it wasn't right. They got to Highway 28 and Mr. Thom stayed on the right side, much to Red's relief. The visibly displayed elk legs told everyone that they had got their elk. Some very surprised and jealous hunters saw the Golden Eagle riding in back and called the Fish and Game Department. No one had ever heard of such a thing before. A Lander Game Warden put the news out on the radio. Joe Charbonneau and the Reservation Police Department heard the description, "Golden Eagle riding in back of Chevrolet Pickup Truck."

It is a federal crime to kill Eagles or sell their feathers, even for a Sundance headress. Joe wondered who in the world would be driving around with a Golden Eagle in the back of their truck. He drove to Red's house, parked and waited.

The Thoms and Red made it safely down the South Pass to Lander. The elk were taken to the Lander Locker to be cured and butchered. At Thoms' house, Red hugged the Golden Eagle like an old friend and lifted him out of the truck. He set him under a canvas leanto so that he could leave any time he wanted. Mrs. Thom said she would feed, water, and take care of the Eagle. Red drove home to Ft. Washakie and saw Joe Charbonneau sitting in his Big Green Game Warden Pickup. He waved at him but Joe didn't wave back.

About two months later, Tom Tom told Red that the Eagle had eventually started eating and drinking water. Then, one day, he jumped up into the air flapping his wings. He circled around higher and higher over their house and finally disappeared high above Lander.

Red was supposed to graduate from Fremont County Vocational High School, Class of '61. The yearbook staff placed a saying under each senior's picture. Underneath Red's photo, it read – "There's not much to do in the Country." Red packed up his things and hawked his pistol, rifles, and shotgun. He hefted his suitcase full of baseball cards and mused out loud that he didn't know what to do with them.

"I know someone who could use those," said Honch, grabbing the case. He set it down in his closet and said goodbye to Red.

As Red left the Reservation the radio in his Jeep played Roy Orbison singing "Only the Lonely" and "Pretty Woman." In his new home he would be listening to "The Wanderer" and "Runaway."

CHAPTER 39 High School Reunion

Red got a Geology Degree from the University of Wyoming. He married and had children. He received an invitation to attend a reunion of his Lander High School Class. He drove from Casper to Shoshoni. All along that 100 miles he drove through areas where he had staked uranium mining claims and worked on oil exploration rigs. He turned north on Highway 20 for a side trip and drove along Boysen Reservoir where he had fished for ling and trout. He loved going through the Wind River Canyon where the Wind River cut through the Owl Creek Mountains and then changed its name to the Big Horn River at the Wedding of the Waters.

The Geological Cross Section from the PreCambrian up was exposed and signs along the highway told each formation's name and age. He had long ago memorized the Geological Ages: PreCambrian, Cambrian, Ordovician, Silurian, Devonian, Mississippian, Pennsylvanian, Permian, Triassic, Jurassic, Cretaceous, and Tertiary.

Red had walked the outcrops and cut drill cores through all the Canyon's formations. The three billion year old rocks of the PreCambrian were here exposed. Then, going upward in time and space: the Flathead Sandstone, Gros Ventre Formation, Gallatin Limestone, Bighorn Dolomite, Darby Formation, Madison Limestone, Amsden Formation, Tensleep Sandstone, Phosphoria Formation. Exiting the Canyon, he drove over the reds and oranges of the Chugwater Group, and then the ever younger Formations: Sundance, Morrison, Cloverly, Thermopolis, Muddy, Mowry, Frontier, Cody, MesaVerde, Meeteetse, and Lance. Lying on top of these were the youngest Tertiary Formations – the Fort Union and the Willwood, only 60 million years old.

Wind River Canyon

Red ran the names over in his mind as he drove along the Canyon's sheer rocks. He drove into Thermopolis and turned around to go back through the canyon and back through time to Lander. He had brought his fishing pole with him and remembered that the Reservation boundary wove through the canyon. The river was deep and well shaded. It looked perfect for big trout. Red kept looking at that perfect fishing river as he curved left and right through the narrow canyon. Finally, he couldn't stand it any longer. There were no signs saying, "No Fishing", so he pulled over past the scenic overlook at The Wedding of the Waters. Red got out his fishing pole, the Wright and McGill fly rod he had bought at Hunt's Trading Post when he started fishing. He walked down on the jumble of giant boulders and found a swirling patch of roaring deep water. Standing on a big boulder at the water's edge, he could not be seen by passing cars.

After just a couple of casts, Red got a powerful strike. He set the hook and tried to reel the fish in. The crashing of the water through the giant boulders made it difficult to work a fish in to the riverbank. He knew he had a big one on the hook and worked it smoothly. When the fish came to the surface it was the biggest Rainbow that Red had ever seen. Its brilliant silver sides and rainbow stripes flashed at him. He wished he had a net, but he didn't. He grabbed the line just above the hook and pulled the fish out of the water. In fear that it might get off the hook, he hopped back on another boulder further from the water. Just then the monster fish made a flip and came off the hook. It landed on the top of the boulder, took a big flop, and fell down in a crack between all the huge chunks of limestone.

"Shit, shit, shit," sang Red to himself. The fear of losing this big beauty choked him up. He set his pole down, fell on his knees, and stuck his head in the crack. He saw the monster down there trapped among the boulders. He tried to reach it. He stuck his butt up in the air, forced his shoulder hard on the boulders, and stretched his arm as far down as he could. He couldn't reach the fish.

Just then, he heard a whistle. He looked up the slope towards the highway and saw a Game Warden standing there. He said something to Red and made a "come here" motion.

"Shit, shit, shit," sang Red to himself again. He wondered if the Game Warden had seen his fish.

Red picked up his pole and climbed up the boulders to the road. There was an Indian Game Warden standing by a big green pickup truck with a red light on top. Red felt like he had been punched in the face. He looked closely at the Warden. Was it Joe Charbonneau?

Red looked him over. It was Joe with white hair! He glanced at the brass nameplate on the uniform – "Joe Charbonneau". Joe apparently didn't recognize Red.

"Do you have an Indian Fishing Permit?"

"No, I didn't see a Reservation sign." Red didn't remember that the entire river belonged to the Shoshones and Arapaho. American legal custom drew deed boundaries to the center of a river. He thought that the lack of Reservation signs showed that the river was outside the Reservation where it wasn't posted.

"Let me see your Driver's License," said Joe.

Red took his License from his wallet and handed it to Joe. He read it and then looked at Red. Then he read it again and looked at Red from head to foot. "Red?"

"Yah," laughed Red.

Joe Charbonneau burst out laughing. He stepped back a couple of paces and slapped his knee. He shook Red's license in the air like it was burning his fingers. "Red!"

"Yah," Red doubled over in laughter and rested his palms on his knees.

When Joe recovered a little, he wiped the tears from his eyes and read the license, "six feet two and 220 pounds. Are you sure that's you?"

They both laughed again. "It's me."

Joe handed the license back to Red. "When I first saw you poachin' at Trout Creek you were only half this size."

"I was just carrying Freckles' backup fishing pole."

"And his .22, and his shotgun!" laughed Joe, "And Alan's, and Beazel's, and Robbie's, and Johnny's!" Joe held out his hand. "How about the thousands of times I saw you out by yourself?"

Red smiled, grabbed Joe's hand and they shook. They leaned against Joe's big green game warden truck and talked about the old days. Joe told Red what all his old buddies were doing. Red told Joe where he had been since he left the Reservation: College in Laramie, a wife and two sons in Casper.

"Why don't you have a Wind River Reservation fishing license, Red?"

"I've got Shoshone Blood."

"I know you do. Get out of here!"

Red put his fishing pole in his car. He started the motor, looked at Joe and waved. Joe took off his hat and slapped Red's rear fender as it went by, "Gittyup!"

Red drove into Lander, dragged Main Street and noticed his old High School had been torn down. He found the new High School building and went in to register for his Class Reunion. At the reception desk in the lobby he was greeted by Miss Stack, his old English and Journalism Teacher.

"Do I ever have something for you!" she beamed and handed him a bulging manila folder.

"What have we here?" asked Red as he flipped open the folder. He saw some faded manuscripts that started his memory churning.

"All those 'Tiger Talk' stories you wrote - here they are!"

"Well, well, well," sighed Red. He picked up the top story and flipped through. It was about eating the liver of the first deer he killed. Miss Stack had written on it, "Show me, don't tell me."

"You need to publish these," she smiled.

"They're pretty sophomorish. It would take a lot of work to polish them up."

"No, no, leave them just the way they are - growing up in the 1950s. Don't change a thing. The only thing you left out was the time you and Beazel started laughing in Miss Kim's class and couldn't stop. She sent you to an empty room where you laughed for the rest of the hour. Have you seen Beazel or Honch?"

"I'm going out right now," smiled Red. He shook Miss Stack's hand, tucked the story collection under his arm and left the school.

Then he started the familiar 16 mile trip North to Fort Washakie. Crossing the North Fork of the Little Popo Agie River, he was safe again on the Wind River Reservation. Still, he drove by White farms where land had been bought from individual Indians.

In doing Title Research on land ownership and mineral interests, Red had learned a lot about Land Law. He had seen the ancient Homestead Patents in the County Courthouses. He saw them lost, abandoned, and slowly accumulating in the hands of the strongest. As he worked over the western states he saw the old, abandoned farmhouses that marked someone's lost dream.

Red drove around the triangle: Hunt's Corner – Wind River – Fort Washakie. He went by Sacajawea's Grave and Roberts Mission. Red was surprised to find the Mission had been razed and both the log St. David's Church and the Church of the Redeemer had been moved here. He saw that time had reduced his paintjob on the logs of St. David's to almost nothing. It looked just like it did before he had started painting. He saw the dent in the side of the Church of the Redeemer where the hot water heater had landed after blowing up and almost hitting Russ Crossman. Red was surprised to also see the house that Russ built for them at Fort Washakie, miles away. He couldn't tell if the house was being lived in. All the presence of the Church had been collected here, except for the Wind River house, which had burned down.

Red drove to the site of the burnt down house where the Church of the Redeemer had once been. They had moved into the new house at Fort Washakie, but Red had a key to the old adobe house at Wind River. A bunch of friends went out walking one night and decided to go inside. Robbie,

Freckles, Dane, and Red went in. Television hadn't arrived in Wyoming yet, so he showed them their old TV, from Walla Walla, stored in a closet.

Red had enjoyed watching Kukla, Fran and Ollie in 1949 and Howdy Doody in 1950. He showed them the strange device stored in the corner of a closet. He told them to climb up on it, which they took turns doing. Then Red said, "Now you can say you've been on T.V."

They went into the living room and wrestled for a while. Then they smoked. Red noticed ashes being flicked into the grate of the floor furnace and that bothered him. A smoking butt might have been dropped through the grate.

The next day, Red stepped out of the bus at Fort Washakie and saw smoke coming from Wind River. Someone told him his old house was on fire. Luckily the house was empty and no one got hurt. A lot of stuff got burnt up, including all the family photos.

Red pulled into Hunt's Corner and entered the Trading Post. Honch said hello with a big grin and they talked about the good old days. They reminded each other of the great adventures they had.

"Red, did you ever tell Ryan that you threw a rod in his Dodge?"

"No, but I'm going to tell him now. It's been 50 years so I should be safe." Red asked about Ronnie.

"Oh, it's bad. He's totally changed. He's holed up in his house and won't talk to anyone. He hates the Whites and blames them for everything."

"I could see him, couldn't I?" asked Red, "Will he talk?" He remembered that when Ronnie went away to Haskell, he never talked to him again.

"Sure, he's still there." Honch pointed down the road.

Red drove to the big windbreak and turned down the dirt road. He drove up to Ronnie's house, knowing that he was seen. He walked up the steps and knocked on the door. It opened and there stood a Ronnie that was 50 years older than the Ronnie he had played hooky with and played baseball with. They still recognized each other. They both smiled and Ronnie waved him in.

"Red!"

"Ronnie!"

They sat at the kitchen table. After some small talk, Red cut right to the point, "Honch says you are angry."

"The White Man took all my money," said Ronnie.

"The White Man took all my money, too," answered Red. He told Ronnie how the oil crash, interest rate spikes and conmen in the '80s had wrecked his business.

"Honch almost went under, too," said Ronnie.

"He survived?"

"Yah, he sold a suitcase full of baseball bubblegum cards for a small fortune. Even had two Pee Wee Reeses."

"I'm glad," smiled Red.

"The White Man almost killed me," said Ronnie.

"The White Man almost killed me, too," answered Red.

They looked at each other with changed eyes.

"The oil companies stole our oil."

"The oil companies steal everyone's oil. I read about you chasing Tanker Trucks and checking their load tickets. At Faults Oil Company they told their Pumpers to 'make your wage' every day."

"The White Man's alcohol is killing us."

"The White Man's alcohol is killing me."

Ronnie looked surprised. He held Red's eyes for a little while. "Smoke?"

"I had to quit. The White Man's tobacco was killing me."

"Me too!" Ronnie smiled. "Hey, wait a minute – the White Man got tobacco from the Indians."

"You're right," nodded Red, tilting his head and squinting while he thought. "So, the Red Man's tobacco was killing me."

"Me too!" Ronnie laughed and felt the tip of his finger where they had cut themselves to be Blood Brothers in the Seventh Grade. He reached across the table and turned Red's finger over. "No scars?"

"No scars," grinned Red. They slid their hands over each other's wrist and made the secret handshake. Ronnie smiled his old smile.

"I'm glad you came."

"Me too."

"Even if you did steal my Culture," laughed Ronnie.

"And you stole mine - no house, no Church, no School, no Mission, no Fort, no swimming hole," laughed Red.

"Let's call it even."

They stood. Ronnie put his hand on Red's left shoulder and walked him toward the door. They knew that this might be the last time they ever saw each other. They passed a wall full of photos where Ronnie stopped and pointed to one of the pictures. "Recognize any of these guys?"

Red saw his classmates sitting on the bleachers in the new gym. His eyes paused on each one and he recalled the great times and the laughs they had. He raised his finger to touch Alan's image, but Ronnie slowly shook his head, stopping Red's roaming thoughts. He wouldn't wade up Trout Creek beside

Alan with fishing poles in hand. A shot would not wobble off the backboard with Freckle's big old basketball. Galloping horses wouldn't carry Robbie and friends in races across the Sundance Grounds. Beazel, with rifle in hand, wouldn't walk beside him on the way to Chalk Butte. Johnny's smiling face wouldn't pop above water at the Little Wind River. Wesley wouldn't hit grounders to him on 1st base. Layman wouldn't spin, jump and dance in Eagle Feathers at the Shoshone Family Dance.

Red and Ronnie had misty eyes. They looked away and could not talk. Red went to the door by himself and walked out.

Red drove around Fort Washakie. He saw the big grassy field where he had played touch football with Buck Elliot, Johnny Rodda, Ronnie Beauclair, Beazel Hardin, Scooter Ferris, Freckles Contado, Honch Hunt, Alan Beauclair, and Robbie Beauclair. They were all his friends and he saw no differences between them. They were all the same. As long as they were children they were all alike and all equal. Only when someone older started talking to them did they start hearing mean things.

Red looked out over the woods that once thrived in the valley where the South Fork and the North Fork of the Little Wind River meet. Here they had fished, swam, hunted, smoked, laughed, built forts,

441

and grew up. He was struck by how decimated the area looked. The area covered by trees was greatly shrunk and the leaves looked dry and unhealthy.

"Something's wrong. I wonder if they had a big fire or flood?" He drove further down Highway 287. "I need to ask Honch if they had a fire."

Red found both the Jail and Hardin's house had disappeared. A newer Highway 287 veered around Ft. Washakie and right through where Hardins had lived. Beazel and his family had evaporated. His eyes swept down toward the old swimming hole. The raccoon tree was gone. Big cottonwoods were replaced by scrub brush. Then he remembered that the Government had channelized the stream.

The Government straightened out the Little Wind River!

Heading east on the Ethete Road and passing the hot springs, Red looked over at the chunk of red Chugwater Formation that is Chalk Butte. He automatically checked his rearview mirror for a big green game warden pickup truck.

The End

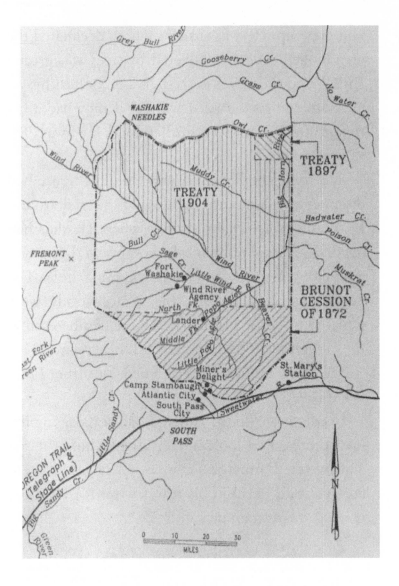

Treaty Map. Used by permission of Linda Marston

Appendix - The Incredible Shrinking Indian Reservation

July 22, 1790, Nonintercourse Act, no sale of Indian Land is valid unless made under Public Treaty. George Washington told the Seneca Nation, "Here then is the security for the remainder of your lands."

1834, 25th section of Act of 30 June, extended U.S. law to Indian Country excepting crimes of Indian vs. Indian.

September 27, 1850, Donation Land Claim Act. Much of the West had once been the Oregon Territory. The DLC Act of 1850 granted 320 acres to single White men or 640 acres if married. The women were thereby also given interests in land. The land would have to be cultivated for 4 years and patents were available for American half-breed Indians. San Francisco was one of the first "DLCs". The Act expired in 1855.

In 1861, President Lincoln appointed James Doty as Superintendant of Indian Affairs for Utah Territory. He negotiated treaties with the Shoshones. He became governor of Utah in 1863.

May, 1862, Homestead Act, required 5 years to occupy and improve 160 acres. It included women, free slaves and immigrants who had applied for citizenship. In 1866 Blacks were included. The cold and dry conditions of the West were not understood by Lawmakers in the East and they never caught up with the realities of farming in the West. The resulting westward expansion pushed trails through Indian Territory. The Kinkaid Amendment of 1904 granted 640 acres in Western Nebraska.

1862, some Shoshones broke with Washakie and raided trails. Punished by General Connor in Battle of Bear Run, January, 1863. 368 Shoshones killed.

In 1863, James Doty had assembled the following map showing areas occupied by the tribes.

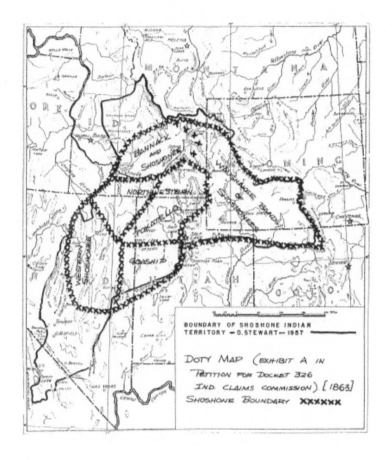

1863, 1st Ft. Bridger Treaty. Article II, Outline of Shoshone Country - "All the country lying between the meridian of Salt Lake City and the line of the North Platte River to the mouth of the Sweetwater and the valley of the Wind River and lands on its tributaries as far east as the Popo Agie." 44,672,000 acres (69,800 square miles) in Colorado, Utah, Idaho, and Wyoming. Never ratified.

July 3, 1868, 2nd Ft. Bridger Treaty. Reservation Boundary, "Commencing at the mouth of Owl Creek and running due south to the crest of the divide between the Sweetwater and Popo Agie Rivers; thence along the crest of said divide and the summit of Wind River Mountains to the longitude of North Fork and up its channel to a point twenty miles above its mouth; thence in a straight line to head-waters of Owl Creek and along middle of channel of Owl Creek to Place of Beginning". 3,054,182 acres.

April 10, 1869, Peace Policy of President Grant. Church groups to help tribes settle down and farm.

1869 to 1909, Ft. Washakie in use by 9th and 10th Cavalry.

1871, 1872, Bannock Shoshone Band on Wind River Reservation. They select lands and move to Ft. Hall, Idaho.

September 26, 1872, Brunot Cession. Cuts 1/4 out of reservation, 710,642 acres, as U.S. falls into the National Panic of 1873. ". . . that portion of their reservation in Wyoming Territory which is situated south of a line beginning at a Point on the eastern boundary of the Shoshone and Bannock reservation, [said Point being due east of the mouth of the Little Popo Agie at its junction with the Popo Agie], and running from said Point west to the mouth of the Little Popo Agie; thence up the Popo Agie to the North Fork, and up the North Fork to the mouth of the canyon, thence west to the western boundary of the reservation." 2,343,000 acres remained. This cut out areas near the Gold Camps of Atlantic City, South Pass and Miners Delight.

1878, Arapaho, under Black Coal and Sharp Nose, come to the Wind River Reservation. Shoshones told it is only temporary. Arapaho given 1/2 undivided interest, equivalent to 1,171,500 acres.

1882, Shoshones kill 2400 buffalo. In 1885, only 10.

1885, Major Crimes Act, gave Federal jurisdiction over Indians, both victims and offenders.

1887, Dawes General Allotment Act, allows tribesmen to acquire individual rights in land similar to the Homestead Act; 80 acres each, 160 acres for the head of a household, 40 acres for those under

18. They then became U.S. citizens, could farm like whitemen and pay taxes. They could not sell for 25 years. Many had to sell to whites. "Surplus" lands not allotted were made available to whites. In the U.S., by 1932, whites had acquired 2/3rds of the 138,000,000 acres that the Indians had in 1887.

1890, Rev. John Roberts' School at Wind River burns down. Builds Roberts Mission further west on Trout Creek on Chief Washakie's gift of 160 acres.

1891, Commission of Indian Affairs with the Woodruff Commission states over Shoshone complaints that the Arapaho have equal rights in the reservation.

1891, John McLaughlin starts negotiating for Indians to cede 1,480,000 acres north of the Big Wind River and east of the Popo Agie. This would leave 490 acres to each of 1,650 Indians.

1896, ratified 1897, Thermopolis Hot Springs being developed by Whites. Shoshones and Arapahos agree to relinquish 64,000 acres at the northeast reservation corner for $60,000.

March 2, 1899, Act to Acquire Rights of Way through Indian Reservations and Allotments.

April 21, 1904, McLaughlin Agreement, ratified by Congress March 3, 1905, negotiated by James McLaughlin, U.S. Indian Inspector, who had arrested Sitting Bull. The reservation lost 1.5 million acres north of the Big Wind River. The Indians were paid $50 per capita, $150,000 for irrigation systems, $50,000 for livestock, and $50,000 to the school fund. 282 of 484 Shoshone adult males signed and 80 of 237 Arapaho. Reverend John Roberts was a witness. The Shoshones accused their leader, George Terry, of deception.

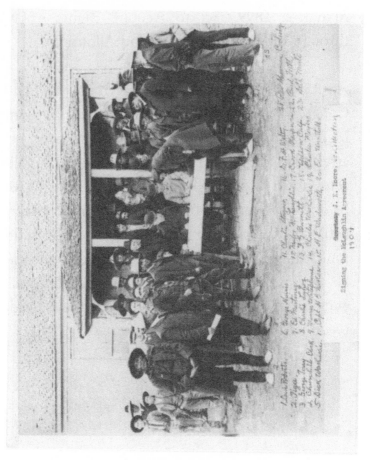

1904 McLaughlin Agreement Signatories

1.Dewi Roberts	13.F.G. Burnett
2.Tigee	14.Charlie Washakie
3.George Terry	15.H.E. Wadsworth
4.Churchill Clark	16.Dr. S.H. Welty
5.Dick Washakie	17.Chief Sharpnose
6.George Harris	18.Yellow Calf

451

7.Ed Martinez   19.Charlie Meyers
8.Charles Lahoe   20.Edw. Wanstall
9.Morris Whiteplume   21.Rev. Sherman
10.Capt. H.G. Nickerson   Coolidge
11.Charlie Stagner   22.Bad Teeth
12.Major McLaughlin   23.Seth Marti

Tribal Councilman, George Terry, had supported the sale of Reservation Lands. His barn was burned down. A Shoshone confessed that he and three others killed Terry on January 11, 1907, but later retracted his confession.

August 5, 1906, State planned to irrigate 265,000 acres in the Midvale Irrigation District. The last land rush, but it was mostly sandy. Heavy clay was a few inches beneath the topsoil, underlaid by sandstone and decomposed shale allowing no drainage and waterlogging easily. The Wind River water had a high alkali content. The sodium prevents the maturation of many crops. The government had to buy back 78 units (22,000 acres) by the 1960s.

1906, Burke Act, modifies the Dawes Act to end the 25 year holding term before Indian land can be sold.

1909, The Enlarged Homestead Act increased the 1862 Act's 160 acres up to 320 acres.

1916, The Stock Raising Homestead Act granted 640 acres.

June 2, 1924, Indian Citizenship Act, 43 Stat 253. Right to vote limited by some state laws until 1957.

1925, Diversion Dam on Wind River irrigates Midvale Irrigation Project taken out of Reservation.

1928, St. Stephens mission church, gym, boys' dormitory and quarters burnt down.

June 18, 1934, Indian Reorganization Act, (Wheeler-Howard Act), prohibits further allotment of Indian Lands. Reversed assimilation programs and increased Indian self government. Attempted to recover sold Allotments and stopped the Dawes General Allotment Act. Did not restore already patented land to Indians. Known as the Indian New Deal and signed by President Roosevelt.

1938, Court of Claims, Washington, D.C. Shoshones receive $4,453,000 for the Arapaho living on the reservation since 1877. Clears title to

2,268,000 acres, surface and minerals. Justice Cardoza said it had been a 5th Amendment taking. Called the "Tunison Money" after Shoshone Tribe's Attorney, George M. Tunison of Omaha, Nebraska.

November 12, 1942, Indian Affairs: Laws and Treaties Vol. 7, restores lands to tribe taken by Act of March 3, 1905 (the McLaughlin Agreement). Returns over 1,000,000 acres not leased or permitted to non-Indians, designated as "undisposed of ceded land". White towns of Riverton, Pavilion, Kinnear, Morton and the Midvale Irrigation District now surrounded by reservation again.

August 13, 1946, President Truman signs Indian Claims Commission Act, encouraging assimilation. Joint Tribal Council Members Nell Scott and Robert Harris object.

1957, Shoshones receive $443,013 for land lost in Brunot Cession. [see Chapter 29 - Payday]

December 22, 1957, KWRB TV Channel 10 starts broadcasting over Fremont County and the Reservation.

1976, The Federal Land Policy and Management Act ended Homesteading except for Alaska (Alaska to 1986). 1.6 million Homesteaders in America had claimed 160 million acres, only 8.4% of U.S. land. There were many unsuccessful Homesteaders whose dreams were lost. Acquiring workable sized farms with water sometimes led to chicanery.

1992, Big Horn #3 Case Final Decision, Wyoming Supreme Court. White Agricultural water use is "Beneficial Right" but Indian "Beneficial Right" does not include fish, wildlife, recreation or groundwater recharge.

2010, Claims Resolution Act, Senate 3754, provides $2 billion for education and to buy fractionalized land for return to community tribal ownership in U.S.

2014, Eastern Shoshone Tribe and Arapaho Tribe share $157 million for mismanaged trust assets and trust funds. In court since 1979.

March 17, 2016, Roberts Mission burns down. The School Building had burned down in 1953 and the Boys Dormitory had burned down in 1956.

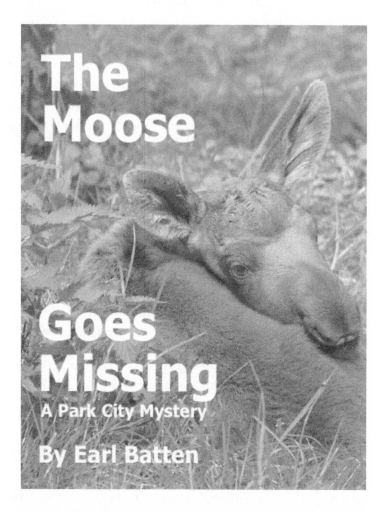

The *Author of Joe and the Preacher's Kid is recycled when his grandchildren become Amateur Sleuths in the historic mining town of Park City, Utah. Join their fun adventure in* The Moose Goes Missing, *available in Amazon Books.*

The Sheriff needs help. The baby moose that was the Park City Zoo's favorite is gone! How do you search for a moose in miles of mountains and old mines? With the help of those who hike, bike, and ski all over the Wasatch Mountains - Haley and Nash Barton. A busy football weekend distracts them and evidence points different directions. A trip to the underground museum refreshes their knowledge of the extensive mine tunnels running through the mountains.

An underground railway in the Spiro Tunnel once delivered miners two miles into the mountain to the Thaynes Hoistway where they rode to the many mine levels. Skiers rode to the Silver King Ski Run on the only ski elevator in the world. The tunnel is maintained by Engineer Craig Maceri and his two motorcycle sidekicks, Wayne and Chuck. The Barton's dog, Eiger, applies his acute senses to the moose trail. The young Investigators are immersed in the mining history of Park City and its change into a skiing and recreation destination. The search is aided by advice from "Grandpa" and his old friends from the mining industry.

Reports in the Salt Lake Chronicle bring the attention of the world. Within the mine, Haley and Nash will face great danger. A rockfall traps them. Invisible carbon dioxide fills the shaft. The hidden secret behind the Missing Moose is untangled in a confidential courtroom showdown only now unsealed and made available to the Public.

Made in United States
Orlando, FL
09 June 2022

18650900R20278